Dodge City, the Cowboy Capital, and the
Great South-west in the Days of the Wild
Indian, the Buffalo, the Cowboy, Dance Halls,
Gambling Halls and bad Men

Dodge City

The Cowboy Capital

AND

The Great Southwest

IN

The Days of
The Wild Indian, the Buffalo, the Cowboy,
Dance Halls, Gambling Halls
and Bad Men

———

BY
ROBERT M. WRIGHT
Plainsman, Explorer, Scout, Pioneer, Trader and Settler

T 68.
· I 64 W 9

R. M. Wright and Son, with Wright Park in Background

PREFACE

Whether a preface is explanatory or apologetic, is material, in the use we make of this one. Local history)oth personal and public; but the narratives of a border ? are from conspicuous events, having an origin and a rpose similar to the discovery of a new country. Local tory is the result of development and progress; and :h city or state history is the example of the whole intry. The history of Dodge City, however, includes a ler environment than the ordinary city or town, :ause it was the focus of a range of country two idred miles, north, south, east, and west. Therefore, center of gravitation was equal in extent to that of a te. Upon this axis revolved and oscillated the bull-acker, the buffalo hunter, the cowboy, the humble izen, and the desperado. The character and life of s mixed class of citizenship was greatly sharpened and ianced by reason of the strenuous and characteristic oulses which governed the circumstances in pursuit l development. There was nothing passive in the life the plainsman. The objective was the supreme motive; he stood in face of danger, and his quickness of uition and sense of warning kept him always alert. character built up under such conditions must have :n able to cope with the dangers and hardships incident a country infested with warlike bands of Indians, and outlaws which followed on the flanks of civilization.

It is the author of this book, Honorable R. M. 'ight, we wish to emphasize in this simple explanation. . Wright came to the plains country a few years 'ore the civil war. As a young man, active and 'orous, he became imbued with a spirit of chivalry l courage, followed by those traits of character inevitable to this kind of life; charity and benevolence. Many of the narratives in this book are largely his own personal experiences; and they are written without display of rhetoric or fiction. In everything, Mr. Wright took the initiative, for he had the ability and had acquired an influence to accomplish whatever he undertook. Possessing wealth, at one time, he fostered every enterprise and gave impetus to its accomplishment. These are living examples of his public spirit and generosity; and these are living memories of his charitable deeds and benevolent gifts. This book is a fitting testimonial to his life and character. Time is generous in its rewards; but no testimony endures which has not a basis upon which to found a character worthy of testimonial. Mr. Wright will give this book as furnishing an example of what constitutes greatness in life; for few men have passed a severer ordeal, in greater hardship, and in more danger to life.

N. B. KLAINE.

INTRODUCTION

At the solicitation of many friends and acquaintances as well as a great many people who are desirous of knowing about early life in the wild west and the Great American Desert, especially in wicked Dodge City, I write these true stories and historical facts. The task is a pleasant one. As I look back and endeavor to recall the events of that period, a kaleidoscopic panorama presents itself to my mind—a picture ever changing, ever restless, with no two days alike in experience. In those days, one lived ten years of life in one calendar year. Indians, drought, buffaloes, bad men, the long horn, and, in fact, so many characteristic features of that time present themselves that I am at a loss where to begin.

I have often thought that did I possess but an atom of the genius of a Kipling, what an interesting narrative might I write of the passing events of that period. It would be another forceful proof of the trite saying that, "Truth is stranger than fiction." Had I but kept a diary of each days events as they occurred, from the first time I entered the great West, what rich food it would be to the novelist, and how strange to the present generation would be the reading.

If you wish to feel yourself more comfortable than a king while listening to the sweetest strains of music, come back into a warm pleasant home with its comforts and listen to the crackle of a cheerful, open wood fire, after being out in cold and storm for a month or two, never, during that time, being near a house or comfortable habitation, while every moment being in terror of Indian attack, or suffering from cold and storm really more terrible than Indian attack, sitting up the greater part of the night to keep from freezing, and riding hard all day on the morrow. In the joy of the change, you will imagine yourself in the heaven of heavens. How many of us have often experienced these feelings on the frontier of Kansas in the early days. Yet this kind of a life gives one a zest for adventure, for it is a sort of adventure to which he not only become accustomed but attached. In fact, there is a fascination about it difficult to resist, and, having once felt its power, one could not permit himself to give it up.

In writing these stories, I have yielded to the request of my friends, principally, for the reason that there are but few men left who saw these things, and I, too, will soon pass away. But before I go, I want to leave behind a feeble description of the greatest game country on earth, as well as of the game that roamed over it, and of its people, and various phases of life.

No doubt, many readers of this book who are reared in Christian homes under proper influences and, by reason of wholesome teachings, parental care and guidance and pure environments, will naturally conclude that Dodge City, in its early period, did not offer the best social climate in the world.

Dodge City has been quoted all over the United States as the most wicked town in existence. The New York papers refer to it as such, the Washington papers do the same—so it goes. From New York to Washington, from Washington to New Orleans, from New Orleans to St. Louis, from St. Louis to Chicago, and from there back to Kansas, if horrible crime is committed, they say, "This is almost as bad, as wicked, as Dodge City."

But, in extenuation of the conduct of her early inhabitants, I plead the newness of the territory, the conditions of life, the dangers and associations of a western frontier, and the daring and reckless spirit that such conditions engender.

BIRD'S EYE VIEW OF DODGE CITY, 1888

I also insist that Dodge City was not the worst place on earth and at last I have heard of a town which was equal to if not worse than Dodge City, and, by way of comparison, I here quote a graphic picture taken from the "Virginia City Chronicle," published in the '70's, of another bad town:

"There are saloons all over the place, and whisky four bits a drink. They put two barrels upon end, nail a board across for a bar and deal out. A miner who wants to treat pours some gold dust on the barrel head and says, "Set 'em up!" They never weigh the dust. Sometimes a man won't put down enough dust, but they never say a word, and if he's a little drunk and puts up ten or fifteen dollars worth they never mention it. They have three faro banks running all the time. They don't use checks, for the boys, when they won a pile of checks they threw them all over the place and some of them were too drunk to handle them. So the checks got played out. Now a man puts a little gold dust on a dollar greenback and it goes for two dollars worth of dust, on a ten dollar greenback goes for twenty dollars, and so on— don't weigh the dust at all but guess the amount. We have a daily newspaper—that is, sometimes it's daily, and then when the compositors get drunk it doesn't come out for several days. If a man wants gun wadding he goes and pays four bits for a newspaper. Whenever they start a new city government they print a lot of city ordinances, then there's a grand rush for the paper. Sometimes it comes out twice a week and sometimes twice a day. Every man in Deadwood carries about fourteen pounds of firearms hitched to his belt, and they never pass any words. The fellow that gets his gun out first is the best man and they lug off the other fellow's body. Our graveyard is a big institution and a growing one. Sometimes, however, the place is right quiet. I've known times when a man wasn't killed for twenty-four hours.

Then again they'd lay out five or six a day. When a man gets too handy with his shooting irons and kills five or six, they think he isn't safe, and somebody pops him over to rid the place of him. They don't kill him for what he has done, but for what he's liable to do. I suppose that the average deaths amount to about one hundred a month.''

CHAPTER I

The Country, Time, and Conditions
that Brought About Dodge City

Dodge City is situated on or near the hundredth meridian. It is just three hundred miles in a direct western line from the Missouri river, one hundred and fifty miles south from the Nebraska line, fifty miles north of the Oklahoma line, and one hundred miles from Colorado on the west. As the state is just four hundred miles long and two hundred wide, it follows that Dodge City is located in the direct center of the southwestern quarter, or upon the exact corner of the southwestern sixteenth portion of Kansas. By rail it is three hundred and sixty-three miles from Kansas City, Missouri, toward the west. Dodge City was laid out in July, 1872, under the supervision of Mr. A. A. Robinson, chief engineer of the Atchison, Topeka & Santa Fe Railroad, and, for many years afterwards, general manager of that road, and a more pleasant gentleman I never met. The town company consisted of Colonel Richard I. Dodge, commander of the post at Fort Dodge, and several of the officers under him. R. M. Wright was elected president of the town company, and Major E. B. Kirk, quartermaster at Fort Dodge, was made secretary and treasurer. Dodge City, was located five miles west of Fort Dodge, on the north bank of the Arkansas river. The Atchison, Topeka & Santa Fe railroad reached Dodge City in the early port of September the same year, and the town was practically the terminus of the road for the next few months, when it reached out to Sargent, on the state line. Meanwhile, what a tremendous business was done in Dodge City! For months and months there was no time when one could get through the place on account of the blocking of the streets by hundreds of wagons—freighters, hunters and government teams. Almost any time during the day, there were about a hundred wagons on the streets, and dozens and dozens of camps all around the town, in every direction. Hay was worth from fifty to one hundred dollars per ton, and hard to get at any price. We were entirely without law or order, and our nearest point of justice was Hays City, ninety-five miles northeast of Dodge City. Here we had to go to settle our differences, but, take it from me, most of those differences were settled by rifle or six-shooter on the spot.

Hays City was also the point from which the west and southwest obtained all supplies until the Atchison, Topeka & Santa Fe railroad reached Dodge. All the freighters, buffalo hunters and wild and wooly men for hundreds of miles gathered there. It was a second Dodge City, on a smaller scale. Getting drunk and riding up and down the sidewalks as fast as a horse could go, firing a six-shooter and whooping like a wild Indian, were favorite pastimes, exciting, innocent and amusing. At this place lived a witty Irishman, a justice of the peace, by the name of Joyce. One day, near Hays City, two section-hands (both Irish) got into an altercation. One came at the other with a spike hammer. The other struck him over the head with a shovel, fracturing his skull and instantly killing him. There was no one present. The man who did the deed came in, gave himself up, told a reasonable story, and was very penitent. Citizens went out and investigated and concluded it was in self-defence. When the Irishman was put on trial, Justice Joyce asked the prisoner the usual question, "Are you guilty or not guilty?" "Guilty, your honor," replied the prisoner. "Shut up your darned mouth," said Joyce; "I discharge you for want of evidence." Many couples did Justice Joyce make man and wife, and several did he divorce. He went on the principle that one who had the power to make had also the power to unmake. Many acts did he perform that, although not legal, were witty, and so

nany snarls were made in consequence that, after the
ountry became civilized, the legislature was asked for
elief, and a bill was passed legalizing Justice Joyce's
.cts.

Such is a sample of early day justice, and a glance at
ither phases of life on the plains, in early days, will make
lear the conditions that made possible a town like
)odge City. During the '50's overland travel had become
stablished, and communication between the Missouri
·iver and Santa Fe, New Mexico, and Denver, Colorado,
vas regularly kept up, in the face of many dangers and
lifficulties. I made my first overland trip with oxen in
he year 1859, reaching the town of Denver in May.
Three times after that I crossed the plains by wagon
ind twice by coach. My second trip was made in war
.imes, in the spring of 1863, when guerrilla warfare was
·ife in Kansas. I witnessed some evidences of the
guerrillas in the work of Jim and Bill Anderson, hard
characters from Missouri who, at the commencement
)f the war, had taken to the brush. It happened like
his:

Traveling along I noticed that the country was dotted
vith bare chimneys and blackened ruins of houses along
he old Santa Fe trail, from a few miles west of Westport
o Council Grove. The day we reached Council Grove,
.wo men rode in on fine horses and, dismounting, one
)f them said: "I expect you know who we are, but I am
suffering the torments of hell from the toothache, and if
γου will allow me to get relief we will not disturb your
:own; but if we are molested, I have a body of men near
1ere who will burn your town." These men, I learned
ifterwards, were Bill Anderson and Up. Hays. A friend
by the name of Chatfield with his family, and I with my
family, were traveling together. We drove about ten
miles from Council Grove that day, and camped with an
ox train going to Santa Fe. Chatfield and I had a very

large tent between us. That night, about midnight, during a heavy rainstorm, these two men with about fifty others rode up and dismounted, and, as many of them as could enter our tent, crowded in and asked for water. We happened to have a large keg full. After they drank, they saw that our wives as well as ourselves were much frightened, and they said: "Ladies, you need not be frightened; we are not making war on women and children, but on 'blue coats.'" When we reached Diamond Springs we saw what their purpose was. They had murdered the people and burned their houses. The place, indeed, presented a look of desolation and destruction. Not a living thing could be seen about the premises and we were too scared to make an investigation. We learned afterward it was an old grudge they had against these people.

Various government posts were established along the trails for the protection of travelers and settlers, and the quelling of numerous Indian outbreaks. Fort Aubrey, Bent's Fort, and Fort Atkinson, were among the earlier posts, and Fort Larned, Fort Supply, Fort Lyon, and Fort Dodge were familiar points to the inhabitants of the plains before the establishment of Dodge City. Fort Lyon was in eastern Colorado, and was first established in 1860, near Bent's Fort on the Arkansas, but was newly located, in 1867, at a point twenty miles distant, on the north bank of the Arkansas, two and one-half miles below the Purgatory River. Fort Larned was established October 22, 1859, for the protection of the Santa Fe trade, on the right bank of the Pawnee Fork, about seven miles above its mouth. Fort Dodge was located in 1864, and the site for its location was selected because it was where the wet route and the dry route intersected. The dry route came across the divide from Fort Larned, on the Pawnee, while the wet route came around by the river, supposed to be about fifteen miles further. The dry route was often without water the whole distance, and trains would lay up to recruit after making the passage, which caused this point on the Arkansas river to become a great camping ground. Of course the Indians found this out, to their delight, and made it one of their haunts, to pounce down upon the unwary emigrant and freighter. Numerous were their attacks in this vicinity, and many were their victims. Men were butchered in the most horrible manner, stock was killed, and women taken into captivity more terrible than death, and even trains of wagons were burned. Some of the diabolical work I have witnessed with my own eyes, and will speak of some of it later.

One day a Mexican Indian, or at least a Mexican who had been brought up by the Indians, came in and said his train had been attacked at the mouth of Mulberry creek, the stock run off, and every one killed but him. This was the first outbreak that spring. We afterward learned that this Mexican had been taken in his youth and adopted by the Indians, and had participated in killing his brothers. In fact, he had been sent to the train to tell them that the Indians were friendly. They captured the train and murdered every one in it, without giving them the ghost of a show. The Mexican was then sent to Fort Dodge to spy and find out what was going on there, because he could speak Spanish. Major Douglas sent a detachment down, and true enough there lay the train and dead Mexicans, with the mules and harness gone. The wagons were afterward burned. The train had passed over the old Fort Bascom trail from New Mexico, a favorite route, as it was much shorter than the Santa Fe trail and avoided the mountains, but scarce of water and very dangerous. At last it became so dangerous that it had to be abandoned. The trail which came into the Arkansas four miles west of the town of Cimarron had to be abandoned for the same reason.

Many attacks were made along the route, and three trains that I know of were burned, and several had to be abandoned and stock driven into the Arkansas river on account of the scarcity of water. The route was called the "Hornado de Muerti" (the journey of death; very significant was its name). At one time you could have followed the route, even if the wagon trail had been obliterated, by the bleaching bones. There are two places now in Grant or Stevens county, on the Dry Cimarron, known as Wagon Bed Springs and Barrel Springs. One was named because the thirsty freighters had sunk a wagon-bed in the quick-sand to get water; and in the other place because they had sunk a barrel. Sixty miles above where this route came into the Arkansas there was another called the Aubrey route, which was less dangerous because less subject to Indian attacks, and water was more plentiful. Colonel F. X. Aubrey, a famous freighter, established this route, and it became more famous on account of a large wager that he could make the distance on horseback, from Santa Fe to Independence, Missouri, in eight days. He won the wager, and had several hours to spare. Colonel Aubrey had fresh horses stationed with his trains at different places along the whole route. He afterwards made his famous trip down through the wilds of Arizona and California, accompanied by a single Indian, and came back to Santa Fe, after a six months' journey, with marvelous stories of the rich finds he had made. He had the proof with him in the shape of quartz and nuggets. When some gentleman questioned his veracity, immediately a duel was fought, in which the Colonel was killed. No money, bribe, threats or coaxing could induce that Indian to go back and show where these riches lay. He said: "No, I have had enough. Nothing can tempt me again to undergo the hardships I have endured from want of food and water and the dangers I have escaped. Death at once would be preferable."

A few miles east of where the Aubrey trail comes into the Arkansas is what is known as the ''Gold Banks.'' Old wagon bosses have told me that along in the early fifties a party of miners, returning from California richly laden, was attacked by Indians. The white men took to the bluffs and stood them off for several days and made a great fight; but after a number were killed and the others starved out for water, they buried their treasure, abandoned their pack animals, and got away in the night, and some of the party came back afterwards and recovered their buried riches. Another version of the story says that they were all killed before they reached the states. At any rate, long years ago there were many searches made, and great excitement was always going on over these bluffs. In 1859 I saw a lot of California miners prospecting in the bluffs and along the dry branches that put into the Arkansas; and I was told they got rich color in several places, but not enough to pay. In this vicinity, and east of the bluffs, is what is named Choteau's island, named after the great Indian trader of St. Louis, the father of all the Choteaus. Here he made one of his largest camps and took in the rich furs, not only of the plains, but of the mountains also.

At this side of the point of Rocks, eight miles west of Dodge City, used to be the remains of an old adobe fort. Some called it Fort Mann, others Fort Atkinson. Which is correct I do not know. When I first saw it, in May, 1859, the walls were very distinct and were in a good state of preservation, excepting the roofs gone. There had been a large corral, stables, barracks for troops, and a row of buildings which I supposed were officers quarters. Who built it, or what troops had occupied it, I do not know. There were many legends connected with old Fort Mann. Some say that a large Mexican train, heavily loaded with Mexican dollars, took shelter there from the Indians, and finally lost all their cattle, and buried their money to keep it out of the hands of the Indians, and got back to Mexico as best they could. When they returned, the river had washed all their cache away, and it was never recovered; but the following is the best information I could gather, and I think it is the most plausible story: In the '50's, and a long while before, the government did its own freighting with ox teams. Many a horn have I seen branded "U. S." One of these trains was on its way back to the states, loaded with ox chains, for the simple reason that the government usually sold its wagons after they had delivered their loads of supplies, at their respective destinations, to the miners, hunters, and trappers, and turned the cattle over to the commissary for beef. This would naturally leave a large accumulation of ox chains. Now, this train loaded with chains met the heavy snowstorm in or near Fort Mann, and they cached their chains at the fort, and went in with a few light wagons, and the river washed the chains away; for the banks have washed in several hundred feet since I have known the place.

There was some inquiry made from Washington about Fort Mann, about thirty years ago, and I remember going with an escort, and, on the sloping hillside north of the fort, finding three or four graves. Of these, one was that of an officer, and the others of enlisted men; also two lime-kilns in excellent condition and a well-defined road leading to Sawlog. In fact, the road was as large as the Santa Fe trail, showing that they must have hauled considerable wood over it. This leads me to believe that the fort had been occupied by a large garrison.

Another story, and a strange one, of very early times deals with the ever interesting subject of buried treasure, hinting of the possibility of companies being organized to dig for such treasure, supposed to have been concealed near Dodge City. About four miles west of Dodge, perhaps many of our readers have noticed a place where the earth seems to have been, a long time ago, thrown up into piles, holes dug, etc., indicating that some body of soldiers, hunters, or freighters had made breastworks to defend themselves against an enemy. We have often noticed this place and wondered if a tale of carnage could not be told, if those mounds only had mouths and voices to speak. But we leave this to be explained, as it will be, in the after part of this article, and will proceed to tell all we have learned of the story, just as it was told in the early days of Dodge.

"In the year of 1853, when this country was as wild as the plains of Africa, only traversed at intervals by tribes of Indians and bands of Mexicans, there were no railroads running west of St. Louis, and all the freight transmitted by government was carried over this country by large freighting trains, such as now run between here and Camp Supply. In the summer of that year, a freighting train consisting of eighty-two men with one hundred and twenty wagons started from Mexico, across these plains, for Independence, Missouri, to purchase goods. The whole outfit was in charge of an old Mexican freighter named Jesus M. Martinez, whom many of the old plainsmen of thirty years ago will remember. They traveled along what is now known as the old Santa Fe trail and every night corralled their wagons and kept guards posted to give the alarm if danger should approach in the way of Indians, bandits, or prairie fires. One evening they halted about sundown, formed the usual corral, and prepared to rest for the night. Little did they think what that night had in store for them. They had observed Indians during the day, but the sight of these children of the plains was no source of annoyance to them, as they had never been troubled and had seen no hostile manifestations. Some time during the night the men who were on watch observed objects not far from camp, the dogs commenced making a fuss, and presently the watchmen became suspicious and aroused old man

Martinez. Martinez, being an old plainsman and understanding the tactics of the Indians, after closely observing through the darkness, came to the opinion that Indians were lurking around, and that their intentions were not good. He awoke some of his men and they held a kind of consultation as to the best course to pursue, and finally decided to prepare for the worst. They immediately commenced digging trenches and preparing for defense. The objects around them during all this time seemed to grow more numerous every moment, and finally could be seen on all sides. The Mexicans waited in suspense, having intrenched themselves as well as possible in ditches and behind piles of dirt. Finally, with yells and shouts, as is always their custom, the Indians made a dash upon the camp from all sides. The Mexicans received them like true martyrs, and being well fortified had every advantage. Their eighty-two guns poured fatal balls into the yelling enemy at every report. The Indians finally fell back and the Mexicans then hoped for deliverance, but it was like hoping against fate. The next day the attack was renewed at intervals, and at each attack the Mexicans fought like demons. For five days the siege continued, a few of the Mexicans being killed, in the meantime, and many Indians. During the time the Mexicans had scarcely slept, but what struck terror to their hearts was the consciousness that their ammunition was nearly gone. On the sixth night the Indians made a more desperate attack than before. They seemed crazed for blood and vengeance for the chiefs they had already lost. As long as their ammunition lasted the Mexicans continued their stern resistance, but powder and lead was not like the widow's oil. It steadily decreased until none was left. Then their guns were still, and they were swallowed up like Pharaoh's hosts in the Red Sea, by wild Cheyennes, Arrapahoes and Kiowas, who made deathly havoc with the little handful of brave Mexicans. We need not dwell upon this scene

— 18 —

of butchery, and it is only necessary to relate that but one man is known to have escaped in the darkness, and that man, somewhat strange to note, was old Jesus M. Martinez. How he managed to secrete himself we can hardly divine, others might have been carried away and held captive until death, but he alone never told the story to the pale-face. The Indians pillaged the train of all the flour, bacon, etc., took the stock, set fire to some of the wagons, and then, Indianlike, immediately left the field of carnage. Old Martinez remained in his hiding place until morning and until the Indians were miles away, then creeping out he surveyed the remains of what a few days ago was his jolly, jovial companions. He was alone with the dead.

"As is nearly always the case with persons when no eye is near, he thought of the valuables, and knowing that quite an amount of silver was stored in one of the wagons, he searched and found a portion of it. As near as he remembered, when he related this occurrence to his son, he found twenty-one small bags, each one containing one thousand silver Mexican dollars. These bags he carried some distance from the camp, we cannot learn exactly how far, or which way, and buried them. He then started out and made his way on foot back to his old home in Mexico, where, it seems, he died soon afterwards. But before he died he told his son what we have related above, and advised him to hunt this treasure. What goes to corroborate this story was the evidence of Dr. Wilber of Kansas City, who sold goods to these Mexicans and knew of their having a considerable quantity of silver in their possession.

"Pursuant to his father's advice young Martinez came up to this country some years after the death of his father for the purpose of following his instructions. There are two men now living in this city to whom he revealed the secret, one of whom assisted him in searching for the buried treasure. From the directions marked out by old Martinez they found the spot where the massacre took place, about four miles west of Dodge City—the spot described above, where the pits and dirt piles are still plainly visible. For days and even weeks young Martinez searched the ground in that vicinity using a sharpened wire, which he drove into the ground wherever he supposed the treasure might lie concealed. But he was not successful, and not being of a persevering nature abandoned the search and remained around Fort Dodge for some time, when he fell into the habit and became a hard drinker. He finally returned to Mexico and has not been back here since, that we are aware of. After he left, one of the men to whom he had revealed the secret (and this man now lives in this city) made a. partial search for the treasure. He hired men and after swearing them to secrecy as to what they were searching for, set them to digging ditches. They found nothing and abandoned the work.''

This story, as told above, is an historical fact, and portions of it have been heretofore published. We can give names of men who know more about it than we do, but by request we do not publish them. This treasure will probably be found some day, and probably will lie buried forever, and never see the light. No eye but the Omnipotent's can tell the exact spot where it lies. As we said above, it is rumored that parties are preparing to institute a search. They may find it and they may not. We hope they will as it is of no benefit to mankind where it is. It certainly exists.

Such were some of the traces which the feet of the white man left behind in their first passing over the plains of the southwest. One almost lost sight of the natural features and attractions of the region, in viewing these intensely interesting evidences of the beginnings of the conquest of the wilds by civilization. Yet the natural beauties and attractions were there in superlative degree.

An old darkey, living in the Arkansas valley, thus explains how it happened that the territory of Kansas exists. On being asked by a land looker what he thought of the country, he said:

"Well, sah, when the good Lord made dis whole world, He found out that He had made a mistake, dat He had not made any garden, so He jest went to work and made Hisself a garden, and we call it Kansas."

And a natural garden, indeed, in many respects, was the Arkansas valley in southwestern Kansas. Pages could be filled with descriptions of its beauties without exhausting the subject. But no less than the charms and interest of its physical features, were the charms and interest of other of its natural attributes, atmospheric peculiarities, for instance, which, as in the blizzard, arose at times to the height of the grand and terrible. Other phases of atmospheric conditions, however, peculiar to the great plains in pioneer days, were very beautiful, and perhaps the best example of such was the mirage.

Mirage, Webster describes as an "optical illusion, arising from an unequal refraction in the lower strata of the atmosphere, and causing remote objects to be seen double, as if reflected in a mirror, or to appear as if suspended in the air. It is frequently seen in deserts, presenting the appearance of water."

If I were gifted with descriptive powers, what wonderful scenes could I relate of the mirage on the plains of Kansas. What grand cities towering to the skies have I seen, with their palaces and cathedrals and domed churches, with tall towers and spires reaching almost up to the clouds, with the rising sun glistening upon them until they looked like cities of gold, their streets paved with sapphire and emeralds, and all surrounded by magnificent walls, soldiers marching, with burnished spears and armor! There would arise at times over all a faint ethereal golden mist, as if from a smooth sea, shining upon the towers and palaces with a brilliancy so great as to dazzle the eyes—a more gorgeous picture than could be painted by any artist of the present, or by any of the old masters. The picture as has presented itself to me I still retain in good recollection, in its indescribable magnificence. At other times the scenes would change entirely, and, instead of great cities there would be mountains, rivers, seas, lakes, and ships, or soldiers and armies, engaged in actual conflict. So real have such sights appeared to me on the plains that I could not help but believe they were scenes from real life, being enacted in some other part of the world, and caught up by the rays of the sun and reflected to my neighborhood, or perhaps that some electrical power had reproduced the exact picture for me.

How many poor creatures has the mirage deceived by its images of water. At times one unacquainted with its varied whims would be persuaded that it really was water, and would leave the well-beaten track to follow this optical illusion, only to wander farther from water and succor, until he dropped down from thirst and exhaustion, never to rise again, never again to be heard of by his friends, his bleaching bones to be picked by the coyote, unburied and forgotten. On other occasions you would see immense towering forests, with every variety of trees and shrubbery. In some places it would be so dark and lowering, even in the daylight, as to appear dangerous, though one could not help admiring its gloomy grandeur. Then there would be fair spots of picturesque beauty, with grottoes and moonlit avenues, inviting you to promenade, where one seemed to hear the stroke of the barge's oars on lake and river, and the play of the fountains, and the twitter of the birds.

With the trail of the plow, followed by immigration and civilization, the wonderful mirage is a thing of the past. It is only now and then that one gets a glimpse of its beauties; its scenes of magnificence, far beyond any powers of description, I will never see again.

CHAPTER II

Travel on Old Trails

On a beautiful spring morning in early May, 1859, I was awakened at the break of day—having gone into camp the preceding evening after dusk—by the singing of birds and lowing of cattle, and last, but not least, the harsh and discordant voice of the wagon boss—of whom I stood in wholesome fear—calling, "Roll out! roll out!" to the men as the cattle were driven into the corral to yoke up and get started. Indeed all nature seemed alive and pouring out the sweetest notes on that lovely morning when I first saw the great Pawnee Rock.

It was, indeed, a curious freak of nature, rising abruptly out of a fertile stretch of bottom land several miles wide, thee or four miles north of the Arkansas river, which flowed sluggishly along its way, its muddy current on its usual spring rise caused by the melting of snow in the mountains. The time of the year, the ideal weather, and the lovely greensward, interspersed with the most beautiful variegated wild flowers, combined to make one of the most beautiful sights I ever witnessed. The scene impressed itself not only upon me, but the other drivers—"Bull whackers," we were called—shared my admiration, and through our united petition to the wagon boss, the train was halted long enough to allow our going to the Rock, from the summit of which I obtained the grand view that so impressed me. It seemed as if I could never tire of gazing on the wonderful panorama that spread before me.

The road, if recollection serves me right, ran only a few hundred feet south of the base of the Rock, parallel to its face. The Rock faced the south, rearing itself abruptly, and presenting almost a perpendicular front with a comparatively smooth surface, having thousands of names inscribed on its face, and also on a great many slabs that had, in the process of time and exposure to the elements, been detached from its top and sides and lay flat at its base. Most of the names were those of "Forty-niners" who had taken that route in their mad rush for the gold fields of California during that memorable year. Among the names cut in the Rock were those of officers and enlisted men in the United States army as well as a number of famous men and frontiersmen.

There were also a great many Indian paintings, or pictographs, and hieroglyphics done by the red man— crude and laughable, and some of them extraordinarily funny, but I have been told since there was a great deal of significance attached to these paintings, some of them portraying important tribal history, others representing brave and heroic deeds, performed by members of the tribes.

Of course, there were a great many stories told of the Rock, romances the most of them, I suppose.

An old plainsman and mountaineer told me that the name "Pawnee Rock" was taken from a great fight lasting several days, between the Pawnees and their life-long enemies, the Plains Indians composed of a mixed band of Cheyennes, Arapahoes, Kiowas, Commanches, and a few Sioux, all pitted against the Pawnees, and numbering more than ten to one. What a desperate battle it was!

The Pawnees had come over to the Arkansas on their usual buffalo hunt, and, incidentally, to steal horses from their enemies, the Plains Indians. They crossed the river and proceeded south, penetrating deep into the enemy's country, where a big herd of ponies grazed and lived in supposed security. The Pawnees reached the herd without arousing the least suspicion of the owners that the animals were in danger. Surrounding and cutting out what they wanted, they started on the return trip, greatly elated over their easy success, and reached the Arkansas river without meeting with the slightest resistance, but found the river very high and out of its banks. The ponies refused to take the river, which delayed them considerably. In the meantime, the band of Indians, composed of Cheyennes, Araphaoes, Kiowas, Comanches, and a few Sioux, was on a buffalo hunt, too, when some of them discovered the trail of the Pawnees and quickly notified the others. They all gave chase, overtaking the Pawnees just as they were crossing the Arkansas. The Pawnees might still have gotten away had they abandoned the stolen horses; but this they refused to do until it was too late.

Finally, pressed on all sides by overwhelming odds, they were glad to retreat to the rock where they made a final stand, fortifying themselves as best they could by erecting mounds of loose rock, and loading and firing from behind this crude shelter with such daring and bravery that their enemies were kept at bay. They were sorely in need of water. Of meat they had plenty, as they lived upon the flesh of their dead horses. At night, some of them usually crept through the line of sentinels that guarded them and made their way to the river, filling canteens of tanned hide or skins and working their way back to their beseiged friends.

The fight was kept up for three days and nights, the Cheyennes and allies making frequent charges during the day, but always being compelled to fall back with severe loss, until they had almost annihilated the little band of Pawnees. On the fourth night they were reduced to three or four men. Knowing their desperate situation and realizing that there was no chance for any of them to escape, they determined to sell their lives as dearly as possible. Every man stripped stark naked, and, watching his opportunity, when the guards were less vigilant than usual, crept stealtthily toward the foes. Having approached as near as they could without detection, the Pawnees burst upon the enemy with all the fury of desperate men going to their death, and, with blood-curdling yells, fought as never men fought before. One of them was armed with a long spear and knife only. (These spears were used in killing buffaloes). Many a man went down before the weapon, but, finally the Pawnee drove it so deeply into one of his victims that he could not withdraw it. Then he fell back on his butcher knife and made terrible havoc with it, until overpowered by numbers, he died a warrior's glorious death, reeking with the blood of his enemies. He certainly had sufficient revenge.

The time we camped at the foot of the Rock we did not go into camp until after nightfall. Another man and I were placed on first guard around the grazing cattle. After being out some time, we were startled by something dropping, zip! zip! into the grass around us and near us. We thought it was Indians shooting at us with arrows. There were all sorts of rumors of attacks from Indians, and this certainly was a great Indian camping ground and country, so we were greatly alarmed and continually on the lookout, expecting at any time to be attacked. We finally concluded to go to camp and notify the wagon boss. He came back with us and for a long time believed that Indians were shooting at us, but the question was, where were they concealed? The mystery was finally solved. The peculiar sound was made by the little birds called sky-larks, flying up and alighting, striking the earth with such force that the noise seemed like that produced by the fall of an arrow or of a stone. The skylarks and meadow larks sang at all hours of the night on the plains.

The great Pawnee Rock has found its way into the history of the west. Around its rugged base was many a desperate battle fought and won; and many a mystic rite, performed within its shadow, has stamped upon the grand old mass the wierd and tragic nature of the children of the plains.

It was in the immediate vicinity of the rock that I inadvertently started one of the most disastrous stampedes in the history of the plains.

In the fall of 1862 I was going back east with one of Major Russell's and Waddell's large ox teams. I think we had thirty or forty wagons, with six yoke of oxen to the wagon. Our wagons were strung five or six together and one team of six yoke cattle attached to each string. It was the latter part of November, and we were traveling along the Arkansas river bottom about ten miles west of where Great Bend is now located. It was a very hot afternoon, more like summer than winter—one of those warm spells that we frequently have in the late fall on the plains. I was driving the *cavayado* (cave-yard—that is, the loose cattle). The Mexicans always drove their *cavayado* in front of their trains, while the Americans invariably drove theirs behind. I had on a heavy linsey-woolsey coat, manufactured from the loom in Missouri, lined with yellow stuff, and the sleeves lined with red; and, as I said, it was very warm; so I pulled off my jacket, or coat, and in pulling it off turned it inside out. We had an old ox named Dan, a big, old fellow with rather large horns, and so gentle we used him as a horse in crossing streams, when the boys often mounted him and rode across. Dan was always lagging behind, and this day more than usual, on account of the heat. The idea struck me to make him carry the coat. I caught him and by dint of a little stretching placed the sleeves over his horns and let the coat flap down in front.

I hardly realized what I had done until I took a front view of him. He presented a ludicrous appearance, with his great horns covered with red and the yellow coat flapping down over his face. He trudged along unconscious of the appearance he presented. I hurried him along by repeated punches with my *carajo* pole, for in dressing him up he had gotten behind. I could not but laugh at the ludicrous sight, but my laughter was soon turned to regret, for no sooner did old Dan make his appearance among the other cattle than a young steer bawled out in the steer language, as plain as good English, 'Great Scott! what monstrosity is this coming among us to destroy us?" and with one long, loud, beseeching bawl, put all the distance possible between himself and the terror behind him. All his brothers followed his example, each one seeing how much louder he could bawl than his neighbor, and each one trying to outrun the rest. I thought to myself, "Great guns! what have I done now!" I quickly and quietly stepped up to old Dan, fearing that he too might get away, and with the evidence of my guilt, took from his horns and head what had created one of the greatest stampedes ever seen on the plains, and placed it on my back where it belonged. In the meantime the loose cattle had caught up with the wagons, and those attached to the vehicles took fright and tried to keep up with the *cavayado*. In spite of all the drivers could do, they lost control of them, and away they went, making a thundering noise. One could see nothing but a big cloud of dust. The ground seemed to tremble.

Nothing was left but Dan and me after the dust subsided, and I poked him along with my *carajo* pole as fast as possible, for I was anxious to find out what damage was done. We traveled miles and miles, and it seemed hours and hours, at last espying the wagon boss still riding like mad. When he came up he said: "What caused the stampede of the *cavayado?*" I replied that I could not tell, unless it was a wolf that ran across the road in front of the cattle, when they took fright and away they went, all except old Dan, and I held him, thinking I would save all I could out of the wreck. There stood old Dan, a mute witness to my lies. Indeed, I thought at times he gave me a sly wink, as much as to say: "You lie out of it well, but I am ashamed of you." I thought that God was merciful in not giving this dumb animal speech, for if He had they certainly would have hung me. As it was, the wagon boss remarked: "I know it was the cussed wolves, because I saw several this afternoon, while riding in front of the train. Well," he continued, "that wolf didn't do a thing but wreck six or eight wagons in Walnut creek, and from there on for the next five miles, ten or twelve more; and most of them will never see the states again, they are so completeely broken up. Besides, one man's leg is broken and another's arm, and a lot of the men are bruised up. Three steers have their legs broken, and the front cattle were fifteen miles from where we are now, when I overtook them."

I have seen many stampedes since, but never anything to equal that. I have seen a great train of wagons heavily loaded, struggling along, drivers pounding and swearing to get the cattle out of a snail's pace, and one would think the train too heavily loaded, it seemed such a strain on the cattle to draw it, when a runaway horse or something out of the usual would come up suddenly behind them, and the frightened cattle in the yoke would set up a bawl and start to run, and they would pick up those heavily loaded wagons and set off with them at a pace that was astonisoing, running for miles and overturning the wagons. The boss in front, where he was always supposed to be, would give the order to roughlock both wheels, which would probably be done to a few of the front wagons. Even these doubly locked wagons would be hurled along for a mile or two before the cattle's strength was exhausted, and apparently the whole earth would shake in their vicinity.

My experience with old Dan and the yellow-lined coat was laughable, with but a touch of the tragic at its

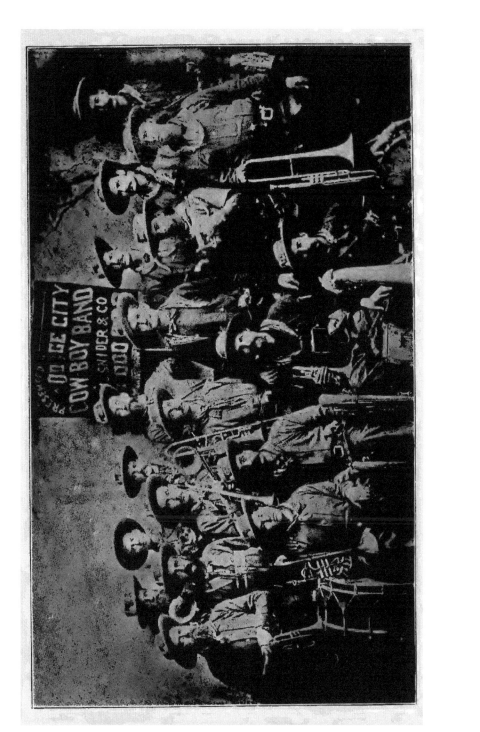

se, but all the travel along the Santa Fe trail and
ge part of it was tragedy from beginning to end,
adred highways, in those old days, had not so happy a
ae, and much of it had a much more tragic ending. A
lightened by any touch of humor. Indeed, had all the
od of man and beast, that was shed beside them, been
ned, unlessened, into the trails, their course across
a plains would have been marked in unbroken crimson,
m Westport to Santa Fe, and from Leavenworth to
nver. Moreover, the tragedy was greater than will
er be known, for mute evidences of mysterious blooded were not wanting along the old trails. Many times,
the early days of Fort Dodge, I have picked up little
nches of cattle wandering on the plains aimlessly that
d been run off by the Indians, as well as horses and
lles, and turned them over to some Mexican train from
uch they had been stampeded. Once I found a buggy
smashed to pieces in the timbered breaks of Duck
ek, but we could never discover whom the unfortunate
upants had been. They had been killed and dumped
t, no doubt, miles from where the vehicle was wrecked.
e day I found one of the most beautiful horses I ever
v, with a fine saddle on his back. The saddle was
npletely saturated with blood.

In 1863, the fall before Fort Dodge was established,
the bluffs where you first get a sight of the Arkansas
the dry route from Fort Larned, a little Mexican train
ten or twelve wagons loaded with corn, groceries and
er goods, many sacks of flour, together with a feather-
d or two, camped one day to get dinner. Soon after
y had corralled a band of Indians rode up, with their
stomary, "How-how, heap Hungry," and wanted some
huck-a-way." After gorging themselves, and had sat
und the small fire of buffalo chips smoking, they
se, shook hands all around, mounted their ponies, and,
they arrived at the rear of the corral, suddenly turned
d killed every one of the Mexicans, excepting the day

— 31 —

herder, who had started off in advance to his animals that were quietly grazing in the grassy bottoms. The moment he heard the firing he lit out mighty lively for Fort Lyon, closely followed by the red devils, but he managed to escape; the only one left to tell the horrid tale.

We camped with the mail en route several times that winter, and fed our mules on corn, and ourselves ate of the canned goods that were scattered all over the trail. It was certainly a curious spectacle, and could be seen for quite a distance, where the savages had cut open feather beds and scattered their contents around, which had caught in the weeds and grass of the prairie. They also emptied many sacks of flour to get the sacks for breech-clouts. In nearly the same spot, and in the vicinity, have I many times helped bury the mutilated and scalped remains of men who had been ruthlessly murdered there by the Indians.

For many years, and several years before Dodge City was started, Barlow, Sanderson & Company ran a tri-weekly stage line through Fort Dodge, over the old Santa Fe trail. They used a large Concord coach, containing three inside seats, capable of holding nine persons comfortably. Then there was a driver's box where three more could be comfortably seated, besides an upper deck where more passengers and baggage could be stowed away; and also what was called a front and hind boot, where still more trunks and baggage could be carried, with a large leather apron strapped down over them, to hold things in place and keep out the weather. There were five mules attached to the coach, two mules on the wheel and three on the lead, and relays were provided from thirty to fifty miles apart, except from Fort Larned to Fort Lyon which were two hundred and forty miles apart. In addition to the stage, a light wagon was taken along to carry grub and bedding. It was seven hundred miles from Kansas City to Santa Fe, and the coach made it is seven days.

One time, before Fort Dodge was established, we had to abandon a big Concord coach, at the foot of Nine-mile Ridge, on account of the muddy condition of the trail, and went on to the stage station with a light spring wagon. On the way we met a band of friendly Indians who were going to Fort Larned, and we told them to haul the coach in. Of course they didn't follow the trail, but struck across the country on to Pawnee Fork. After a long time had elapsed, Little Raven, the chief, rode into the fort and told us he had left the coach twenty miles up the creek, and blessed if he could get it any farther, as he had pulled the tails out of nearly every one of his herd of ponies to get it that far. You see their method of hauling the coach was by tying it to the tails of their ponies.

The summer of 1866, I was closing up my business at Fort Aubrey, preparatory to moving to Fort Dodge, where I had a contract to fill for wood, with the army quartermaster at that post. For a few years previous to this, I had been ranching at the abandoned government post of Fort Aubrey (which I had strongly fortified against the Indians), and erecting stage stations every thirty-five or forty miles, wherever a suitable location could be found, about that distance apart, for the overland stage line of Barlow, Sanderson & Company. This line started from Kansas City, Missouri, but branched off at Bent's old fort, the main line going to Santa Fe, New Mexico, and the branch to Denver, Colorado. After crossing the Arkansas river, the former wended its way southwest, over the Raton mountains, while the branch, following up the Arkansas to Pueblo, and from thence, the Fountain Gulch to Colorado Springs, crossed over the divide to Denver.

I was also furnishing these small stations with hay, cut in the river bottoms near each station, and I kept a small mule train constantly on the road, hauling grain from the Missouri river (we simply called it "the River" those days, every one knowing, as a matter of course, that we meant the Missouri) to keep the stations supplied with feed for the stage stock. This is the way we built these stations. We first hunted a steep bank facing the south and the river—as the Arkansas ran east and west—and dug straight into this bank a suitable distance, wide enough to suit our convenience, and ten or twelve feet deep at the deepest place, with a gradual slope to the south of seven or eight feet. Now this formed three sides of an excavation, you understand, and only left the south opening exposed. This we built up with sod or adobes. The top we covered with poles laid across, and on the poles we placed hay, covering the whole business with dirt, and sloping it down with the natural fall of the ground.

I had hard work to get men to keep these stations, as it was dangerous as well as lonely work. Indians were bad—not in regular open warfare, but occasionally murdering small parties, and we had to keep constantly on the lookout for them. One of the stations about twenty-five miles west of Aubrey, was called Pretty Encampment. After much persuasion, I got a Dutchman by the name of Fred to keep this station. Fred was a big, burly devil, strong as an ox, but a big coward. He continually sent me word, by drivers, that he was going to quit, and, in consequence I had to ride up twenty-five miles every few days, to brag on him and encourage him to stay. Well, the Indians had lately been committing little devilments, and one morning I met Fred, a half-mile from the station, a horrible looking sight, blood all over him, his dirty shirt bloody and torn, and a big, sharp butcher-knife in his hand. He was terribly excited and almost raving, going on at a terrible rate, in broken English and

Dutch, flourishing his bloody knife and saying, "G— d— him, the son of a b—; I killed him—I cut his throat and his guts out!" I was sure he had killed an Indian. I said, "Fred, you have raised the devil. This will bring on an Indian war. Don't you know it is against orders from headquarters and the commander of the fort to kill an Indian or shoot at him first, under any circumstances? (And so it was, a standing order). Let's go see about it."

We went up, and the house looked like a tornado had struck it. The roof was torn partly off, the room covered with blood, the bed broken down, the old furniture smashed, and everything in disorder, while in the midst of all this lay a big dead bull buffalo. You see, there was some hay sticking up from the covering of the roof, and some time before day, an old bull had crept down on this roof after the hay, and had broken through, one foot first. It struck Fred, who was soundly sleeping, and, with the noise and dirt falling upon him, suddenly awakened him. He grabbed the foot and leg and, feeling the hair on it, it scared him to death, and being a powerful man, he held on to the leg and foot, like grim death to a nigger's heel, thinking the devil had got him. Then they fought and struggled in the dark, until, at last, the buffalo fell through, and still Fred did not know what it was. But his butcher-knife was under his pillow, and he grabbed it and went to cutting and slashing.

Whenever I thought of it afterwards, I had to laugh at his actions and looks when he met me. But I could get him to stay at Pretty Encampment no longer, and well he did not, for, less than a week afterwards, two drivers of teams I had just sold, for the purpose of hauling supplies to these ranches, were killed within two miles of this ranch, and the mules and harness stolen. Fortunately, Fred had not yet been replaced with another stock tender or he would have been killed.

Not among the least of the hardships and dangers incident to the early pioneer of the southwest was the

"Kansas blizzard;" like all the storms in the arid belt, a great majority of them were local, but nevertheless severe and terrible in their destructive fury. A blizzard is defined as "a fierce storm of bitter, frosty wind, with fine, blistering snow." No definition, however, save that of actual experience, can define its terrible reality. I have witnessed a change in temperature from seventy-four degrees above zero to twenty degrees below in twenty-four hours, and during this time the wind was blowing a gale, apparently from the four points of the compass. The air was so full of the fine, blistering snow and sand that one could not see ten feet in advance. Turn either way, and it is always in front. The air is full of subdued noises, like the wail of lost spirits; so all-absorbing in its intensity is this wailing, moaning, continuous noise, that one's voice cannot be heard two yards away. The historical blizzards of 1863, 1866, 1873 and 1888, were general, embracing a very large area of country. The early pioneers were, of necessity, nomadic, and were in no way prepared for these sudden changes; and hundreds have lost their lives by suffocating in blizzards when the temperature was not zero, it being a physical impossibility to breathe, the air being so full of fine, blistering snow and said.

The spirit of the blizzard, as the background to pictures of the wild west, in early days, is well brought out in Eugene Ware's vivid little poem, "The Blizzard."

"The fiddler was improvising; at times, he would cease
    to play,
Then, shutting his eyes, he sang and sang, in a wild,
    ecstatic way;
Then, ceasing his song, he whipped and whipped the
    strings with his frantic bow,
Releasing impatient music, alternately loud and low;
Then, writhing and reeling, he sang as if he were dream-
    ing aloud,

and wrapping the frenzied music around him like a
shroud;
and this is the strange refrain, which he sang in a minor
key,
No matter how long the river, the river will reach the
sea.'

It was midnight on the Cimarron, not many a year ago;
The blizzard was whirling pebbles and sand, and billows
of frozen snow:
He sat on a bale of harness, in a dugout roofed with clay;
The wolves overhead bewailed, in a dismal, protracted
way;
They peeped down the 'dobe chimney, and quarreled and
sniffed and clawed;
But the fiddler kept on with his music, as the blizzard
stalked abroad;
And, time and again, that strange refrain came forth in
a minor key,
No matter how long the river, the river will reach the
sea.'

Around him, on boxes and barrels, uncharmed by the
fiddler's tune,
The herders were drinking and betting their cartridges
on vantoon;
And, once in awhile, a player, in spirit of reckless fun,
Would join in the fiddler's music, and fire off the fiddler's
gun.
An old man sat on a sack of corn and stared with a
vacant gaze;
He had lost his hopes in the Gypsum Hills, and he thought
of the olden days.
The tears fell fast when the strange refrain came forth
in a minor key,
No matter how long the river, the river will reach the
sea.'

"At morning the tempest ended, and the sun came back
    once more;
The old, old man of the Gypsum Hills had gone to the
    smoky shore;
They chopped him a grave in the frozen ground where the
    Morning sunlight fell;
With a restful look he held in his hand an invisile
    asphodel;
They filled up the grave, and each herder said, 'Good-by
    till the judgment day.'
But the fiddler stayed, and he sang and played, as the
    herders walked away—
A requiem in a lonesome land, in a mournful minor key—
'No matter how long the river, the river will reach the
    sea.'"

As an illustration of the terrible nature of a Kansas
blizzard in early times, another poem may be quoted,
which describes a real experience, in the neighborhood
of Dodge City, by some cowboys on the trail. This poem
is written by Henry C. Fellow, the cowboy poet of
Oklahoma, and is used in this work by special permission
of the author.

PASSING OF THE WRANGLER.

"Wrangle up yer broncks, Bill,
    Let us hit the trail;
Cinch 'em up a knot er two,
    'Fore there comes a gale.

"Fill the wagon full o' chuck,
    'Fore we cut adrift;
Fer we'll have a time, Bill
    With this winter shift.

"My bones they feel a blizzard
    A hatchin' in the west,
An' I must load my gizzard
    With some pizen-piker's best.

TRAIL HERD IN SOUTHWEST KANSAS, JUST STARTING FROM THEIR NOON GROUNDS

"Sam, git yer chips together,
 An' stack 'em in a box;
An' gether up the tether,
 Ropes, shirts, an' dirty socks,

"An' lash 'em to the cayuse,
 An' strap 'em tight an' strong;
Fer we given to ha'f t' ride, Sam,
 Kase 'tseems they's sumthin' wrong.

"Pards, see the clouds a shiftin';
 They's given to turn a trick,
An' make us go a driftin',
 Afore we reach the crick.

"It's a hundred miles, ye know, boys,
 To reach the O X camp,
An' we'll ha'f to keep a rollin'
 Er we'll ketch a frosty cramp.

"So skin the mules a plenty,
 With yer double triggered crack;
An' keep the broncks a goin',
 Jist so ye know the track."

So with a whoop an' holler,
 The rounders, full o' pluck,
An' tanked up to the collar—
 With their wagon load o' chuck,

They left the Dodge behind 'em,
 An' started fer the South,
With the wind a blowin'
 A peck o' dirt a mouth.

They skase could see the other
 Feller, lopin' through the cloud;
Er hear nothin' but the thunder,
 An' the flappin' o' their shroud.

Tumble weeds a rollin',
 With a forty minit clip,
An' the clouds a pilin'
 Up like a phantom ship.

With 'er double triggered action,
  The wind she turned her tail,
An' kicked out all the suction
  Fer the souther's gale.

She started into rainin',
  An' follered with a sleet;
An' kept 'er speed a gainin',
  A throwin' down 'er sheet;

Till everything wuz covered,
  A frozen glare o' ice;
Yet still she closter hovered,
  An' pinched us like a vise.

That blizzard came a peltin'
  With 'er frozen shot;
An' sich snow a driftin',
  I never have forgot!

We couldn't see a nothin',
  Ner hear a rounder croak;
But the gurgle o' the pizen
  A puttin' us to soak.

We kept the broncks a movin',
  Frum bein' froze to death;
While waitin' fer the mornin'
  To thaw us with his breath.

But when the snowy mornin'
  Had come in with his smile,
He'd left a ghastly warnin'
  Fer many and many a mile.

A thousand head of cattle,
  Caught driftin' with the storm,
Were frozen, while a millin',
  A tryin' to keep warm.

Poor Sammy, with the wagon,
  Wuz found a mile alone;
Wuz stuck adrift, an' frozen,
  An' harder'n a stone.

Ol' Bill, he froze his fingers,
　　An' blistered up his face,
Tryin' to pitch his ringers,
　　An' a fightin' fer the ace.

I fell into a canyon,
　　With my cayuse an' my traps,
An' shuffled fer the joker,
　　With the cinchin' straps.

I warmed myself a plenty
　　A keepin' up the fight,
A skinnin' ol' McGinty,
　　Till a comin' of' the light.

Poor Sam! he boozed a plenty,
　　To stack 'im in a heap;
An' the devil swiped his ante,
　　When he went to sleep.

So Bill an' me together,
　　Stood in silence by the wag-
On, not a knowin' whether
　　To swig another jag,

'Er cut the cussed pizen
　　That had foggled up our breath,
An' kept our spirits risin',
　　Without a fling o' death.

So me an' Bill, we tackled
　　The job without a drop,
An' in the hill we hackled
　　A grave with icy top,

An' shuffled Sammy in it,
　　An' banked 'im in with snow,
An' 'rected up a monument,
　　To let the Nesters know

We done our solemn dooty,
　　An' planted 'im in style,
With the whitest snow o' heaven
　　Heaped on 'im in a pile.

Poor Bill! he sniffed a little
  When I lifted up my hat,
An' let some weepin' splatter
  On Sammy's frozen mat.

Sam wan't no idle rustler;
  No one could ride the range
Better'n he, ner brand 'em,
  Ner dip 'em fer the mange.

His check book showed a balance,
  Fer a wrangler o' the stuff,
Fer a hilpin' o' his mither
  No one could spake enough.

His heart wuz where God put it;
  His blood was always red;
His mouth he alluz shut it,
  When troubles wuz ahead.

An' if the storm wuz ragin',
  He rode the line alone,
An' never once a stagin'
  Some other's stunt his own.

Fer his larnin' he wuz known,
  Figgered with the letter X;
Never had to once be shown;
  Wuz no mangy maverick.

Set an' count a herd o' stars,
  Driftin' frum the hand o' God;
Tell us all about the flowers
  Playin' bo-peep in the sod.

Hope the jedge will let 'im thru,
  When he rounds up at the gate;
But, ol' pard, I'm fearin', though,
  Sam'll be a little late.

Peace be then to Sammy's ashes,
  Till the round up o' the race,
When each wrangler's check book cashes
  What it's worth, an' at its face.

Speaking of blizzards, makes me think of John Riney who was one of the very first citizens to settle in Dodge City. He helped build the Santa Fe road into-Dodge, and was also the first toll-gate keeper for the only bridge over the Arkansas for miles each way; which position he held for many years and was always found strictly honest in his receipts. Before this he was a freighter and froze both of his feet in our big blizzard of 1873, which crippled him for life. He now, (1913), resides peacefully on his big alfalfa farm, a short distance west of Dodge, and has raised a large family, all of whom are much respected citizens of Dodge City.

As a closing word in this brief discussion of the blizzard in pioneer days, I will narrate one of the many experiences I have had with them. In the summer and fall of 1872 I was freighting supplies from Fort Dodge to Camp Supply, I. T. Up to the middle of December we had had no cold weather—plenty of grass all along the route. I loaded some twenty-mule wagons with corn, along about the twentieth of December, and the outfit crossed the river at Fort Dodge, and went into camp that night at Five-mile Hollow, about five miles from Fort Dodge. It had been a warm, pleasant day, and the sun disappeared in a clear sky. Along in the night the wind whipped around in the north, and a blizzard set in. By morning the draw that they were camped in was full of snow, and the air so full that one could not see from one wagon to the other. The men with the outfit were all old, experienced plainsmen, but the suddenness and severity of the storm rendered them almost helpless. They had brought along only wood enough for breakfast, and that was soon exhausted. They then tried burning corn, but with poor success. As a last resort they began burning the wagons. They used economy in their fire, but the second day saw no prospect of a letting up of the storm, in fact, it was getting worse hourly. It was then that P. G. Cook, now living at Trinidad, and another whose name escapes me, volunteered to make an effort to reach Fort Dodge, only five miles distant, for succor. They bundled up in a way that it seemed impossible for them to suffer, and, each mounting a mule, started for the fort. The first few hours, Cook has told me, they guided the mules, and then recognizing that they were lost, they gave the animals a loose rein and trusted to their instinct. This was very hard for them to do, as they were almost convinced that they were going wrong all the time, but they soon got so numbed with the cold that they lost all sense of being. They reached the fort in this condition, after being out eight hours. They each had to be thawed out of their saddles. Cook, being a very strong, vigorous man, had suffered the least, and soon was in a condition to tell of the trouble of his comrades. Major E. B. Kirk, the quartermaster at the fort, immediately detailed a relief party, and, with Cook at their head, started for the camp. The storm by this time had spent itself, and the relief party, with an ample supply of wood, reached them without great hardship, and the entire outfit, minus the three wagons which had been burned for fuel, were brought back to the fort. Cook's companion was so badly frost-bitten that amputation of one of his limbs was necessary to save his life.

In the winter of 1869 I made a contract with the settlers at Camp Supply to freight a trainload of goods from Dodge to that point. I hurriedly caught up my cattle, and picked up what drivers I could find. So little time had I to prepare, and so scarce were hands, that I was glad to get anyone that could handle a whip. Of course I had a motley crew—some good men and a few very worthless. Among the latter was one Jack Cobbin. Now Jack had been a scout during the war, down around Fort Gibson and Fort Smith, and was as great a drunkard as ever drank from a bottle. The first night out we camped at Mulberry, about fifteen miles from Dodge. A little snow had fallen, and the night herders lost about half the cattle. Of course the cattle drifted back to Dodge. Next morning I sent my extra hand and night herder back on the only two horses I had, and pulled one wing of the train ten miles on the divide half way between Mulberry and Rattlesnake creek, and went back and pulled the other wing up about nightfall. That night these cattle got away, but I found them next day and drove them over on a little spring creek three miles from the main road, where there was plenty of water, grass and shelter, and placed a guard with them.

I will here have to anticipate a bit. I was loaded with several wagons of liquor. Jack Cobbin had been drunk ever since we had left Dodge, and I had broken every pipe-stem, quill or straw I could find, as this was the only means he could use to get the liquor out of the barrels, after drilling a hole in the top, so I concluded that I would take him along that night to relieve the guard and keep him sober. About two hours before sundown he and I started out to the cattle. The Indians were at war and killing everybody; so I supplied each man with a dozen rounds of cartridges, in case of a sudden attack, to be used until our ammunition could be got out of the mess wagon, with strict orders not to fire a gun, under any circumstances, unless at an Indian. Well, we had gone about two miles in the direction of the cattle when Jack began to lag behind, and pretty soon a jackrabbit jumped up and Cobbin blazed away at it. I went back to chide him, when I found he had something slushing in the coffee pot he was carrying with his blankets. I asked him what it was, and he said water. I said: "Throw it out; you are a bright one to carry water to a creek." He said: "Maybe we won't find any creek." I told him that if we did not find the creek we would not find the cattle. So he went on with the coffee pot slushing, slushing, and I cursing him, and ordering him to throw it out. At last we reached the creek and relieved the other boys. I went at once to round up the cattle.

When I got back it was late and very dark and the fire nearly out. Jack was sound asleep. I built up a big fire and sat down to enjoy it. After sitting some time I awakened Jack, but he refused to go out to the cattle. I felt very uneasy and went again myself. I found that the cattle had stopped grazing and wanted to ramble. I stayed with them several hours, until it was almost impossible to hold them alone, and then went back after Jack, but found him too drunk to be of any assistance. Then I found out what was in the coffee pot. It was whisky which he had drawn with his mouth out of the barrels and spit into the coffee pot. I kicked the pot over, which very much enraged him and he tried to kill me, but I was too quick for him and disarmed him. I went back to the cattle, and after awhile got them quiet and they lay down. I then went back and rebuilt the fire. When I had my back turned to get some more wood the devil threw a handful of big cartridges on the fire. Part of them exploded almost in my face, and the creek being situated in a little canyon with high rocky walls on each side, it sounded like heavy cannonading. I was frightened, for I thought if there were Indians in five miles they would certainly hear this and pounce down upon us next day. I did not feel like killing Jack when he tried to shoot me for kicking his pot of whisky over, but I was sorely tempted then. I said to him: "My hearty, I won't kill you now, but I will surely get even with you."

Next morning we drove in by daylight and strung out one wing of wagons for Rattlesnake creek. When they were about three miles away, Major Dimond came along, in command of several companies of the Nineteenth Kansas cavalry and asked for whisky. I said: "You are too late; yonder go the wagons containing all the whisky. I sent them off on purpose to keep my friend Jack Cobbin sober," pointing to Jack, who replied: "Major Dimond, how are you? I was your old scout at Fort Gibson. If you will loan me your horse and canteen I will get you some whisky." Nearly a dozen of the officers unstrung their canteens and handed them to Jack, and the column was halted until his return, and he came back with every canteen loaded. Each officer took a hearty pull and asked me to join them, but I said I never drank when I was out in the cold. I thought, "Where ignorance is bliss, 'tis folly to be wise."

We drew up the other wing that afternoon in a nice little sheltered, heavily wooded grove, under the bank of the creek, where the cook had stretched wagon-sheets and prepared a nice dinner, in the midst of a terrible snow-storm. The lost cattle arrived at the same time we did; so I put Cobbin on one of the horses and sent him out on day herd, while we sat down to dinner. Along in the afternoon I sent a man to relieve him. One of the men saw him coming and dropped a couple of cartridges in the fire just where he thought Jack would hover over to warm; and sure enough he hardly spread his hands to the cheering fire when one cartridge went off and as he turned, the other gave him a parting salute. That night, just as supper was ready, Jack retaliated by throwing another handful of cartridges into the fire, and blew our supper all to flinders. We held a council of war, and a majority decided to kill him. The extra hand and cook swore they would. The extra said he would take it upon himself to do the shooting, but I finally persuaded them out of the notion.

That night it cleared off, and we pulled over to Bluff Creek, at the foot of Mount Jesus, only a few miles away. I again put Cobbin on night herd. The clouds had rolled away and the new moon was shining brightly. The air was balmy and springlike. My extra hand and I were sitting up, smoking and enjoying the fine night, with a nice fire on the side of the bank, and the creek below us, when we heard a disturbance at one of the whisky wagons. The extra hand went to see about it, and brought in Cobbin, pretty full, as usual. I upbraided him for not being with the cattle, but to no use, and finally he lay down in front of the fire on the bank above and went to sleep. The extra said: "Now is the time." Jack wore a long, blue, homespun coat, which reached nearly to his heels, with pockets as far down as the coat, in which he kept his cartridges. We gently pulled the tails out from under him and built a fire of dry cottonwood chips on top of his cartridges, and placed a big wet rag above this, so that the fire would be cut off from the balance of his clothing. In course of time the chips were live coals, and then the cartridges began to explode and awaken him. He rolled from the top of the bank right through that fire and plumb into the creek. Scrambling out, he said, "I reckon I laid most too close to the fire." The extra hand told him, "He reckoned he did," and what was more, "if he ever caught him at those barrels again he would kill him;" and the extra being a very determined man, Jack knew he would. We had no more trouble with him on the trip.

ROBERT M. WRIGHT, 1880

CHAPTER III

Ranching in Early Days

The ranches in those days were few and far between. Beyond the Grove were Peacock's ranch, at Cow creek, Alison's ranch, at Walnut creek, and also that of William Griffinstein, with whom I afterward had the pleasure to serve in the house of representatives. The following is a true story of the fate of Peacock, as related to me a few years after his death. Peacock kept a whisky ranch on Cow creek. He and Satank, the great war chief of the Kiowas, were great friends and chums, as Peacock knew the sign language well. He had quite a large ranch and traded with the Indians, and, of course, supplied them with whisky. In consequence, the soldiers were always after him. Satank was his confidential friend and lookout. He had to cache his whisky and hide it in every conceivable manner, so that the troops would not find it. In fact, he dreaded the incursions of the soldiers much more than he did the Indians. One day Satank said to him: "Peacock, write me a nice letter that I can show to the wagon bosses and get all the chuck I want. Tell them I am the great war chief of the Kiowas, and ask them to give me the very best in the shop."

Peacock said, "All right, Satank," and sat down and penned this epistle: "This is Satank, the biggest liar, beggar, and theif on the plains. What he can't beg of you he will steal. Kick him out of your camp, as he is a lazy, good-for-nothing Indian."

Satank presented his letter several times to passing trains, and, of course, got a very cool reception, or rather a warm one. One wagon boss blacksnaked him, after which indignity he sought a friend, and said to him: "Look here! Peacock promised to write me a good letter, but I don't understand it. Every time I present it the wagon boss gives me the devil. Read it, and tell me just what it says.'' His friend did so, interpreting it literally. ''All right,'' said Satank, and the next morning at daylight he took some of his braves and rode to Peacock's ranch. He called to Peacock, ''Get up; the soldiers are coming.'' The summons was quickly obeyed. Seizing his field-glass, Peacock ran to the top of his lookout, and the instant he appeared, Satank shot him full of holes, exclaiming as he did so, ''Good-by Mr. Peacock; I guess you won't write any more letters.''

Then they went into the building and killed every man present, except one, a sick individual, who was lying in one of the rooms, gored through the leg by a buffalo. All that saved him was that the Indians were very superstitious about entering apartments where sick men lay, for fear they might have the smallpox, which disease they dreaded more than any other.

I came from the mountains in the spring of 1864 to Spring Bottom, on the Arkansas river. The Cheyennes, Arapahoes and Kiowas were committing many depredations along the Arkansas that summer.

Shortly after our arrival, my partner, Joe Graham, went to Fort Lyon after supplies to stand a siege, as we expected daily to be attacked, the hired man and myself remaining at the ranch to complete our fortifications. On the night of Graham's return I started for Point of Rocks, a famous place on the Arkansas, twenty miles below our ranch, to take a mule which he had borrowed to help him home with his load.

The next morning at daylight our ranch was attacked by about three hundred Indians, but the boys were supplied with arms and ammunition, and prepared to stand a siege. After they had killed one Indian and wounded a number of their ponies, the savages became more careful; they tried by every means in their power to draw the boys outside; they even rode up with a white flag and wanted to talk. Then they commenced to tell in Spanish, broken English, and signs, that they did not want to hurt the boys; they simply wanted the United States mail stock; and if it was given up they would go away. When this modest demand was refused, they renewed their attack with greater fury than ever before.

My wife and two children were with me at the ranch at the time, and, at the commencement of the fight, Mrs. Wright placed the little ones on the floor and covered them over with feather beds; then she loaded the guns as fast as the boys emptied them. She also knocked the clinking from between the logs of the building, and kept a sharp lookout on the movements of the Indians. Often did she detect them crawling up from the opposite side to that on which the boys were firing. Upon this information the boys would rush over to where she had seen them, and by a few well-directed shots make them more than glad to crawl back to where they had come from. This was long before the days of the modern repeating rifle, and of course they had only the old-fashioned muzzle-loaders.

For about seven hours the Indians made it very warm for the boys; then they got together and held a big powwow, after which they rode off up the river. The boys watched them with a spy-glass from the top of the building until they were satisfied it was not a ruse on the part of the savages, but that they had really cleared out.

Graham then took my wife and two children, placed them in a canoe, and started down the Arkansas, which was very high at the time. The hired man saddled a colt that had never before been riden, and left for the Point of Rocks. Strange as it may seem, this colt appeared to know what was required of him, and he ran nearly the whole distance—twenty miles—in less than an hour and a half. He was the only animal out of sixteen head that was saved from the vengeance of the Indians. He was a little beauty, and I really believe that the savages refrained from killing him because they thought they would eventually get him. He was saved in this manner: After the attack had been progressing for a long time and there came a comparative lull in the action, my wife opened the door a little to see what the Indians were up to, while the boys were watching at the loopholes; the colt observed Mrs. Wright, made a rush toward her, and she, throwing the door wide open, the animal dashed into the room and remained there quiet as a lamb until the battle was over.

The Indians killed all our mules, horses and hogs— we had of the latter some very fine ones—a great number of our chickens, and shot arrows into about thirty cows, several of which died. The majority of them recovered, however, although their food ran out of the holes in their sides for days and weeks until the shaft of the arrows dropped off, but, of course, the iron heads remained in their paunches; still they got well.

I had just saddled my horse, ready to start back to the ranch, when the hired man arrived, bringing the terrible news of the fight. He told me that I would find my wife and children somewhere on the river, if the savages had not captured them. "For my part," he said, "I am going back to my people in Missouri; I have had enough." He was a brave man, but a "tenderfoot," and no wonder the poor fellow had seen enough. His very soul had been severely tried that day. I at once called for volunteers, and a number of brave frontiersmen nobly responded; there were only two or three, however, who had their horses ready; but others followed immediately, until our number was swelled to about a dozen. A wagon and extra horses brought up the rear, to provide means of transportation for my wife and little ones.

When we had traveled thirteen miles, having carefully scanned every curve, bend, and sand-bar in the stream, we discovered Graham, Mrs. Wright, and the children about two miles ahead, Graham (God bless him!) making superhuman effort to shove the boat along and keep it from upsetting or sinking. They saw us at the same moment, but they immediately put to cover on a big island. We shouted and waved our hats, and did everything to induce them to come to us, but in vain, for, as they told us afterwards, the Indians had tried the same maneuvers a dozen times that day, and Graham was too wary to be caught with chaff. At last Mrs. Wright recognized a large, old, white hat I was wearing, and she told Graham that it was indeed her husband, Robert. When they reached the bank, we took them out of the canoe more dead than alive, for the frail, leaky craft had turned many times; but Graham and Mrs. Wright, by some means, had always righted it, and thus saved the little children.

A party went with me to our ranch the next day, and we witnessed a scene never to be forgotten; dead horses, dead hogs, dead cows and dead chickens piled one upon another in their little stockade. Two small colts were vainly tugging at their lifeless mothers' teats; a sad sight indeed, even to old plainsmen like ourselves. Both doors of the building were bored so full of bullet holes that you could hardly count them, as they lapped over each other in such profusion. Every window had at least a dozen arrows sticking around it, resembling the quills on a porcupine. The ceiling and walls inside the room were filled with arrows also. We thought we would follow up the trail of the savages, and while en route we discovered a government ambulance, wrecked, and its driver, who had been killed, with two soldiers and citizens, so horribly butchered and mutilated that the details are too horrible and disgusting to appear in print. They had also captured a woman and carried her off with them, but the poor creature, to put an end to her horrible suffering, hung herself to a tree on the banks of a creek northeast of where the Indians had attacked the ambulance. In consequence of her act, the savages called the place White Woman. The little stream bears that name today; but very few settlers, however, know anything of its sad origin (it was on this creek, some years later, that the gallant Major Lewis met his death wound at the hands of the Indians, while bravely doing his duty).

After the fight at Spring Bottom, I moved down to Fort Aubrey, where, in conjunction with Mr. James Anderson, I built a fine ranch. At that place we had numerous little skirmishes, troubles, trials, and many narrow escapes from the Indians. While at Aubrey, I had my experience with Fred and the bull buffalo, as described in a previous chapter.

Just before I moved from Aubrey, J. F. Bigger and I had a sub-contract to furnish hay at Fort Lyon, seventy-five miles west of Aubrey. While we were preparing to move up to go to work, a vast herd of buffalo stampeded through our range one night and took off with them about half of our work cattle. The next day the stage-driver and conductor told us they had seen a few of our cattle about twenty-five miles east of Aubrey. This information gave me an idea in which direction to hunt for them, and I started after the missing beasts, while my partner took those that remained and a few wagons and left for Fort Lyon.

I will interpolate here the statement that the Indians were supposed to be peaceable, although small war parties of young men, who could not be controlled by their chiefs, were continually committing depredations, while the main body of the savages were very uneasy, expecting to go out any day. In consequence of this threatening aspect of affairs, there had been a brisk movement of troops

Cowboy Band on the Round-up, Indian Territory

stationed at the various military posts, a large number of whom were supposed to be on the road from Denver to Fort Lyon.

I took along with me some ground coffee, filled my saddle-bags with jerked buffalo and hardtack, a belt of cartridges, my rifle and six-shooter, field-glass and blankets, and was ready for any emergency. The first day out I found a few of the lost cattle, and placed them on the river bottom, which I continued to do as fast as I recovered them, for a distance of about eighty-five miles down the Arkansas, where I met a wagon train. The men told me I would find several more with the train that had made the crossing of the Cimarron the day before. I came up to this train in a day's travel south of the river, got my cattle, and started next morning for home. I picked up my cattle on the river where I had left them, as I went along, and, having made a tremendous day's travel, about sundown concluded to go into camp. I had hardly stopped before the cattle began to drop down, so completely tired out were they, as I thought.

Just as it was growing dark, I happened to look toward the west, and saw several fires on a big island near what was called the Lone Tree, about a mile from where I had halted for the night. Thinking they were camp-fires of the soldiers I had heard were on the road from Denver, and anticipating and longing for a good cup of coffee, as I had had none for five days, and besides feeling very lonesome, knowing, too, the troops would be full of news, I felt good, and did not think or dream of anything else than my fond anticipation; in fact, was so wrapped up in my thoughts I was literally oblivious to my surroundings. I was wild to hear the news and wanted a good supper, which I knew I would get in the soldiers' camp.

— 55 —

The Arkansas was low, but the bank was steep, with high, rank grass growing to the very waters' edge. I found a buffalo trail cut through the steep bank, very narrow and precipitous. Down this I went, and arrived within a little distance of my supposed soldiers' camp. When I got in the middle of a deep cut I looked across to the island, and saw a hundred little fires and something less than a thousand savages huddled around them.

I slid back off my horse and by dint of great exertion worked him up the river bank as quietly and quickly as possible, then led him gently away out on the prairie. My first impulse was not to go back to the cattle; but we needed them very badly; so I concluded to return to them, putting them on their feet mighty lively, without any noise. Then I started them, and, oh, dear, I was afraid to tread on a weed lest it would snap and bring the Indians down on my trail. Until I had put several miles between them and me I could not rest easy for a minute; and tired as I was, tired as were my horse and the cattle, I drove them twenty-five miles before I halted. Then daylight was upon me and I lay down and fell asleep. I was at what is known as Choteau's Island, a once famous place on the old Santa Fe trail.

Of course I had to let the cattle and my horse rest and fill themselves until the afternoon, but I did not sleep any longer myself. As I thought it was dangerous to remain too near the cattle, I walked up a big, dry sand creek that ran into the river at that point, and, after I had ascended it a couple of miles, found the banks very steep; in fact, they rose to a height of eighteen or twenty feet, and were sharply cut up by narrow trails made by the buffalo. Here I had an exciting adventure with a herd of buffalo, but will reserve the account of it for another chapter. Nothing further, of note, happened during the afternoon, and, resuming my journey, I finally arrived at the ranch without mishap.

The day after I arrived at home I was obliged to start to Fort Lyon with fourteen or fifteen yoke of cattle and four or five wagons. A Mr. Ward volunteered to accompany me; and let me say right here, he was as brave a young man as it has ever been my fortune to know. He was true blue; a chip of the old block; a nephew of General Shelby; he might well be proud of his pluck. I coupled all the wagons together and strung all the fifteen yoke of oxen to them, and as young Ward could not drive the cattle he went along for company and helped me yoke up. We made eighteen miles the first day and stopped at Pretty Encampment, one of the most celebrated camping places on the old Santa Fe trail, located at the foot of Salt Bottom. We yoked up the next morning several hours before daylight, as the moon was shining brightly; we wanted to cross the bottom before we ate breakfast. A few miles from the head of the bottom the trail diverges, one cutting across the bluff and the other following the Arkansas; we were on the lower one. Presently the stage came along, lumbering over the bluff, stopped, and called to us. I went to it, only a few hundred yards over to the other trail, when who should I see but my partner, Mr. B. F. Bigger, and four or five other men in the coach, besides the driver. They all at once cried out, Bigger leading: "Go back with us, go back with us, or you will both be killed." I said: "Bigger, be a man; stop with us and defend your property; a lot of these cattle here belong to you; and besides you have a splendid rifle." He replied: "No, I must go to Aubrey to protect my wife and child." I answered: "My wife and children are there too, in one of the strongest little forts in the country, six or eight men with them, and plenty of arms and ammunition; all the Indians on the plains cannot take them." He said: 'You don't know how many Indians there are; they stopped the coach, took what they wanted in the way of blankets and ammunition, two or three six-shooters they found on the front seat, besides other things." I asked him why they didn't take his rifle, and he replied: "I reckon they would have done so, but we hid it." I said: "I wish they had; if you won't stop with us, loan us your gun; we have only one rifle and a six-shooter." He said: "No, leave the cattle and go back with us; they will be down on you in a little while." "Well, wait until I see Ward," I answered. "Be quick about it then," replied he.

I went back to Ward and asked him what he wanted to do. I said: "You have nothing to gain and all to lose. The people in the coach yonder say there are several hundred Indians above the bend; and while they are not actually on the warpath, they stopped the coach and robbed it, whipped the mules with their quirts until they got them on a dead run, then fired at them, and shot several arrows into the coach; some are still sticking into the back of it." Ward asked me what I was going to do. I said that a man might as well be dead as to lose his property, and I proposed to stay with it; "Maybe we won't see an Indian." He replied: "I am going to stay with you." "God bless you for it," I said, "but it is asking too much of you." "Well, I am going to stay with you, anyhow." Then I motioned to the stage-driver to go on, and he did so right quickly. The cattle had all laid down in the yokes while we halted, but we soon hustled them up and started, feeling pretty blue. We first held a little consultation, and then moved all the ammunition to the first wagon, on which Ward was to sit. I gave him the rifle; I had on a six-shooter and a belt full of cartridges, and we agreed to let the Indians take the grub and the blankets if they came, but that we would stay by our guns and ammunition. Ward said he would never get off the box containing the ammunition.

We had proceeded about two miles, were awfully tired and hungry, had just driven out of the road to

ake a temporary camp, congratulating ourselves that
e had missed the Indians, when here they came, two on
teir ponies at first. I said to Ward that we would lick
tese two; they dare not tackle us, but we had better
eep right on and not go into camp. Ward raised his
tm and motioned for them to keep off. They circled and
ent to the rear, when just over a little rise the whole
usiness of them poured. I pounded away and yelled
t the cattle to keep them moving, but there were so many
tdians they blocked the road, and we came to a stand-
till. They swarmed around us, and on all the wagons,
ut the front one; this Ward kept them off of. They took
ll of our grub and rope, but nothing else. After string-
tg their bows and making lots of threats and bluffs at
s, they dropped a little behind and we drove off and left
tem. We hustled the cattle along five or six miles,
hen we came to a good place to water. Ward ran up
n a bluff to see what had become of the savages, while
drove the cattle chained together to the river. Ward
ommenced to shout just as I reached the bank. The
xen got no water that day. I turned them around in a
urry, hitched on, and started. Ward said that the
tdians were not more than three miles off, coming our
ray. We never made another halt until we were in sight
f the lights on Commissary Hill, at old Fort Lyon,
thich we reached about one o'clock that night. I
eported to the commanding officer the next morning,
nd we learned afterwards that these Indians had been
n Sand creek to bury the bones of their dead who were
illed in the Chivington fight several years before.
)nly a week after our escape there was a general out-
reak and war.

In 1866 I went to Fort Dodge. Now, one might be
tclined to think that the kind of life I had been leading—
he hard experience—that a person would be anxious to
bandon it at the first favorable opportunity; but this
s not so. It gives one a zest for adventure, for it is a

scrt of adventure that you become accustomed to; you get to like it; in fact, there is a fascination about it no one can resist. Even to a brave man—God knows I make no pretension to that honor—there is a charm to the life he cannot forego, yet I felt an irresistible power and could not permit myself to give it up.

Mr. A. J. Anthony and I bought out the Cimarron ranch, twenty-five miles west of Fort Dodge. The company of which we purchased were heartily tired of the place, and eager to sell, for two of their number had been brutally murdered by the Indians while attempting to put up hay. Anthony was an old "Overland stage messenger," had seen lots of ups and downs with the Indians on the plains, and rather enjoyed them. So we got together some of the old-timers and went to making hay. Right there our troubles commenced. We both had seen a great deal of the Indians and their methods before; but we didn't realize what they could and would do when they took the notion. If we didn't see some of the savages every day it was a wonder; and once that summer they actually let us alone for four weeks. I remarked to my partner: "There is something wrong in this; they must be sick." So they were. When they came in that winter and made a treaty, they told us the cholera had broken out among them, and the reason for their remaining away for so long a time was on account of the scourge. The cholera was perfectly awful that summer on the plains; it killed soldiers, government employees, Santa Fe traders and emigrants. Many new graves dotted the roadsides and camping places, making fresh landmarks.

I remember two soldiers coming up with the mail escort one night, who were severely reprimanded by their sergeant for getting drunk, at which they took umbrage, stole two horses and deserted the next day. One of them returned on foot about noon, stating that the

Indians had attacked them early in the morning, got their animals from the picket line, and shot his partner through the right breast; that he had left him on an island twelve miles up the river. Our cook had been complaining a little that morning, and when I went to his room to see him he said that he had dinner all ready, and would like to go along with us after the wounded soldier. I told him no; to stay at home, go to bed, keep quiet, and above all else to drink very little cold well-water. The sergeant took six men and the escort wagon with him, and I followed on horseback.

When we arrived opposite the island we hailed the soldier, and he came out of the brush. He walked up and down the river bank, and made signs to us that his right arm was useless, and he seemed to be in great pain. The sergeant called for volunteers, but not a man responded. The Arkansas was swimming full and the current was very swift in one place for about three hundred yards. It appeared that none of his comrades liked the fellow very well, one of them saying, when the sergeant asked for some one to go over, "If he don't swim, or at least make an effort, he can stay, and I hope the Indians will get him." I said, "Boys, this won't do; I will get him," and after him I went. When I reached the island I sat down and reasoned with him; told him exactly what I required him to do. He seemed very grateful, and knew that I was risking my own life on him. He was a powerfully built fellow, and his wound had almost paralyzed his right side. He said: "Mr. Wright, I appreciate what you have done for me, and what you are about to undertake; now, before God, I will let go my hold if I see you cannot make it." He stayed nobly by his promise. When we had gone under water several times, and the current was bearing us down, and it appeared that every minute would be our last, he said, in the despair of death: "I am going; let me go." I replied, "For God's sake, no; hold on." I then felt inspired. I said to myself, this man has a grand nature; I am going to save him or sink with him. Indeed, all these thoughts flashed through my mind, and, as God is my judge, I would have done it, as at that moment I had no fear of death whatever. When I reached the bank I was completely exhausted and had to be helped out of the water. I was awfully sick; it seemed that my strength had left me absolutely. It was fully an hour before I was strong enough to ride.

Strange to say, I lay side by side with this poor man in the hospital at Fort Dodge, after his rescue. He was excessively kind and attentive, and when I began to convalesce—for the same night I was stricken down with cholera—we exchanged drinks; he took my brandy, I his ale. He would insist in saying that the cause of my sickness was the terrible exertion I had made that day in his behalf; but it was not so. When I got back to the ranch, after our ride up the river, our poor cook was in a terribly bad fix. I knew that he was gone the moment I saw him, although he was still sitting up and appeared cheerful, except when the cramps would seize him. I asked him what he had been drinking. He replied that his thirst was so intolerable that he drank a whole bucketful of canned lemonade. I said to him, "My poor boy, make your peace with God; tell me the address of your parents or friends." He answered: "I have none; it makes no difference; I think I will pull through all right." In an hour he was dead. We were laying him out in the shade on the east side of the house, and I was in the act of tying up his jaws, when a breeze from the south seemed to enter his mouth and was wafted back into mine. I said then, "There, boys, I have tasted the cholera from this poor fellow," and at once set about making my preparations as to my business affairs and other matters. Before two o'clock in the morning I was down with the dreadful disease. Barlow, Sanderson, & Company, the proprietors of the "Overland Stage," to whom I had shown many

These Indians Would Only be Photographed in Company with the Interpreter. They Were Afraid the Camera Would Shoot Them.

favors, the moment they heard of my illness, sent an ambulance and escort of soldiers, and I was conveyed to the hospital at Fort Dodge. There, under the kind and careful treatment of Doctors De Graw and Wilson, I recovered.

I must go back to the haymaking at the ranch. Day after day the Indians would harass us in some manner, but they had not yet succeeded in killing any of our men, although they repeatedly ran off our stock, fired into and broke up our camp, until even the old-timers, men in whom we had placed the utmost confidence and depended upon in case of emergency, began to grow tired. They said it was too monotonous for them. I don't think they really understood the true definition of the word. Still we persisted, were hopeful, and continued to hire new men at from seventy-five to a hundred dollars a month for common hands; we had to have hay. We considered it no more than just to tell these new men, when we hired them, they would have to take desperate chances, and that was the reasons we were paying such large wages. Well, the Indians finally exhausted us of our horse stock, and we had to resort to ponies; but they were too small and we got along very slowly. We were compelled to purchase a big span of mules of the United States mail company, for which we paid six hundred dollars. Mr. Anthony was very proud of them, as he often sat behind them when he was a messenger on the overland routes. They were named Puss and Jennie. The first morning they were sent to the haystack Anthony was in the corral stacking. After a while he came to the house, looking as proud as a peacock, and said to me: "Hear that machine? Ain't Puss and Jennie making it hum?" But the sound did not seem natural to me, so I grabbed a spy-glass and ascended to the lookout on top of the building. Sure enough, just as I expected, I saw two Indians come up, one on each side of the mules, pounding them over the back with their bows, and they were making it hum, while the boys in the camp were shooting as fast as they could load and fire, protecting the poor driver, who was running toward them for his life, with about two dozen of the red devils after him, whooping, yelling, and shouting as they charged upon him. The two Indians who attacked the driver of the mowing-machine had watched their opportunity, rushed out of the brush on the bank of the river, and were upon him before he had the slightest idea of their presence, and running off with the mules. His two revolvers were strapped upon the machine, and he could do nothing but drop off behind from his seat, leave his weapons, and run for his life.

The government had ten men and a sergeant stationed at the ranch, on escort duty with the United States mail. One day while the men were at dinner, and a soldier was on guard outside, whom I suspected was asleep at the time, two Indians, who had stolen a couple of old mules from the stage station forty miles above, rode by and fired at the sentinel, just for fun, I believe, or at least to wake him up, and then dashed down to the river, cross-ing close to a Mexican train. Quicker than thought they unsaddled their mules, threw them upon the backs of two freight horses that were picketed near, mounted them, and jumped off a steep bank five feet deep into the Arkansas and were over on the other side before the astonished Mexicans really knew what was going on.

The day before the same train had left a lame steer out in the sand hills, and the wagon boss sent one of the hands back after it that morning. As soon as the two Indians crossed the river they spied the Mexican with the lame ox and immediately took after him. From the top of my building, with an excellent glass, I could plainly see their whole maneuverings. The savages circled around the poor ''greaser'' again and again; charged him from the front and rear and on both sides, until I actually thought they had ridden over him a dozen times, emptying their revolvers whenever they made a charge. They would only halt long enough to reload, and then were after him again. During all these tactics of the Indians, the Mexican never made any attempt to return their fire; that saved his life and scalp. They wanted to compel him to empty his revolvers, and then they could run up and kill him. Of course, from the distance, nearly two miles, I could not hear the report of the Indians' weapons, but I could see the smoke distinctly, and I knew that the Mexican had not fired a shot. Presently the poor fellow's horse went down, and he lay behind it for awhile Then he cut tthe girth, took off the saddle, and started for the river, running at every possible chance, using the saddle as a shield, stopping to show fight only when the savages pressed him too closely; then he would make another stand, with the saddle set up in front of him. After a few more unsuccessful charges, the Indians left him. When he had arrived safely at the train, they asked him why he had not fired a shot when the Indians rode so close to him. He stated if he had a thousand shots he would have fired them all, but in crossing the river that morning his horse had to swim and his revolver got wet (the cartridges were the old-fashioned kind, made of paper, and percussion caps the means of priming). It was fortunate, perhaps; for if the Indians had surmised that his revolver would not go off, they would have had his scalp dangling at their belts in short order.

The Indians had given us a respite at the ranch for awhile (I refer to the time I have mentioned when they were attacked by the cholera). We had recruited up considerably, were in high hopes, and had started in fresh, as it were, when one morning they swooped down upon us again to the number of two thousand, it appeared to me; but there was not that many, of course; still they were thick enough. It looked as if both of the banks of the Arkansas were alive with them, as well as every hill and hollow. There were Indians everywhere. Our men were all in the hay field, with the exception of two, and my partner, Mr. Anthony, was with them. Anthony was a cool, brave man; knew exactly what to do and when to act. I think that his presence saved the party. I could see the whole affair from the lookout. As soon as the firing began we could see our watchman, who was stationed on a bluff, and his horse ran away and threw him, but he managed to get to the boys in the field. We were using two wagons with four yoke of cattle to each. The wagons were about half loaded, and the boys had to fly and leave them standing. The Indians set the hay on fire, then opened with a shower of arrows upon the steers, and started them on a run, scared out of their senses. We found them after the thing was over, all dead in a string, chained together as they had been at work. The savages had lots of fun out of their running the poor brutes around the bottoms while the hay on the wagons was burning. At the first attack the men all got together as quickly as possible and made for the camp, which was on the bank of the river. A hundred or more Indians charged them so close that it appeared they would ride over them, but whenever our boys made a stand and dropped on their knees and began to deliberately shoot, they would shy off like a herd of frightened antelope. This, they kept up until they reached the river, over half a mile from where they started in the field, then they made for a big island covered with a dense growth of willows; there they hid, remaining until after dark. We at the ranch formed little parties repeatedly and tried to go to their relief by hugging the river bank, but at every attempt were driven back by an overwhelming number of savages.

The Indians charged upon our men in the willows many times during the day, in their efforts to dislodge them, and so close did some of them come on their ponies

R. M. WRIGHT. 1875

that any of the boys by a single spring could have grabbed their bridle-reins. Although they might have killed several of the savages, the latter would have eventually overpowered them, and cruelly butchered the last one of them. To show how cool and brave a man old Anthony was, and what stuff the men were made of, he passed many a joke around among the boys. There was a stern, reticent veteran in the group, whose pipe was seldom out of his mouth excepting when he was asleep. Anthony would repeatedly hand him his pipe and tobacco, and say: "Brother Tubbs, take a smoke; I am afraid there is something wrong with you; have you given up the weed?" Tubbs would reply: "If we don't be getting out of here, we won't be making those ten loads of hay today, and you will lose your bet." Anthony had wagered with some one that they would haul ten loads of hay that day. These and similar jokes passed between them all the while, while they were surrounded by hundreds of savages, many of them within five or six steps very frequently; the least false move on the part of the besieged, and none of them would have lived as long as it takes me to write this. About three o'clock that afternoon we heard firing both above and below us. The Indians had attacked the United States paymaster coming up the river, and several companies of soldiers coming down, and gave them a hot fight, too, compelling them to go into corral, and holding them for several hours.

These constant swirmishes kept up till late in the fall; in November and December, 1868, the Indians made a treaty. I then sent for my family, who were in Missouri. A short time after their arrival, one Sunday morning, during a terrible snowstorm, and no help at the ranch but two stage drivers and a Mexican boy, I threw open the large double doors of the storeroom, and, before I could even think, in poped forty Indians, all fully armed, equipped, and hideous with their war paint on. I thought to myself, "Great God, what have I done; murdered my wife and little ones!" We had to use strategem; resistance would have been useless. The stack of guns was in the corner behind the counter, in a passageway leading to the dwelling-house, or in the part of the building in which I lived. I called to the Mexican boy, in an adjoining apartment, to get his revolver and hold the door at all hazards; to put the guns one at a time inside of the sitting room, and to shoot the first Indian who attempted to get over the counter; to tell the savages what I had ordered, in Spanish, and that I would remain with them and take my chances. Everything worked to a charm, except that the Indians commenced beating the snow off of them and laying aside their accouterments. I said to the boy: "Tell them, in Spanish, this won't do; they could not stay in here; this is the soldiers' room; but they must follow me out into a larger, warmer room where we would cook them some chuck." This he accomplished by signs and in Spanish, as rapidly as God would let him. I said: "When the last one is out, jump quickly and double-bar the door; it is our only chance." I thought the reason why the Indians acted so coolly was that they believed they had a "dead cinch" on us, and were in no hurry to commence action.

As soon as the boy had finished talking to them they turned and followed me out. One of them took hold of me with many a sign and gesture, but as I could only understand the sign language a little, barely enough to trade with the Indians, I was at this moment so excited that I hardly understood English. The savage then led me back to the door and signed for me to open it. I shook my head and said: "Oh, no, old fellow; not for all the gold in the Rocky Mountains would I open that door again; my dearest treasures on earth are in there, and as long as these doors are closed that long they are safe; but God only knows how long they will remain so." At my refusal he immediately began to abuse me most outrageously; spat in my face, and went on like a madman;

more than once he reached for his revolver, and, of course, I thought my time had surely come. The Mexican boy, having heard the rumpus, slipped out of the back door and came around the house to see what was up. I said to him: "Placido, what does he mean?" Placido commenced to smile (the first beam of sunshine I had seen since the entrance of the savages), and he replied: "Oh, that is all right; he left his bow in there, and because you won't open the door thinks you want to steal it." "Tell him I will get it; and, now you have got him in good humor, ask him what they all want and what they are after, and tell me." When I returned Placido and the savages were talking like old chums. The boy said: "No danger, we are all right; this is a party of young bucks going to the mountains to steal horses from the Utes." This intelligence was a burden lifted, and I felt as if I could fall down and worship the great God who created me. I said: "Bring out the fatted calf; feed them to their hearts' content, and until their bellies pop out like pizened pups; until their very in'ards are made to cry, 'Enough!' and want no more." Instead of the fatted calf we cooked them several camp kettles full of bacon and beans, many of the same full of coffee, two gallons of black molasses, plenty of sugar, and a box of hardtack. They feasted, and went on their way rejoicing.

The ultimate fate of the old ranch was, that the Indians burnt it, together with several hundred tons of hay, the day after Mr. Anthony abandoned it, by order of Major Douglas, commanding Fort Dodge.

CHAPTER IV

The Greatest Game Country on Earth

Of course, it was not always fight and run, run and fight; we had our fun, too. One day a stage driver, Frank Harris, and myself started out after buffalo. They were very scarce, for a wonder, and we were very hungry for fresh meat. The day was fine, and we rode a long way, expecting sooner or later to rouse up a bunch. Late in the afternoon we gave it up, and started for home. Of course, we did not care to save our ammunition; so we shot away at everything in sight—skunks, rattlesnakes, prairie dogs, and so on—until we had only a few cartridges left. Suddenly up jumped an old bull that had been lying down in one of those sugar-loaf shaped sand hills, with the top hollowed out by the action of the wind. Harris emptied his revolver into him, and so did I, but the old fellow stood suddenly still on top of the sand hill, bleeding profusely at the nose, but persistently refusing to die, although he would repeatedly stagger and nearly topple over. It was getting late, and we could not wait for him, so Harris said: "I will dismount, creep up behind him, and cut his hamstrings with my butcher knife," the bull by this time having laid down. Harris commenced his forward movement, but it seemed to infuse new life into the old fellow; he jumped to his feet, and, with his head down, away he went around the outside of the top of the sand hill. It was a perfect circus ring, and Harris, who had gotten him by the tail, never let go his hold; he did not dare; it was his only show. Harris was a tall, lank fellow, and his legs were flying higher than his head, as round and round he and the bull went. I could not help him in the least, but had to sit and hold his horse and judge the fight. I really thought that the old bull would never weaken. Harris said to me, after it was over, that the only thing he

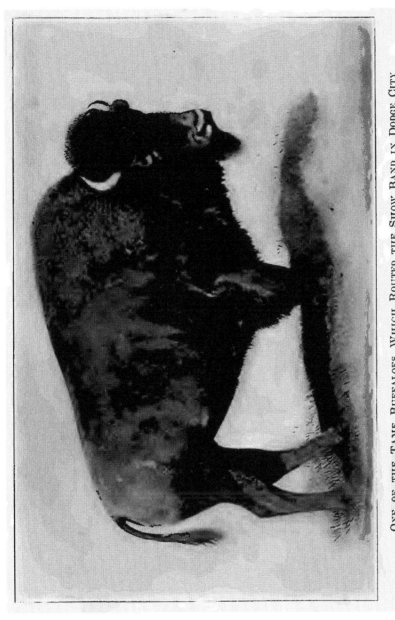

One of the Tame Buffaloes Which Routed the Show Band in Dodge City

feared was that he would pull the bull's tail out by the roots, and if he did he was a goner. Finally the ring performance began to grow slower and slower, and Harris at last succeeded in cutting his hamstrings, when down went the bull. We brought in his tongue, hump, and hindquarters, and, at a glorious feast that night, had a big laugh with the boys over Harris's comical adventure.

I wish here to assert a few facts concerning game, and animal life in general, in early days, in the vicinity of Fort Dodge and Dodge City. There were wonderful herds of buffalo, antelope, deer, elk, and wild horses. There were big gray wolves and coyotes by the thousand, hundreds of the latter frequently being seen in bands, and often from ten to fifty grays in a bunch. There were also black and cinnamon bears, wild cats and mountain lions, though these latter were scarce and seldom seen so far from the mountains. Then there was the cunning little prairie dog—millions of them; and next in number to them was the little swift, similar to a fox in shape and color, but much prettier, and it could run like a streak, which gave it the name of swift. They were very susceptible to poison, and soon vanished from the face of the earth, as did the black croaking raven. I have seen the ground literally covered with dead ravens, for the space of an acre, around the carcasses of dead wolves that had been poisoned; having eaten of the flesh of the poisoned wolves, it affected the ravens the same as if they had eaten the poison direct.

One terror of the plains was mad wolves. Several times were the different forts visited by them, and they not only did great damage to stock, but frequently to human beings. One ran into Fort Larned one night, bit the officer of the day, Lieutenant Thompson, and two soldiers, and I think two or three employees of the government. Thompson went east and put himself under treatment, but he never was the same man afterward. It is doubtful whether it was the treatment he underwent that affected him, or the continual dread. The others all died.

Now I wish to give an idea of the great number of water-fowl and amphibious animals, such as the otter, beaver, muskrat, weasel, and mink, that were found on the southwestern plains. Up to about 1870 the beavers were plentiful, and there was also quite a number of otter; but neither of these animals could stand civilization, and both were soon wiped out of existence, on account of the high price of their fur, and too many trappers.

For some years after Dodge was established, our rivers, streams, ponds and lakes were covered with wild fowl—ducks, geese, swans, brants, pelicans, cranes and every species of water-fowl known to this continent. It was a poor day or a poor hunter who could not kill a hundred ducks and geese in a day, and sometimes several hundred were killed in a day, so one can judge by this how plentiful they were. Then turkeys and quails— there was no end to them. Their numbers were countless; one could not estimate them. Indeed, I am almost ashamed to state how many I have seen, but what I am going to say about their number is no exaggeration. I have seen thousands of turkeys in a flock, coming in to roost on the North Fork and the main Canadian and its timbered branches. Several times, at a distance, we mistook them for large herds of buffalo. They literally covered the prairie for miles, with their immense flocks, and, more than once, we saddled our horses to make a run for them, thinking they were buffalo. If my recollection serves me right, about ninety miles down the North Fork of the Canadian from Fort Supply, is what is called, Sheridan's Roost, named for the large number of wild turkeys, killed in a single night, by Major-General Sheridan's escort, who made camp there one night. I had passed by the place before, and several times after the big killing, and I should think it was rightly named, for, in my trips through that country, I thought I saw, with my own eyes, more wild turkeys than there were tame ones in the whole United States put together; and there were just as many quails in the sand hills, bordering on these streams.

I must not fail to mention, among our game birds, the pretty prairie plover, which, for about three months in the years, came in great numbers and dotted the prairie everywhere. It was a most beautiful game bird and considered by epicures to be very fine eating, superior to quail in flavor and juiciness. I have often gone out and killed from one hundred to two hundred, and back to Dodge, inside of four hours. It was beautiful sport. The bird would arise singly, when you approached it within forty of fifty yards, and sail gently away from you; and before you could reach your first dead bird, you would oftentimes have three or four more down. Army officers, and distinguished sportsmen and our governors and congressmen would come here to hunt them. But, like the wild turkey and other game, the prairie plover, too, has almost ceased to appear. Civilization or settlement of the country has sounded its death note.

I have spoken about the great number of wild animals, but have failed to mention the skunks. They, too, were very numerous, in the early days, at and around Dodge City, and, strange to say, their bite was almost always fatal. At least eight or ten persons died here from their bite, the first season Dodge started. We supposed they were mad skunks, or affected with hydrophobia. Every one, of course, slept out of doors, and skunks would crawl right into bed with the men, and bite. Some were bitten on the nose, some on the lip, some on the hand or finger, and one man had his toe bitten almost off. One man who was bitten through the nose, had the skunk hold on to him, while he ran through the camp in the night, beating with both hands at Mr. Skunk, and he had a time getting rid of the beast. The man whose toe was bitten was George Oaks, partner, at the time, of our fellow townsman, Mr. George Richards. After he was bitten he determined to have revenge, so he camped his train (and he had quite a large mule train) and waited for, some say, four nights, before Mr. Skunk came back. Anyhow, he laid his train up for a day or two. But finally, one night, he blew Mr. Skunk's head off with a double-barreled shotgun, and, not satisfied with emptying both barrels into his victim, reloaded and shot him again. He sure got his revenge. Some people were mean enough to say that Mr. Skunk would have died anyway, after biting Mr. Oaks, and that Mr. Skunk only came back to apologize, after he found out whom he had bitten, but I think different; this was a joke, for George Oaks was my friend and a big hearted, noble fellow, even if a little eccentric, and some people could not appreciate him.

The creeks, when the fort (Dodge) was first started, were all heavily wooded with hackberry, ash, box-elder, cottonwood, and elm. We cut fifteen hundred cords of wood almost in one body on a little creek six miles north of the fort, all hackberry. There were a good many thousand cords cut on the Sawlog, which stream is properly the south fork of the Pawnee, but the soldiers would go out to the old Hays crossing, chop down a big tree, hitch a string of large mules to it, haul it up on the bank near the ford, and, after stripping off its top and limbs, leave its huge trunk there. In consequence thousands of immense logs accumulated, making the place look as if a sawmill had been established; and these great trunks were sawlogs ready to be cut into lumber. The early buffalo hunters called the creek Sawlog, which name it bears to this day.

Just above the crossing was a great resort and covert for elk. I have seen as many as fifty in a single band at one time. Every spring we would go out there and capture young ones. That region was also the heart of the buffalo range as well as that of the antelope. I have seen two thousand of the latter graceful animals in a single bunch driven right into Fort Dodge against the buildings by a storm. I have shot buffalo from the walls of my corral at the fort, and so many of them were there in sight it appearerd impossible to count them. It was a difficult problem to determine just how many buffalo I saw at one time. I have traveled through a herd of them days and days, never out of sight of them; in fact, it might be correctly called one continuous gathering of the great shaggy monsters. I have been present at many a cattle round-up, and have seen ten thousand head in one herd and under complete control of their drivers; but I have seen herds of buffalo so immense in number that the vast aggregation of domestic cattle I have mentioned seemed as none at all compared with them.

In writing this brief description of animal life along the old trails, I have purposely left till the last the mention of the buffalo for it is the animal to which it is hardest to do justice. The southwestern plains, in early days, was the greatest country on earth, and the buffalo was the noblest as well as the most plentiful of its game animals. I have indeed traveled through buffaloes along the Arkansas river for two hundred miles, almost one continuous herd, as close together as it is customary to herd cattle. You might go north or south as far as you pleased and there would seem no diminution of their numbers. When they were suddenly frightened and stampeded they made a roar like thunder and the ground seemed to tremble. When, after nightfall, they came to the river, particularly when it was in flood, their immense numbers, in their headlong plunge, would make you think, by the thunderous noise, that they had dashed all the water from the river. They often went without water one and two days in summer, and much longer in winter. No one had any idea of their number.

General Sheridan and Major Inman were occupying my office at Fort Dodge one night, having just made the trip from Fort Supply, and called me in to consult as to how many buffaloes there were between Dodge and Supply. Taking a strip fifty miles east and fifty miles west, they had first made it ten billion. General Sheridan said, "That won't do." They figured it again, and made it one billion. Finally they reached the conclusion that there must be one hundred million; but said they were afraid to give out these figures; nevertheless they believed them. This vast herd moved slowly toward the north when spring opened, and moved steadily back again from the far north when the days began to grow short and winter was setting in.

Horacre Greeley estimated the number of buffaloes at five million. I agree with him, only I think there were nearly five times that number. Mr. Greeley passed through them twice; I lived in the heart of the buffalo range for nearly fifteen years; now who do you think would be the best judge of their number? I am told that some recent writer, who has studied the buffalo closely, has placed their number at ninety millions, and I think that he is nearer right than I. Brick Bond, a resident of Dodge, and old, experienced hunter, a great shot, a man of considerable intelligence and judgment, and a most reliable man as to truthfulness and honesty, says that he killed fifteen hundred buffaloes in seven days, and his highest killing was two hundred and fifty in one day, and he had to be on the lookout for hostile Indians all the time. He had fifteen skinners, and he was only one of many hunters.

Charles Rath and I shipped over two hundred thousand buffalo hides the first winter the Atchison, Topeka & Santa Fe railroad reached Dodge City, and I think there were at least as many more shipped from there, besides two hundred cars of hind quarters and two cars of buffalo tongues. Often have I shot them from the walls of my corral, for my hogs to feed upon. Several times have I seen wagon trains stop to let the immense herds pass; and time and time again, along in August or September, when putting up hay in the Arkansas bottom, would we have to put out men, both night and day, to keep them out of our herd of work cattle. We usually hunted them on horseback; that is, we would single out one animal in a herd, and ride along by the side of it, and shoot it with a six-shooter. Sometimes we would kill several buffalo on a single run, but very few white men killed them wantonly.

There was great antipathy between the hunters and the Indians; they cordially hated each other. This hatred between them was greatly on account of their different manner of killing the buffalo. The Indian hunted the buffalo altogether on horseback, with bow and arrow, or else with a long spear or lance, which they planted in the side of the animal by riding up alongside of him. By either means, they had to ride up close to the buffalo, scattering the herd and running them out of the country or off the range entirely. The Indians claimed they only killed for meat or robes, and, as soon as they had sufficient, they stopped and went home, the herds of buffalo soon getting together again and recovering from their panic. Whereas, the hunter never knew when to quit or when he had enough, and was continually harassing the buffaloes from every side, never giving them a chance to recover, but keeping up a continual pop-pop from their big guns. The Indians further claimed that the hunters' mode of killing was not only unfair, but it was cowardly, and downright murder, pure and simple, for they did not give the buffaloes the ghost of a show for their lives. They would get a stand on a herd by shooting the leader, at the great distance of a mile, clear out of scent and sound of the gun, and almost out of sight, and, in a short time, would annihilate the entire bunch, whilst the bewildered animals would wander around, taking their deaths, ignorant of what was the source of danger or how to get away. Besides, many of them, wounded, would wander off, out of sight and reach, and were not found until they were unfit for market; and the Indians claimed that the noise of the hunters' guns and their mode of killing would soon drive the buffalo out of the country or annihilate them. Time has proved that the Indians were correct.

A band of hunters cared no more for Indians, than Indians did for foot soldiers, and, unless they greatly outnumbered the hunters, and then only under the most favorable circumstances, the Indians would not attack the hunters. They were afraid of the hunter's big guns, his cool bravery, and, last but not least, of his unerring, deadly aim. Then, too, the hunter had but little plunder that was dear to the Indian, after the fight was won— only a team of work horses, and the redskin cared much more for riding ponies than for work animals.

I want to say something of the buffalo and its habits The buffalo-wallow is caused by the buffalo pawing and licking the salty alkali earth, and when the sod is once broken the dirt is wafted away by the action of the wind; then, year after year, by more pawing and licking and rolling or wallowing by the animals, more wind wafts the loose dirt away, and soon there is a large hole in the prairie. Now there is a much more curious spectacle to be seen every year when the grass starts up; is even plainly to be seen yet when springtime arrives. These are rings on the prairie; and there are thousands of them— yes, millions. From the first of April and until the middle of May was our wet season on the plains; this was always the case; you could depend upon it with almost the certainty of the sun and moon rising at the proper time. This was the calving season of the buffalo; the buffalo, not like domestic cattle, only rutted one month, neither more nor less, then it was all over. I want to interpolate a statement here, that no man living I ever heard of or saw witnessed the act of copulation by the buffalo. It was all done after night. Then was the only time that the buffalo made any noise or fuss; but at this season they would keep up a low roaring sound all night, and, as a consequence, the cows all calved in a month. At that time there were a great many gray wolves in the country as well as the little coyote. While the cows were in labor, the bulls kept guard to drive off the wolves, and, in their beat, made the rings referred to. I have had people argue to me that they were caused by lightning striking the earth; but it is certainly strange that lightning should only strike at these breeding places and nowhere else. Others would argue that the Indians had their war dances there, which is just about as absurd a statement as the other. Others even say that two bulls get their heads together in battle and push each other round and round in a ring until a circle is formed. Buffaloes live to a great age. I have heard it from best authority that some of them live to be seventy-five or eighty years old, and it is quite common for them to live thirty or forty years; in fact, I think I have seen many a bull's head that I thought to be over thirty years old. After a storm, when we would go in search of our lost cattle, we could tell the buffalo tracks from our cattle tracks because the buffalo tracks would be going against the storm every time, while our domestic cattle would invariably go with it. You see the buffalo is much more thinly clad behind than in front; nearly all of his coat is on his head, shoulders and hump, and, when our cattle would turn tail, the buffalo would naturally face the storm.

In another paragraph, mention has been made of the terrific noise and quaking of ground, resulting from a stampeding herd of buffaloes. I will now remind the reader of my exciting adventure with buffaloes, referred to in another chapter, and which I promised to relate. It will be remembered that, after a forced march in flight from Indians, I was allowing my horse and cattle to rest and graze a few hours, before proceeding on our way to the ranch at Aubrey. While waiting for the animals, and for greater safety to myself away from them, I ascended a dry sand creek a couple of miles, where the banks rose very steeply to the height of eighteen or twenty feet, and were sharply cut up by the narrow trails made by the buffalo.

The whole face of the earth was covered with buffalo; they were grazing slowly toward the river. As it was a warm day, and getting on in the afternoon, all at once they became frightened at something and stampeded pell mell toward the very spot where I was. I quickly ran into one of the precipitous little paths and up on the prairie to see what had scared them. They were fairly making the ground tremble, as in their mighty multitude they came on running at full speed; the sound of their hoofs resembled thunder, only a continuous peal. It appeared to me that they must sweep everything in their path, and for my own preservation I ran under the banks; but on they came like a tornado, with one old bull in the lead. He held up a second to descend the deep, narrow trail, and when he got half way down the bank I let him have it— I was only a few steps from him—and over he tumbled. I don't know why I killed him—out of pure wantonness, I expect; or perhaps I thought it would frighten the others back; not so, however: they only quickened their pace over the dead bull, and others fell over them. The top of the bank was actually swarming with them; they leaped, pitched and rolled down. I crouched as close to the bank as possible, but numbers of them just grazed my head, knocking the sand and gravel in great streams down my neck; indeed, I was half buried before the last one had passed. The old bull was the last buffalo I ever shot wantonly, excepting once from an ambulance, to please a distinguished Englishman who had never seen one killed. Then I did it only after his hard persuasion.

Jack Bridges, a scout of some fame in eastern Kansas during the war, said to me one day: "I see you always hunt buffaloes on horseback. If you will take a needle-gun (that was an improved Springfield) and go with me, you will never hunt on horseback again." And I never did. We usually hunted the calves only in the fall and winter, as all we cared for was the meat. It was wonderful to see how strong the mother's instinct was to protect her young. The calf would invariably run on the opposite side of its mother. One day I had taken a knee rest, and waited and waited for the calf to run ahead of its mother as they ascended a hill together. At last I saw a dark spot just ahead of the cows breast and fired, killing both caw and calf, breaking the cows neck as she had it distended ascending the hill, and shooting the calf dead, as I supposed. Just then a soldier came along and asked permission to have their tongues. We told him yes. On coming back with a wagon, picking up the dead calves, we found this one gone. Bridges said to me: "See, the d— soldier has stolen the calf." We saw the soldier soon after coming to us. He said: "After I cut the tongue out of the calf, he got up and ran over the hill a quarter of a mile." Sure enough, there he lay dead, with his tongue cut out. Two other soldiers verified this ones story.

Notwithstanding this abundance of game and the general pursuit of it, for a white man to go south of the Arkansas river to hunt was considered suicidal until after 1870. The south side of the Arkansas was considered sacred to the Indians, or at least this was their view of it, and no one ventured across the Arkansas except the old

— 81 —

traders, unless under a good escort of soldiers. The more daring of the hunters would take desperate chances to hunt pelts and furs in winter, south of the river, but they were very few, and some of them never returned, and they would go singly, never more than two together. It was considered an unknown quantity, and so it was. Rich in furs and pelts, game everywhere, no wonder it was watched by the Indians with such jealous care. With longing eyes the daring hunters would gaze across; it was forbidden fruit, and their curiosity and hankering would be increased all the more for this reason. Curly Walker and Jack Pratt were two who ventured down into that country every winter, sometimes in partnership, but most generally alone, with a strong light wagon, two good draft horses, and a good and tried saddler. They always returned loaded to the brim with the richest furs, beaver, otter, big grey wolves, and sometimes a silver fox. The little coyote was too insignificant, and only caught to make up the load. These men made their headquarters at Dodge. They traded with the writer, and I seldom paid them less than six dollars apiece for their grey wolf skins, and their load never netted them less than a thousand dollars and sometimes double that amount.

A game animal of the utmost practical value was the wild horse, which was hunted in a manner very different from that in which other game was hunted, and which was attended by peculiar difficulties and dangers. In the summer of 1878, Mr. J. T. Elliott, of Dodge City, in company with I. M. Henderson and F. C. Foxworthy, started in pursuit of wild horses. An account of their experience, as related at the time, runs as follows:

"They struck a band of about two hundred head of the finest wild horses they ever saw. After following them on horseback and afoot for nine days and nights, they finally succeeded in corralling forty-eight head.

They were thirty-six hours without water, and came near perishing for want of it. Finally the herd struck the Arkansas river, just at the time when they were ready to give up further pursuit, as they felt they could go no farther and must surely perish for want of water. New courage overtook them, however, and they stuck to their little band until the river was reached. They are holding these horses at Lakin. Mr. Elliott was in Dodge a few days ago, purchasing supplies for another trip after wild horses.''

Wild horses were numerous on the plains. These horses were the progeny of abandoned horses by plainsmen, and they were harmful to range stock. The capture of the stallions was necessary, so as to corral and capture the mare herds. The increase of the wild bands was made, yearly, by the escape of horses from the stock herds. The wild stallions could not be secured by a cowboy on horseback. A winter's campaign was necessary to accomplish the capture of the wild horses. The stallions were shot, by getting in close range by the cowboy, from time to time, and the mares were secured alive.

A horse belonging to a cattleman by the name of E. Clemence, was being saddled with a cowman's saddle, made by R. E. Rice, when it broke away from its owner, and was not seen until two years afterwards, when it was discovered with a drove of wild horses, the saddle still being in proper position on the back of the horse. The owner never recovered the animal.

Among the many things that young Dodge City took great pride in and excelled in, was one pertaining to her great game resources and the chase, and that was her dogs. They were known far and wide; every one was singing the praises of Dodge City's dogs, and justly, too, for they were the best bred of their kind in the world. I mean the pure bred greyhound, and there were several large packs of these hounds. I expect the greatest pack and the largest was one owned by Mayor James H. Kelly, and, for that reason the "gang" christened him "Dog" Kellly.

The first winter of Dodge's existence there came a deep snow, the latter part of November, which drove the antelope off the hills into the river bottom, where they bunched up by the thousands. Kelly started out, the morning after the storm, with a lot of sports and a big pack of greyhounds, and just a half mile west of Dodge they struck a big band of antelope, and the dogs soon caught all they could carry home. The snow was deep and the morning turned out to be very warm. They were all true sports and did not wish to kill for useless slaughter, and the dogs were warm and tired, so they called them off and started back to town. When they got in, Kelly missed a favorite hound by the name of Jim, only a pup six months old, but a monster. He was extraordinarily large for his age, big boned and well muscled, and gave promise of making a fine animal when he got age. So back went Kelly after Jim-dog. A mile or two from where they quit the hunt, he found a dead antelope; a few miles farther along the Santa Fe trail, he found another; and on he went, finding dead antelope until he got to the foot of Nine-mile Ridge, twenty miles west of Dodge City. There he found Jim-dog lying by the side of his last kill. I know Kelly told me there were at least a dozen antelope killed by this same dog in the twenty mile run. You see, the old Santa Fe trail ran along the river, and the wind had swept the snow, to a great measure, out of the trail, and the herd of antelope they started that morning kept the trail because it was easier traveling for them. The dog kept after them, and when he would kill one, would leave it and go after the others, until he was completely used up and worn out. Kelly brought him home in front of his saddle, and no money could buy Jim after this exploit.

Many times afterwards, when the dog got age, and they would be on a hunt twenty or thirty miles away, the other dogs would all quit and the hunters return home, when Jim-dog would be missing, sometimes it would be two or three days before his return, and he would eventually stagger in all tired out, as lank as a shad, and it would be days before he would notice anything but water and food, he would be so completely done up and worn out. We would kid Kelly by saying, "Jim has quit." "Not until the antelope does," would be his reply.

In this connection, a story entitled, "A Race to Death," clipped from the "Dodge City Times," of September 15, 1877, is of decided interest. It seems there was great rivalry between Lieutenant Gardener, of Fort Dodge, and Mr. James Kelly, as to who had the best pack of hounds. The story continues:

"The dogs of both of these gentlemen are known to be the best in the land and were eager for the contest, so they made up a race, which, from its tragic termination, will not soon be forgotten. On the morning of the 14th, together with a large party of friends and sports, they crossed the Arkansas four miles from Dodge, in the lower hills that skirt the river, and started two fine antelope. Then followed a race after the flying dogs and antelope, that for excitement and reckless enjoyment makes the finest sport in the world. The antelope, clearing away over the prairie with flying feet, almost seemed for awhile to outdo the sleek graceful hounds, who, with ears laid low and tails straight out and active muscles, dashed after the beautiful fugitives. It was a beautiful sight, the antelope, the hounds, and the huntsmen. A mile and a half of breakneck speed told the story, and just as that wonder of modern speed and ugliness, Yclept, Old Calamity (this was the name of a famous hunter), carried this deponent over the brow of a hill, the hounds brought the tired creatures to the ground. It was a victory dearly won, and the dead antelope were soon to be followed by their captors, in a chase through animal paradise.

"The last of the huntsmen had hardly reached the finish when it became apparent that the faithful dogs had given their lives for the game. Unable to stand, they were taken upon the saddles before the hunters and hurriedly carried toward the river, three miles away. Poor Fly, a most beautiful animal, never reached the water. The others were taken to the river, bled, and rubbed, but to no purpose. Rowdy soon followed Fly, and, to close the scene, Kate, an elegant imported hound of Lieutenant Gardener—both animals, for grace, beauty and speed, probably have no peers in western Kansas—paid the debt of nature. The best dogs die first, and the latter two were very king and queen. It is not everybody that enjoys this kind of sport, but, once a participant, there are but few who will not admire the graceful animals, and, after so noble an effort, be sorry to see them die." The loss of dogs was great in hot weather hunts. Kelly never sold a dog but would occasionally give one away to a dear friend, and, when parties would come to Dodge and bring their dogs for a grand hunt, Kelly would often buy one, no matter what the price. He paid one hundred dollars for a dog, and often fifty dollars, and I have known him to pay two hundred dollars when he saw an extra good one. A few days after the race, Lieutenant Gardener lost two more of his dogs. One was his favorite hound, Omar, who died of congestion of the lungs, brought about by the last day's sport. Omar had an unblemished pedigree. I could mention a great many more exciting races if I had the space.

OLD COURT HOUSE

CHAPTER V.

Indian Life of the Plains.

Upon the loss of our ranch (at Cimarron), Mr. Anthony and I thought we would take our chances again, and burn lime on the Buckner, or middle branch of the Pawnee, about thirty miles north of Fort Dodge. We were well aware that the government could not furnish us with a guard. But the Indians were now supposed to be peaceable and not on the warpath. They had only captured a few trains, burnt a number of ranches, and murdered small parties of defenseless emigrants on the trail; still they were not considered at war. All the whites were forbidden to kill or molest an Indian in any manner, although it was perfectly legitimate for them to murder us.

Under such conditions we started to work to fill our public lime contracts; we were receiving big prices for it, however, comparable to the supposed risk, getting three or four dollars a bushel. Our positive instructions from the commandant at Fort Dodge were: "Under no circumstances, no matter how aggravated, you must not kill an Indian first; let them kill you; then it will be time enough to retaliate."

Late one night, the quartermaster, Lieutenant Bassett, and his chief clerk rode into our camp, and told us that the Indians were killing everybody over in the Smoky Hill country. They had traveled all night, and laid by during the day, as they were unable to get any escort, all the troops being out in the field after savages. They left for Fort Dodge early the next morning, warning us to take the utmost precaution against surprise and attack. After the departure of Lieutenant Bassett and his clerk, Jim Wrighting, an old wagon boss, and I started for a load of wood. We had to go about four miles down the creek for it, but still in plain view of our camp. Suddenly we saw a dozen bucks, each with a led horse, rise over the top of the hill. The creek was between us, and we knew it was exceedingly boggy; it could only be crossed at certain places; if these places were missed, it would mire a saddle-blanket. I said to Jim: "What shall we do? There are some of the very lads who have been murdering the women and children over on the other river; shall we try to make it back to camp, or go right ahead, and pretend that we don't see them, or don't care for them if we do see them?" He replied: "We will take our chances, and go ahead. I hate to run, and have the boys laugh at us." "Here's with you," I answered.

We had only revolvers with us, and away they came lickety brindle. I thought: "Laddie bucks, you are tenderfeet, or young ones, or you would not come tearing down the hill that way. You don't know the creek like your forefathers, and if you keep at that gait, and don't tumble into a mire-pit up to your necks, never to get out again, then you can call me a horse thief. Then Jim Wrighting and I will go down and chop off your heads just even up with where the mire strikes them, as did Jack the Giant Killer." They left their led horses back on the hill with two guards, so they were free to ride at will. But when they arrived at the creek, they stopped short with a little jerk-up, and I think one or two of them—those in the lead—got a taste, and the others had to pull them out. Now they began to slowly and carefully hunt a crossing, which was difficult to find. Then they tried other tactics; they rode along and commenced yelling and gesticulating, motioning for us to stop, but our eyesight was not very good in that direction, and then we lost them altogether. I said: "Jim, these fellows have given us up, or else have tumbled into one of these mire holes, and we will have a time chopping their heads off when we go back." Jim answered: "No, them 'ere fellows was born on the prairie, and is as true to instinct as a buzzard is to scent carrion. They are sure to find a crossing, and be down on us in a holy minute, like a hawk on a chicken, and we are bound to have fun." You see I was beginning to get very ticklish myself—scared nearly to death—but did not want to let on for fear Jim would get scared too. I knew I must try to keep my courage up by keeping up his, and I said to him: "Jim, maybe they are only youngsters, and don't know how to shoot; they appear to be by the way they charged the creek." Jim replied: "Youngsters! nothing; them is the worst kind." Said I: "Jim, perhaps they only want to pay us a friendly visit, and want us to go to camp with them and help eat their grub; what do you think?" Jim answered: "More than likely they will take us into camp, but I will be at the taking."

This was just what I wanted. Jim's metal had "riz," and I knew he was ready to fight a stack of bobtailed wildcats. As the savages reappeared, I turned to Jim and said: "Here they come." "I knowed it," he replied. "Don't waste any ammunition; we have got twelve loads apiece, and there are only eight of them." Four of their number had remained in the rear to guard the led horses, and the eight had only delayed to find a crossing; but they trimmed themselves up besides, to be ready for any emergency. Four of them now dashed ahead, two to the right of us and two to the left, making a detour wide enough to keep out of range of our pistols, which they could plainly see in our hands. Then the first four came in, while the others closed up behind. We kept right on, however, until they finally surrounded us, and we were obliged to stop. They held their six-shooters in front of them, but we had a decided advantage of them, for we were in a thick, heavy wagon box. They wanted to know where the main big camp of the Indians was. We told them that they had been camped at the Cimarron crossing, but the soldiers had got after them and they had gone south. Then we pointed out our tents—we had five of them and they made quite a respectable figure at a distance—and told them it was the soldiers' camp. They evidently did not believe us, for they went over to the camp, bound the cook securely, whom they found asleep (why they did not kill him is a mystery), cut open every valise and took several revolvers from our tenderfeet, who had left them in their grips instead of strapping them on their persons. They carried off all the ammunition they could find, all the horses, mules, ropes, and everything else that seized their fancy. Mr. Anthony and the remainder of our men were quarrying rock up in the bluffs, and had their rifles with them.

These young bucks were certainly of those who had been concerned in the murder on the other river, for we noticed dry blood on their hands and clothing, and, as there was not an antelope or buffalo in the country then, it could not have been the blood of game in which they were ensanguined. They had evidently strayed away from the main band and were very anxious to find them, or get back south of the Arkansas river, where they were better acquainted with the country. They were a little out of their regular beat where they now found themselves,, and that fact undoubtedly deterred them from committing further acts of deviltry.

I have seen with my glass from the lookout on top of my building at the ranch (Cimarron) two hundred or three hundred wagons and two thousand head of mules and oxen, all waiting for the river to go down, so that they could cross; and I have watched a band of Indians charge upon them like an avalanche, kill the poor, panic-stricken Mexican drivers as easily and unmercifully as a bunch of hungry wolves would destroy a flock of sheep. Then the savages would jump off their horses long enough to tear the reeking scalps from their victims' heads and dash away after fresh prey. They, of course, drove off many of the horses and cattle. Sometimes the owners would succeed in getting the majority of their stock into the corrals, and for days and weeks afterward the miserable mutilated oxen would struggle back to the river for water, some with their tails cut off close, some with ears gone, some with great strips of hide stripped from their bodies, others with arrows sticking out of them, the cruel shafts sunk deep into their paunches half way up to the feathers. The Indians did not care anything for the cattle as long as there was plenty of buffalo; they mutilated the poor creatures to show their damnable meanness. The horses, of course, they valued.

Once, while a train of wagons was waiting to cross, three or four of them having already made the passage, leaving the Mexican drivers on this side with the wagons loaded with loose wool, a lot of Indians swooped down upon them. When the men saw the savages, the poor defenseless wretches made for their wagons and concealed themselves under the wool, but the Indians followed them in and killed the last one with an old camp ax belonging to the train, afterwards mutilating their bodies in their usual barbarous manner.

Satank was chief of the Kiowas when I first knew him, but was deposed because he ran away from camp and left the women and children. Satanta took his place. The Indians were camped in a large bottom called Cheyenne bottom, about eight miles north of old Fort Zarah, and the same distance from where the town of Great Bend now is. All of the bucks were out on a hunt, or on the warpath excepting Satank. The soldiers from Fort Larned suddenly surprised them in their camp, when Satank jumped on his pony and skipped. He certainly would have been killed or captured had he remained; so Satank, deeming discretion the better part of valor, lit out. His tribe, however, claims that it was his duty to have died at his post in defense of the women and children, as they had left him back for that purpose, to guard the camp.

Satanta was considered the worst Indian on the plains, and for a long time the most dreaded. He was war-chief of the Kiowas. There were many stories afloat about his doings at Fort Dodge, some of which are true, others not. In 1866 a committee was sent from Washington to inquire into the causes of the continued warfare on the border, and what the grievances of the Indians were. Of course Satanta was sent for and asked to talk his mind freely. He was very pathetic. He had "no desire to kill the white people, but they ruthlessly killed off the buffalo, and let their carcasses rot on the prairie, while the Indian only killed from necessity. The whites had put out fires on the prairie and destroyed the grass, which caused their ponies to die of starvation, as well as the buffalo. They cut down and destroyed the timber and made large fires of it, while the Indian was satisfied to cook his 'chuck' with a few dry limbs. Only the other day," continued he, "I picked up a little switch in the road and it made my heart bleed to think that small limb so ruthlessly torn up and thoughtlessly destroyed by the white man would have in the course of time become a grand tree, for the use and benefit of my children and my grandchildren." After the powwow, and when he had a few drinks of red liquor in him, he showed his real nature, and said to the interpreter: "Now, didn't I give it to those white men in good style? The switch I saw in the road made my heart glad instead of sad, for I knew there was a tenderfoot ahead, because an old plainsman never would have anything but a quirt or a good pair of spurs. I said, 'Come on, boys; we have got him;' and we came in sight of him, pressing him closely on the dead run; he threw his gun away and held tight onto his hat, for fear he might lose it."

Another time, when Satanta had remained at the fort for a long time and had worn out his welcome, so that no one would give him anything to drink, he went up to the quarters of his friend, Bill Bennett, the stage agent, and begged him for liquor. Bill was mixing a bottle of medicine to drench a sick mule, and the moment he set the bottle down to do something else Satanta picked it up and drank most of its contents before stopping. Of course it made the savage dreadfully sick, as well as angry. He then went up to a certain officer's quarters and again begged there for liquor, to cure him of the effects of the previous dose, but the officer refused. Still Satanta persisted; he would not leave; and after awhile the officer went to his closet and took a swallow of balsam copaiba, placing the bottle back. Satanta watched his opportunity and, as soon as the officer left the room, seized the bottle and drank its contents. That, of course, was a worse dose than the horse medicine, and the next day the wily Satanta called his people together, crossed the Arkansas, and went south. Before leaving, however, he burnt all of Mr. Coryell's hay, which was stacked opposite the fort. He then continued on to Crooked creek, where he killed three wood-choppers, all of which he said he did in revenge for trying to poison him twice at Fort Dodge.

In the fall the Indians would come in, make a treaty, and draw rations, and break the treaty as soon as the grass was green in the spring. I have seen the Arkansas bottom for miles above and miles below Fort Dodge covered with Indians' tepees and ponies—thousands of the former and many thousands of the latter—the Indians all drawing rations, and the whole country full of game, black with buffalo and large bands of antelope, with deer on the islands and in the brush, and not a few elk in the breaks and rough country.

I think it was in 1867 our government got a very liberal streak, and sent the Indians thousands of sacks of flour, pantaloons in abundance, and a big lot of stiff-rim hats, bound around the edge with tin or German silver, to hold the rim in shape. They also sent them a few light-running ambulances. The savages, to show their appreciation of these magnanimous gifts from the "Great Father," threw the flour on the prairie in order to get the sacks for breech-clouts. They cut out the seats of the pantaloons, as they said an Indian's posterior was too warm anyhow; they cut the crown off the hats and used them as playthings, shying them in the air like a white boy does a flat stone, to see them sail away. The ambulances they were very proud of. The government neglected to send any harness with them, so the Indians manufactured their own. They did not understand anything about lines, and, instead, they drove with a quirt or short whip; when the near horse would go too much gee, they whipped up the off horse, and when he would go too much haw, they pounded away at the near horse again, and vice versa, all the time. This unique manner of driving kept the poor animals in a dead run most of the time. I remember taking a ride with Little Raven, chief of the Arapahoes. At first we started off gently; but the ponies did not go straight, so he kept tapping them, now the off horse, then the near, until finally he got them on a rapid gallop, and I thought, at one time, that my head would surely pop up through the roof of the ambulance. The country was very level, fortunately, or I don't know what would have been the outcome.

In the fall of 1869 Mr. Anthony and I were filling a hay contract at Camp Supply. Our camp was about ten miles up the Beaver. One afternoon I started from Camp Supply for my own camp, after having partaken of an excellent dinner at the officers' mess. It was issuing day to the Indians; I think the first time that live beef was ever distributed to them. Several hundred big, wild Texas steers were turned over to them, but the Indians didn't care for the meat; they could always get plenty of buffalo, which they infinitely preferred, but they took

reat delight in the sport of killing them after their
anner of hunting buffalo. They ran the frightened
eatures on horseback, lanced them with their spears,
id shot them full of arrows, until the last one was dead.
he whole trail was strewn with dead steers, though
arcely one of them was touched for food. Occasionally
would notice one whose skin was covered with pretty
hite spots, and this fact having struck the savage fancy,
ey had peeled off the most beautiful of them to make
livers for their arrows.

As I was approaching my camp, yet some two miles
stant, a large, fat Indian rode out of the brush on a
eculiar piebald pony, and by signs indicated to me that
e wanted to swap. I asked if he meant that pony; he
iswered, "Not my pony." "What is it, then?" said I.
e tried hard to make me understand, but I could not
lk. He finally motioned for me to ride into the brush,
it I said: "Here, old fellow, none of your tricks; I
in't want any squaws." He said: "No squaw," so I
ide in, and saw a fine dog with his hindquarters gone.
said to him: "You go to ———; what do you take me
ir?" He replied: "Your'e a fool; you don't know
hat is good." I answered him: "Eat it yourself, if you
link it is so nice." He then said he had just traded the
iddle to some white folks, and wanted to trade me the
her part. The skin was still hanging on, attached to
ie body of the dog where he had stripped it from the
iddle, but I looked at him in disgust and rode off.

When I arrived at my camp Mr. Anthony and the
iys were eating supper. I threw my bridle-reins over
ie front standard of a wagon and walked up to the
re where they were eating. They said to me, "Come and
et some supper." I told them no; I had partaken of a
earty dinner at the officers' mess just before I left
upply. Anthony said: "You better have some; I
ought the saddle of an antelope from an Indian this

— 95 —

afternoon; its the sweetest and juiciest meat I eve
tasted." So did all the men urge me to try it. Indeed
they were lavish in the praise of their antelope meat.
said: "Are you sure that is antelope meat? Antelop
are very scarce; I haven't seen one for a long time.'
They were certain it was antelope; it tasted like antelope
they knew it was antelope, and remarked it was a goo(
one. After they had finished supper, I said: "Fellows
do you know what you have all been eating so heartily?'
They all answered antelope, of course; nothing else.
told them **it was dog!** They would not believe me, and
jumped on my horse, rode back, threw my lariat over th
dog's head and pulled it into camp. "Now," said I, ":
big, fat Indian, on a piebald pony, tried to trade me th
balance of this carcass." Anthony said: "That's him
sure," and then he tried to vomit. The others poked thei
fingers down their throats to coax up the obnoxious meat
but I interrupted them with: "It's no use, boys; he i
down deep in your stomachs; let him stay there."

As an interesting picture of another phase of India
life on the plains, I quote the following early day descrip
tion of an Indian duel and their death songs:

"Two Indians came forth from different lodges, eacl
with a gun in his hand. They walked some little distanc
from the rest of the Indians and took post distant fron
each other about fifty yards. At a given signal the
turned, raised their rifles to their faces, and fired. Botl
fell wounded, one fatally. They were immediately sur
rounded by friends who made no effort to bind thei
wounds but simply stood around, talking among them
selves and gesticulating, while the wounded Indians, a
soon as they fell, began the death song. There was littl
music in it. It was a sort of deep-down unnatural tone o
voice, kept up for half a minute or so at a time, when i
would cease and the sufferers would, in the interim, mak
a confession of all the evil deeds that they had done

They would tell of the massacres in which they had been engaged, how many scalps they had lifted from the heads of white people, the number of ponies they had stolen, together with all sorts of important and unimportant evil doings in their lifetime. This accomplished, they were ready to give up the ghost.''

This is what the great chief, Spotted Tail, told the President, when he visited Washington, many years ago, with a lot of other chiefs. It is so much like the wants of Indians who visited Fort Dodge in early days, that I can't help relating it here.

"We want our provisions sent to the agencies that I have mentioned. You told us your nation increases; we want to increase, too, in prosperity and in numbers. You said you wished us to be like white men, and so we are here today, dressed in white men's clothes. I want the kind of cattle the white men have, short horns. I want everything in writing, before I go home, so there be no mistake. We want teachers of English; we want Catholic priests to teach us. We should like saw mills and grist mills and agricultural instruments and seeds. We want five or six stores; then we could buy cheaper from one than at another. I am very well dressed and so are the others. They want forty dollars apiece to buy things for their women and children, and they would like to have a trunk apiece to carry their clothing in. As the weather is getting a little cold, we should like to have an overcoat apiece. We see you wearing overcoats, and we should like to have them.''

Some of them, who came to Fort Dodge to state their grievances, wanted more than these. They wanted even the earth and it fenced in.

Continual danger from the Indians made the pioneers of early days continually apprehensive of Indian attack and continually on their guard against surprise, and keenly watchful when any suspicious move on the part of the Indians was observed. Naturally, this caution and watchfulness were, at times, somewhat overdone, Indian alarms sometimes proving groundless, and precautions, against seemingly threatened outbreak, proving needless, or even laughable.

In the fall of 1874 I went to Texas, and when I came home I found my partner, Mr. H. L. Sitler, who was interested with me in a government hay contract, laid up with a bad flesh wound he had received in a fight with the Indians only the day before, and the men in camp thirty miles west of Fort Dodge badly demoralized, as the Indians had jumped them a time or two very recently. I mounted a good horse, taking with me a fine rifle and two revolvers, and started for camp, where I arrived about sundown that night. I had a long talk with the boss, and I promised to stay right with them, which promise and my cheering conversation soon placed them in good humor, and they declared their intention to keep on at work. In the night there came on one of our late, cold, misty, drizzling rains, The tent was leaky and the next morning we all got up feeling wet and generally miserable. The storm looked as if it had set in for the week. Of course, I did not want to remain there, but the only compromise, after my promise of the evening before, was to leave with the boss my fine rifle, as well as my horse, and ride back in its place an old, wornout one. I thought that anything was better than staying there; so I exchanged horses, left my rifle, and started for Fort Dodge.

The misty rain was constantly beating in my face, so that it almost blinded me. I left the main road and took the trail, or near cut-off, around by the river, and when I got about ten miles from camp, and at nearly the place where Mr. Sitler was shot, up jumped, as I thought, a lot of Indians, yelling and shouting. They seemed to be traveling in Indian file, one right behind the other, as

I had often seen them. Thinks I to myself, I will just fool you; I will make a long detour around the hollow and come back into the trail about two miles below here, and you fellows are trying to cut me off. When I don't come out below, as you expect me to do, you will go over to the main road and watch there. So I carried out my plan and came back to the place two miles below, but they were again running and yelling ahead of me, it seemed, worse than before. I tried it again, with the same result. Then I went out to the main road, chose my position, and waited for their coming, intending to shoot my old horse and then lie behind him. How many times I wished I had not left my good horse in camp, as I coulld easily have run away from the Indians; and I further cursed my luck that I was so foolish as to give up my rifle also. After waiting and waiting in the rain, until I was completely soaked and tired out, expecting them to be on me every minute, I thought I would go back to the trail along the rough breaks by the river and take my chances. When I got back the last time, up they jumped again; but the wind and rain had let up a little and I saw what I had taken for Indians was nothing but a fllock of blue cranes. You see the wind and rain were so blinding— one of those awfully cold, misty storms—that when I approached the river the birds would rise and merely skim along through the willows, one after another, and so I kept chasing them down stream a mile or more every time I scared them up; but they scared me worse than I scared them; they chased me back to the main road nearly frightened to death. We had many a hearty laugh over my fright from the cranes.

CHAPTER VI

Wild Days With the Soldiers

As has been stated, the site of Fort Dodge was an old camping ground for trains going to New Mexico. The government was obliged to erect a fort here, but even then the Indians struggled for the mastery, and made many attacks, not only on passing trains, but on the troops themselves. I witnessed the running off of over one hundred horses, those of Captain William Thompson's troop of the Seventh United States Cavalry. The savages killed the guard and then defied the garrison, as they knew the soldiers had no horses on which to follow them. Several times have I seen them run right into the fort, cut off and gather up what loose stock there was around, and kill and dismount and deliberately scalp one or more victims, whom they had caught outside the garrison, before the soldiers could mount and follow.

Early one very foggy morning they made a descent on a large body of troops, mostly infantry, with a big lot of transportation. At this time the government was preparing for a campaign against them. It was a bold thing to do, but they made a brave dash right into and among the big mule trains. It was so dark and foggy that nothing was seen of them until they were in the camp, and they made a reign of bedlam for a short time. They succeeded in cutting about fifty mules loose from the wagons and getting away with them, and killing, scalping, and mutilating an old hunter named Ralph, just as he was in the act of killing a coyote he had caught in a steel trap, not three hundred yards from the mule camp. Of course they shot him with arrows, and then speared him, so that no report should be heard from the camp. "Boots and saddles" was soon sounded, and away went two companies of cavalry, some scouts following, or at

DODGE CITY, 1878

east acting as flankers, I among the latter. The cavalry kept to the road while we took to the hills. In the course of time we came up to the Indians—the fog still very heavy—and were right in among them before we knew it. Then came the chase. First we ran them, and then they turned and chased us. They outnumbered us ten to one. More than once did we draw them down within a mile or two of the cavalry, when we would send one of our number back and plead with the captain to help us; but his reply was that he had orders to the contrary, and could not disobey. I did not think he acted from fear or was a coward, but I told him afterward he lost an opportunity that day to make his mark and put a feather in his cap; and I believe he thought so, too, and regretted he had not made a charge regardless of orders.

In a previous chapter, the account was given of the massacre of the little Mexican train and the scattering of their flour and feather beds upon the bluffs near the site of Fort Dodge, but before the fort was established. On the bottom immediately opposite is where Colonel Thompson's horses of the troop of the Seventh Cavalry were run off by the Indians. One of the herders on duty jumped into the river and was killed; the other unfortunately or fortunately was chased by the savages right into the parade ground of the fort before the last Indian leaving him, grabbing at his bridle-rein in his determined effort to get the soldier's horse. The persistent savage had fired all his arrows at the trooper, and the latter, when taken to the hospital, had two or three of the cruel hafts stuck in his back, from the effect of which wounds he died in a few hours.

Major Kidd, or Major Yard, I do not remember which just now, was in command at Fort Larned, and had received orders from department headquarters not to permit less than a hundred wagons to pass the fort at one time, on account of the danger from Indians, all of whom were on the warpath. One day four or five ambulances from the Missouri river arrived at the fort filled with New Mexico merchants and traders on the way home to their several stations. In obedience to his orders, the commanding officer tried to stop them. After laying at Larned a few days, the delay became very wearisome; they were anxious to get back to their business, which was suffering on account of their prolonged absence. They went to the commanding officer several times, begging and pleading with him to allow them to proceed. Finally he said: ''Well, old French Dave, the guide and interpreter of the post, is camped down the creek; go and consult him; I will abide by what he says.'' So, armed with some fine old whisky and the best brand of cigars, which they had brought from St. Louis, they went in a body down to French Dave's camp, and, after filling him with their elegant liquor and handing him some of the cigars, they said: ''Now, Dave, there are twenty of us here, all bright young men who are used to the frontier; we have plenty of arms and ammunition, and know how to use them; don't you think it safe for us to go through?'' Dave was silent; they asked the question again, but he slowly puffed away at his fine cigar and said nothing. When they put the question to him for a third time, Dave deliberately, and without looking up, said: ''One man go troo twenty time; Indian no see you. Twenty mans go troo one time and Indian kill every s— o— b— of you.''

General Sheridan was at Fort Dodge in the summer of 1866, making every preparation to begin an active and thorough campaign against the Indians. One day he perceived, at a long distance south, something approaching the post which, with the good field-glass, we took to be a flag of truce—the largest flag of the kind, I suppose, that was ever employed for a like purpose. Little Raven had procured an immense white wagon-sheet and nailed it to one of his long, straight tepee poles, and lashed it upright to his ambulance. He marched in with a band of his warriors to learn whether he was welcome, and to tell the big general he would be in the next sleep with all his people to make a treaty. Sheridan told him that maybe he could get them in by the next night, and maybe he had better say in two or three sleeps from now. Little Raven said: "No; all we want is one sleep." The time he asked for was granted by the general, but this was the last Sheridan ever saw of him until the band made its usual treaty that winter. The wary old rascal used this ruse to get the women and children out of the way before using hostilities. The first time he came after peace was declared he was minus his ambulance. I asked him what had become of it. He replied: "Oh, it made too good a trail for the soldiers; they followed us up day after day by its tracks. Then I took it to pieces, hung the wheels in a tree, hid the balance of it here and there, and everywhere, in the brush, and buried part of it."

During the same expedition, after the main command had left the fort with all the guides and scouts, there were some important dispatches to be taken to the command. Two beardless youths volunteered to carry them. They had never seen a hostile Indian, or slept a single night on a lonely plain, but were fresh from the states. I knew that it was murder to allow them to go, and I pitied them from the bottom of my heart. They were full of enthusiasm, however, and determined to go. I gave them repeated warnings and advice as to how they should travel, how they should camp, and what precaution to take, and they started. They never reached the command, but were captured in the brush on Beaver creek about dusk one evening—taken alive without ever firing a shot. The savages had been closely watching them, and when they had unsaddled their horses and gone into the brush to cook their supper, (having laid down their arms on their saddles), the Indians jumped them, cut their throats, scalped them, and stripped them naked.

Drunken Tom Wilson, as he was called, left a few days afterward with dispatches for the command, which he reached without accident, just as French Dave had intimated to the New Mexico merchants about one man going through safely. It made Tom, however, too rash and brave. Give him a few canteens of whisky and he would go anywhere. I met him after his trip at Fort Larned one day when he was about starting to Fort Dodge. I said: "Tom, wait until tonight and we will go with you," but he declined; he thought he was invulnerable and left for the post. On the trail that night, as I and others were going to Fort Dodge, under cover of darkness, our horses shied at something lying in the road as we were crossing Coon creek. We learned afterwards that it was the body of drunken Tom and his old white horse. The Indians had laid in wait for him there under the bank of the creek, and killed both him and his horse, I suppose, before he had a chance to fire a shot.

Two scouts, Nate Marshall and Bill Davis, both brave men, gallant riders, and splendid shots, were killed at Mulberry creek by the Indians. It was supposed they had made a determined fight, as a great many cartridge shells were found near their bodies, at the foot of a big cotton-wood tree. But it appears that was not so. I felt a deep interest in Marshall, because he had worked for me for several years; he was well acquainted with the sign language, and terribly stuck on the Indian ways—I reckon the savage maidens, particularly. He was so much of an Indian himself that he could don breech-clouts and live with them for months at a time; in fact, so firmly did he think he had ingratiated himself with them, that he believed they would never kill him. Ed. Gurrier, a half-breed and scout, had often written him from Fort Lyon not to be too rash; that the Indians would kill anyone when they were at war; they knew no friends among the white men. Marshall and Davis were ordered to arry dispatches to General Sheridan, then in the field. They arrived at Camp Supply, where the general was at hat time, delivered their dispatches, and were immediately sent back to Fort Dodge with another batch of lispatches and a small mail. When they had ridden to vithin twenty miles of Fort Dodge, they saw a band of Arapahoes and Cheyennes emerging from the brush on he Mulberry. They quicklly hid themselves in a deep ut on the left of the trail as it descends the hill going outhwest, before the Indians got a glimpse of them, as he ravine was deep enough to perfectly conceal both hem and their horses, and there they remained until, s they thought, the danger had passed.

Unfortunately for them, however, one of the savages, rom some cause, had straggled a long way behind the aain body. Still the scouts could have made their escape, ut Marshall very foolishly dismounted, called to the ndian, and made signs for him to come to him; they vould not hurt him; not to be afraid; they only wanted o know who were in the party, where they were going, nd what they were after. Marshall imposed such mplicit confidence in the Indians that he never believed or a moment that they would kill him, but he was mistaken. The savage to whom Marshall had made the sign o come to him was scared to death; he shot off his pistol, vhich attracted the attention of the others, who immediately came dashing back on the trail, and were right ipon the scouts before the latter saw them. It was then . race for the friendly shelter of the timber on the creek iottom. But the fight was too unequal; the savages etting under just as good a cover as the scouts. The ndians fired upon them from every side until the unforunate men were soon dispatched, and one of their horses illed; the other, a splendid animal, was captured by the Cheyennes, but the Arapahoes claimed him because they aid there were twice as many of them. Consequently,

— 105 —

there arose a dispute over the ownership of the horse, when one of the more deliberate savages pulled out his six-shooter and shot the horse dead. Then he said: "Either side may take the horse that wants him." This is generally the method employed by the Indians to settle any dispute regarding the ownership of live property.

As an example of the encounters the soldiers had so frequently with the Indians, in frontier days, there cannot be a better than that of the battle of Little Coon creek, in 1868. I did not take part in this fight, but I was at Fort Dodge at the time, knew the participants, and was present when the survivors entered the fort, after the fray was over. One of the scouts who took part, Mr. Lee Herron, still lives, at Saint Paul, Nebraska, and I am indebted to him for the following account of the fight and the copy of the accompanying song, which he compiled for me, very recently, with his own hand.

FIGHT AT LITTLE COON CREEK.

During 1868 the Indians were more troublesome than at any previous time in the history of the old Santa Fe Trail—so conceded by old plainsmen, scouts and Indian fighters at that time. It was a battle ground from old Fort Harker to Fort Lyon, or Bent's Old Fort at the mouth of the Picketware, near where it empties into the Arkansas river. The old Santa Fe Trail had different outfitting points at the east, and at different periods. At one time it started at Westport, now Kansas City, at an earlier date at Independence, Missouri, and at one time— in the fore part of the nineteenth century—at St. Louis, Missouri; but from 1860 to 1867 the principal outfitting point was at Leavenworth, Kansas, and its principal destination in the west was Fort Union and Santa Fe, New Mexico. But Fort Dodge and vicinity was the central point from which most of the Indian raids culminated and depredations were committed. The Indians became so annoying in 1868 that the Barlow Sanderson

tage line, running from Kansas City, Missouri, to Santa
?e, New Mexico, found it necessary to abandon the line
ıs there were not enough soldiers to escort the stages
hrough. Also the Butterfield stage line on the Smoky
Iill route was abandoned. Several of the southern tribes
ıf Indians consisted of Kiowas, Comanches, Arapahoes,
Jheyennes, Apaches and Dog Soldiers. The Dog Soldiers
onsisted of renegades of all the other tribes and were a
lesperate bunch, with Charley Bent as their leader. Also
he Sioux, a northern tribe, was on the warpath and allied
hemselves with the southern tribes. In all some five
housand or more armed Indians joined forces to drive the
vhite people off the plains, and it almost looked for a
ime as though they would succeed, for they were in
arnest and desperate. Had they been better armed, our
osses would have been much heavier than they were as
hey greatly outnumbered us. It was a common occur-
ence for us to fight them one to ten, and often one to
wenty or more, but the Indians frequently had to depend
ntirely upon their bows and arrows, as at times they
lad no ammunition. This placed them at a disadvantage
ıt long range as their bows and arrows were not efficient
ıver two hundred feet, but at close range, from twenty-
ïve to one hundred feet, their arrows were as deadly as
ıullets, if not more so. So after the stage line was dis-
:ontinued, a detail was made of the most fearless and
letermined men of the soldiers stationed at Fort Dodge,
ıs a sort of pony express, which was in commission at
ııght time, as it would be impossible to travel in the day-
ïme with less than a troop of cavalry or a company of
nfantry, and they had no assurance of getting through
vithout losing a good part of the men, or perhaps the
ıntire troop, and the entire troop would stand a big
:hance of being massacred. Indeed, in the fall of 1868—
)ctober, I think—I joined Tom Wallace's scouts and
vent with the Seventh United States Cavalry and several
:ompanies of infantry, Wallace's scouts and a company

of citizen scouts, with California Joe in command, all unde
command of General Alfred Sully, a noted Indian fighte
of the early days. The command started south, crossin
the Arkansas river just above Fort Dodge. From th
time we left the Arkansas river it was a constant skirmisl
until we reached the Wichita mountains, the winter hom
of the southern tribes. After we got into the mountains
the Indians crowded us so hard that the whole comman
was compelled to retreat, and had not the comman
formed in a hollow square, with all non-combatants i
the center, it might have proved disastrous. As it was,
number were killed and some were taken prisoners an
burned at the stake and terribly tortured. A very inter
esting article could be written about this expedition, an
I think but a very little is known of it, as there is bu
a sentence relating to it in history.

Fort Dodge was the pivot and distributing base o
supplies in 1868, and thrilling events were taking plac
all the time. All trains were held up and some capture
and burned, and all who were with the train were kille
or captured, and the captured were subjected to th
most excruciating torture and abuse. I saw one part
which was massacred up west of Dodge. Not a soul wa
left to tell who they were or where they were going, an
no doubt their friends looked for them for many years
and at last gave up in despair. I served in the Civil Wa
in Company C, Eighty-third Pennsylvania Volunteers, an
we sustained the heaviest losses numerically of any
regiment in the entire Union army, except the Fifth Nev
Hampshire. This is according to war records compile
by Colonel Fox. But there were many times along th
old Santa Fe trail where the percentage of losses wa
greater than in the Civil War. However, there is n
record kept of it that I am aware of. Of course in thes
fights there were but a few men engaged, where in th
Civil War there were tens of thousands and many thou
sands lost their lives, and a few hundred men who los

their lives out on the great plains was scarcely known except to those in the vicinity—hundreds of miles from civilization.

On the night of September first, 1868, I was coming from Fort Larned with mail and dispatches when I met a mule team and government wagon loaded with wood, going to Big Coon creek, forty miles east of Fort Dodge, as there was a small sod fort located there, garrisoned with a sergeant and ten men. These few men could hold this place against twenty times their number as it was all earth and sod, with a heavy clay roof, and port-holes all around, and they could kill off the Indians about as fast as they would come up, as long as their ammunition held out. But they were not safe outside a minute. They had been depending on buffalo chips for fuel, as there was no other fuel available, and as soon as the men would attempt to go out to gather buffalo chips, the Indians lying in little ravines of which there was a number close by, would let a shower of arrows or bullets into them. The reason why the men with the wagon whom I have mentioned were going to Big Coon Creek was to take them wood. I told the boys who were with the wagon to under no consideration leave Big Coon creek, or Fort Coon as we called it, until a wagon train came by, and if they would not wait for a wagon train, by all means to wait until it got good and dark, as the Indians are inclined to be suspicious at night time, and not so apt to attack as in daytime. The men, whose names were Jimmy Goodman, Company B, Eeventh United States Cavalry, Hartman and Tolen, Company F, Third United States Infantry, and Jack O'Donald, Company A, Third United States Infantry, imagined I was over-cautious, and started back the afternoon of September fourth, 1868.

I, after parting with them, continued on towards Fort Dodge, where I arrived just before daylight, the morning of September second. After lying down and having a

— 109 —

much needed sleep, and rest, I, in the evening, went up to Tapan's sutler store. I noticed the Indians' signals of smoke in different directions, and I knew this foreboded serious trouble. They signaled by fire at night and smoke by day, and could easily communicate with one another fifty or sixty miles. I had not been at the sutler store long, where I was in conversation with some of the scouts. There were a number of famous scouts at Fort Dodge at that time consisting of such men as California Joe, Wild Bill Hickok, Apache Bill, Bill Wilson and quite a number of others whose names I have forgotten, but I noticed the enlisted men had to stand the brunt of the work. I never could understand why this was and it is a mystery to me, except these scouts of fame were too precious, and soldiers didn't count for much for there were more of them. While I was standing talking, an orderly came up to me and said the commanding officer wanted to see me at once. It was nearly night at this time. I at once reported to the commanding officer. He informed me that he wanted me to select a reliable man and be ready to start with dispatches for Fort Larned, seventy-five miles east on the wet route, or sixty-five miles east on the dry route. As I had just come in that morning, I thought it peculiar he did not select some of those noble spirits I had just left at the sutler's store, but it was possible he was saving them up for extreme emergency, but I could not see from the outlook of the surroundings as the emergency would be any more acute than at the present time, as the terms of the dispatch we were to take, if I remember right, were for reinforcements. I selected a man of Company B, Troop Seven, United States Cavalry, named Paddy Boyle, who had no superior for bravery and determination when in dangerous quarters, on the whole Santa Fe Trail. Paddy sleeps under the sod of old Kentucky. For many years he had no peer and few equals as a staunch, true friend and brave man. As luck would have it on this night Boyle selected one of the swiftest and best winded

Dr. T. L. McCarty
One of the Seven Old Timers of Dodge City

horses at the fort, and only for that I would not have been permitted to ever see Fort Dodge again, for that horse, as later will be seen, saved our lives. We had our canteens filled with government whisky before we started, as a prevention for rattlesnake bites, as rattlesnakes were thick in those days, or any other serious event which might occur, and often did occur in those strange days on the Great Plains.

I felt a premonition unusual and Boyle did too, and several of our friends came and bade us good-bye, which was rather an unusual occurrence. I don't think the commanding officer thought we would ever get through, for Indian night signals were going up in all directions, which indicated that they were very restless.

When we arrived near Little Coon creek we heard firing and yelling in front of us. We went down into a ravine leading in the direction we were going, cautiously approaching nearer where the firing was going on, and made the discovery that the Indians had surrounded what we supposed to be a wagon train. We knew somebody was in trouble and could at this time see objects seated all around on the nearby plains, which proved to be Indians, but as yet we had not been seen by the Indians or, if they did see us, they took us for some of their own party as it was night. They were so busy with the wagon train that they didn't know we were whites until we went dashing through their midst, whooping and yelling like Comanches, and firing right and left. Instead of being a wagon train as we thought it was, it proved to be the party we last met at or near Big Coon creek with the wood wagon, and we arrived just in time to save them from being massacred. At this time the Indians made a desperate charge, but were repulsed and driven back in good style. When I looked the ground over and saw what a poor place it was to make a fight against such odds, I knew that as soon as it got daylight we were sure to lose our scalps, and that at any moment they might get in some good shots on one of their desperate charges, and disable or kill all of us. I suggested that either Boyle or myself try and cut his way through the Indians and go to the fort for assistance. As Boyle had the best horse in the outfit—a fine dapple-grey, the same horse previously mentioned in this article—Boyle said he would make the attempt.

He took a sip from his canteen and then handed it to me, saying we would probably need it more than he would, as he didn't propose to be taken alive and that if he got through he could drink at the other end of the line. It always seemed to me this noble horse understood the situation and knew what was wanted of him. Our horses had a terrible dread of Indians. When Boyle started it needed no effort to induce the noble dapple-grey to go, for he darted away like a shot out of a gun. When Boyle left us, he had to go down in a deep ravine which was the bed of Little Coon creek, and where the main trail weaved to the right for a distance of perhaps two hundred yards in order to again get out of the ravine, as the banks were very steep and not prarcticable to go straight across. At this time some of the Indians attempted to head him off, and did so far as following the main trail was concerned, as I had a fairly good view of the top of the hill where Boyle should come out. At this time several shots were fired at Boyle, and not seeing him come out I supposed he was killed and told the men so, and there was no possible chance of us ever getting out that I could see. Up to this time we had been behind the wagon, but the Indians were circling all around us, and I could see we had to get into more secure shelter as all the protection we had was the wagon which was very poor protection from arrows and bullets. Within a short distance of us there was a deep buffalo wallow. When the Indians had quieted down a little, we, by strenuous efforts, pushed the wagon so it stood over the buffalo wallow. After getting into the wallow we found conditions much improved so far as shelter from the firing was concerned and if our ammunition was more plentiful we would have felt much more encouraged, but we knew unless relief came before daylight they would get us. But I will mention a little matter that perhaps many of the good people of Kansas would not approve of, as Kansas is a prohibition state. The canteen full of whisky did a lot to keep up our spirits. Occasionally I would give each one a small amount and did not neglect myself. This little bit of stimulant, under these extremely unpleasant conditions had a very good effect, and I believe our aim was more steady and effective.

The Indians charged repeatedly, uttering the most blood curdling yells. Most of the time they would be on the side of their horses so we could not see them, but hitting their ponies, the bullets would go through and occasionally get one of them. They several times charged up within a few feet of the wagon, but the boys were calm and took deadly aim and would drive them back every time. There were some of their ponies lying dead close to the wagon. It was seldom the Indians would make such desperate and determined efforts when there was nothing to gain except to get a few scalps, but I think at that time, in fact, at all times when they were on the warpath, a scalp-lock was more desirable to an Indian warrior than anything else their imagination could conceive. It was the ones who got the most scalps that were the most honored, and promotion to chiefs depended on the amount of scalps secured while out on expeditions on the warpath. I have known Indians to be cornered when they would make the most desperate fight, and fight until all were killed.

At this time our ammunition was getting low and we saw we couldn't hold out much longer. Goodman had been wounded seven times by arrows and bullets, Jack O'Donald had been struck with a tomahawk and received other wounds, Nolan was wounded with arrows and bullets. This left Hartman and myself to stand off the Indians, and towards the last Hartman was wounded but not seriously disabling him. I would load my Remington revolver and hand it to Nolan, who was obliged to fire with his left hand, his right arm being shattered. The Indians charged right up to the wagons more than once. At one time O'Donald had a hand to hand encounter with one, and was struck on the head with a tomahawk. It was only by the most desperate exertions that anyone escaped. The party were entirely within their power more than once, but they would cease action to carry off their dead—which lost the Indians many a fight, as they thought if one of their number lost his scalp he could not enter the Happy Hunting Grounds.

Finally we saw the Indians apparently getting ready for another rush from a different direction, fully expecting that they would get us if they did. At about the same time I noticed a body of horsemen coming out of a ravine in another direction. We supposed this was another tactful dodge of the Indians and they would come at us from two ways. At this time we hadn't any prospect or hope of saving our lives. Had we had plenty of ammunition we could have probably held them off for awhile, but ammunition we did not have, perhaps not over a dozen rounds. It was understood by all of us that we would not be taken alive, but that each one's last shot was to be used on himself.

What seemed extremely mysterious was when the body of horsemen, just previously mentioned, came out of the ravine, the men on the horses seemed to be dressed in white, and as they came on to high ground, deployed a skirmish line. I had seen Indians form a line of battle occasionally, but it was not common for them to do so.

After they had advanced within three hundred or four hundred feet of us we were still undecided who they were, but they acted and had more the appearance of white men than Indians. But relief we hadn't the least hope of. It was hard to realize that any assistance could possibly reach us, as there were no scouting parties out that we knew of, and we had every reason to believe Boyle was killed and never reached the fort. This body of men dressed in white halted about three hundred feet from us and stood there like a lot of ghosts. (The reader must remember this was in the night time and we could not make out objects plainly. Had it been daytime we could of course readily have seen who they were).

The suspense at this time was becoming very acute. I told the men I would risk one shot at them and end the suspense. But at this Goodman raised his head and looking in the direction of the horsemen remarked, "I believe they are our own men; don't fire." I was about of the same opinion, but the Indians were always resorting to some trickery. I had about made up my mind they were trying to deceive us and make us think they were white men. Finally one of them hollered, speaking in English, that they were friends. But that didn't satisfy me as the renegade Bent boys were with the Dog Soldiers and could speak good English, and were always resorting to every conceivable form of fraudulent devices to get the advantage of white people. They had been the means of causing the deaths of scores of people in this way.

At this time each one of our party was prepared to take his own life if necessary, rather than to be taken prisoner, for being captured only meant burning at the stake, with the most brutal torture conceivable. We knew we did not have sufficient ammunition to resist another charge, and if we fired what little ammunition we had we would have none to take our own lives with. I hollered to one of the horsemen for one of them to advance. At once a horseman came riding up with his carbine held over his head, which those days was a friendly sign. After he came up within about fifty feet, I recognized Paddy Boyle, as though he had risen from the dead. The whole command advanced then and it was a squadron of the Seventh United States cavalry. The joy experienced in being relieved from our perilous position may be imagined. Shaking hands and cheering and congratulations were in full force. Soon after the cavalry arrived, it might have been an hour, another command of infantry came in on a run with wagons and ambulances, and accompanying them was a government doctor; I think his name was Degraw, post surgeon, and a noble man he was. He had the wounded gently cared for and placed in the ambulances and they received the kindest of attention and care in the hospital at Fort Dodge until able to be around, but I don't think any of them ever recovered fully.

It might be of interest to the reader to know why these horsemen were dressed in white, as I have previously mentioned. It was an ironclad custom in those strenuous and thrilling times for every man to take his gun to bed with him or "lay on their arms," as the old army term gives it, loaded and ready for action at a moment's notice, with their cartridge box and belt within their reach. The men those days were issued white cotton flannel underclothes, and as the weather was warm, no time was taken to put on their outside clothes, but every man immediately rushed to the stables at the first sound of the bugle which sounded to horse, and mounted at one blast. When this call was sounded it was known that an extreme emergency was at hand and men's lives in jeopardy. This white underclothing accounts for the mysterious look of the troopers when they made their appearance at Little Coon Creek, and the mysterious actions of the squadron in not advancing up to us when they first arrived, can be explained that they did not know the situation of affairs, as there was no firing at that particular time, and they were using extreme caution for fear they would run into an ambush, of part of the Indians. I think, if I remember rightly, there were four Indians who followed Boyle right up to the east picket line at the fort, and had he had to go a mile farther he never could have made it to the fort. The noble dapple grey horse, if I remember rightly, died from the effects of the fierce run he made to save our lives.

General Alfred Sully who was at that time in command of the troops in the Department, and who was an old and successful Indian fighter, issued an order complimenting the party on their heroic and desperate defense that they made and also for mine and Boyle's action in charging through the Indians to their assistance. As there were scores of little skirmishes, and some big ones taking place on the old Santa Fe trail all the time at some portion of it, it was generally conceded that the Little Coon Creek engagement was the most desperate fight for anyone to come out alive. There were probably as desperate ones fought, but none ever lived to tell it. This is the only instance I know of where a General United States Officer had an order issued and read publicly to the troops of the different forts in the Department, commending the participants of a small party in an Indian fight for heroic action. How any of the party ever escaped is a mystery to me today and always has been. It was reported after peace was declared that Satanta, head chief of the Kiowas, admitted that in the Little Coon Creek fight the Indian warrior losses were twenty-two killed besides a number wounded. I did not count the number of times the wagon was struck with arrows and bullets, but parties who said they did count them reported the wagon was struck five hundred times, and I have not a doubt that this is true, for arrows were sticking out like quills on the back of a porcupine, and the sideboards and end of the wagon was perforated with bullets. The mules were riddled with bullets. Two pet prairie dogs which the boys had in the wagon in a little box were both killed. The general order which was issued by General Alfred Sully, only mentions four Indians being killed, but these being left on the ground were all that could be seen. It is well known among old Indian fighters that Indians on the war-path and losing their warriors in battle will always carry off their dead if possible. It is very often their custom to tie their buffalo hide lariats around their body or connect with a belt and the other end fastened to their saddle when going into battle, and then if they are shot off their ponies, their ponies were trained to drag them off, or at least until some of their brother warriors came to his assistance; then two would come up, one on each side, on a dead run, reach down and grab him. If he was attached to a lariat, they would cut it in an instant and off they would go, but it was a common thing for the rescuers to get shot in their heroic efforts to save their comrades. I have witnessed proceedings of this kind a number of times, and there have been many instances where two or three warriors would be shot trying to rescue a comrade.

*   *   *   *   *   *   *   *

The writer saw the above-mentioned wagon after it was brought into Fort Dodge, and it was literally filled with arrows and bullet holes, and the bottom of the wagon bed was completely covered with blood as were the ends and sides where the wounded leaned over and up against them. I never saw a butcher's wagon that was any bloodier.

Mr. Herron concludes the story of the fight as follows:

DODGE CITY IN 1872—SOUTH SIDE

SONG

Calm and bright shone the sun on the morning,
    That four men from Fort Dodge marched away,
With food and supplies for their comrades—
    They were to reach Big Coon Creek that day;
'Tis a day we shall all well remember,
    That gallant and brave little fight,
How they struggled and won it so bravely—
    Though wounded, still fought through the night.

Chorus:

So let's give three cheers for our comrades,
    That gallant and brave little band,
Who, against odds, would never surrender,
    But bravely by their arms did they stand.
Fifty Indians surprised them while marching,
    Their scalps tried to get, but in vain;
The boys repulsed them at every endeavor,
    They were men who were up to their game.

"Though the red-skins are ten times our number,
    We coolly on each other rely."
Said the corporal in charge of the party,
    "We'll conquer the foe or we'll die!"

Still they fought with a wit and precision;
    Assistance at last came to hand,
Two scouts on the action appearing,
    To strengthen the weak little band.
Then one charged right clear through the Indians,
    To Fort Dodge for help he did go,
While the balance still kept up the fighting,
    And gallantly beat off the foe.

A squadron of cavalry soon mounted,
    Their comrades to rescue and save.
General Sully, he issued an order,
    Applauding their conduct so brave.
And when from their wounds they recover,
    Many years may they live to relate,
The fight that occurred in September,
    In the year eighteen sixty-eight.

This song was composed by Fred Haxby, September, 1868, on the desperate fight at Little Coon creek, about thirty miles east of Fort Dodge, on the dry route, September second, 1868. Fred Haxby, or Lord Haxby, as he was called, was from England, and at the time of the fight was at Fort Dodge.

The song gives fifty Indians comprising the attacking party. This was done to make the verses rhyme, as I am sure there were many more than this.

The tune this song was sung by, nearly a half a century ago, was the same as the one which went with the song commonly known at that time, "When Sherman Marched Down To The Sea." Not, "Sherman's March Through Georgia." "Sherman's March Through Georgia," and "Sherman's March To The Sea," were different songs and different airs.

*   *   *   *   *   *   *   *

The author of this work is further indebted to Mr. Herron for another interesting story of soldier life in the wild days. It runs as follows:

CAPTURING THE BOX FAMILY.

Capturing the Box family from the Indians was one of the interesting events which took place at Fort Dodge, although the rescue of the two older girls took place south of Fort Dodge near the Wichita mountains, perhaps near two hundred miles. But the idea of getting the girls away from the Indians originated at Fort Dodge, with Major Sheridan, who, at the time, October, 1866, was in command of the fort. At this time, the troops garrisoning the fort consisted of Company A, Third United States infantry, of which I was a member, holding a non-commissioned officer's rank.

On a sunshiny day about the first of October, 1866, the sentinel reported what appeared to be a small party of mounted men, approaching the fort from the south side of the Arkansas river, perhaps two miles away, and just coming into sight out of a range of bluffs which ran parallel with the river. They proved to be Indians and the glittering ornaments with which each was decorated could be seen before either the Indians or their ponies. After the Indians came down to the river and were part way across, a guard, consisting of a corporal and two men, met them at the north bank of the river, just below the fort, and halted them. It was noticed they carried a pole to which was attached an old piece of what had at one time been a white wagon cover, but which at this time was a very dirty white. This was to represent a flag of truce and a peaceful mission, which idea they had got from the whites, though the Indians were very poor respecters of flags of truce. When approached with one by white men, they, on several occasions, killed the bearers of the flag, scalped them, and used their scalps to adorn their wigwams. They considered the flag a kind of joke and rated the bearer as an easy mark.

The guard learned from the Indians that they were Kiowas, old chief Satanta's tribe. Fred Jones, who was Indian interpreter at Fort Dodge, was requested to come down and ascertain what was wanted. The Indians informed Jones that they had two pale-faced squaws whom they wished to trade for guns, ammunition, coffee, sugar, flour—really, they wanted about all there was in the fort, as they set a very high value on the two girls.

By instructions of the commanding officer, they were permitted to come into the fort to talk the matter over. After passing the pipe around and each person in council taking a puff, which was the customary manner of procedure, they proceeded to negotiate a "swap," as the Indians termed it. The Indians wanted everything in sight, but a trade or swap was finally consummated by promising the Indians some guns, powder and lead, some coffee, sugar, flour and a few trinkets, consisting mainly of block tin, which was quite a bright, glittering tint. This was used to make finger rings, earrings and bracelets for the squaws. The bracelets were worn on both ankles and arms of the squaws and, when fitted out with their buckskin leggings and short dresses, covered with beads, they made a very attractive appearance.

The Indians knew they had the advantage and drove a sharp bargain—at least, they thought they did. They insisted on the goods being delivered to their camp near the Wichita mountains, which was quite an undertaking, considering that a white man had never been in that section except as a prisoner, a renegade, or possibly an interpreter. Two wagons and an ambulance were ordered to be got ready, and the wagons were loaded. Our party consisted of Lieutenant Heselberger of Company A, Third United States infantry, an old experienced Indian fighter, one non-commissioned officer, (myself), and seven privates, with Fred Jones as interpreter. We crossed the river about a half mile below Fort Dodge and took a southerly course, traveling for days before we came to the Kiowa camp. One evening, just as the sun was going down, we came to a high hill, and as we gained the crest, going in a southeasterly direction, I witnessed the most beautiful sight I ever saw.

The whole Kiowa tribe, several thousands in number, were camped on the banks of a beautiful sheet of water, half a mile away. The sun setting and the sun's rays reflecting on the camp, gave it a fascinating appearance. Hundreds of young warriors, mounted on their beautiful ponies, and all dressed in their wild, barbaric costume, bedecked with glittering ornaments, were drilling and going through artistic maneuvers on the prairie, making a scene none of us will ever forget. There were about three hundred lodges, all decorated as only an Indian could decorate them, being painted with many gaudy

City Hall

colors. Many pappooses were strapped upon the more docile ponies, and, under the guidance of some warriors, were getting their first initiation into the tactics necessary to become a warrior; while squaws were engaged in tanning buffalo skins and going through the different movements necessary to a well organized wild Indian camp. Small fires were in commission in different parts of the camp, with little ringlets of smoke ascending from them, which, in the calm, lovely evening, made an exceedingly interesting scene, while off on the distant hills thousands of buffalo were peacefully grazing.

Right here let me say that I have seen the Russian Cossacks on the banks of the river Volga, in southern Russia, and, while they have the reputation of being the finest and most graceful riders in the world, they did not compare, for fine horsemanship, with the American Indian of fifty years ago.

As we halted and took in this beautiful panorama, a bugle call sounded, clear and distinct, in the Kiowa camp. Three or four hundred young warriors mounted their ponies, the charge was sounded, and they came dashing towards us. On they came, keeping as straight a line as any soldiers I ever saw. When about three hundred feet from us and just as we were reaching for our carbines (for everything had the appearance of a massacre of our little party, and we had determined when starting on this venturesome errand that if the Indians showed treachery, we would inflict all the punishment on them we possibly could before they got us, and would shoot ourselves rather than be captured alive; for being captured meant burning at the stake and the most excruciating torture), the bugle sounded again, the Indians made a beautiful move and filed to right and left of us, half on each flank, and escorted us to their camp which was but a short distance away. The bugler was a professional but we never knew who he was as he never showed himself close enough to us to be recognizable, but he was supposed to be some renegade. On other occasions, when a battle was going on, these bugle calls were heard. At the battle of the Arickaree where Roman Nose, head chief of the Cheyennes attacked Forsythe's scouts, the bugle was heard sounding the calls all through the battle.

The night we arrived at the Kiowa camp we were located on the banks of a creek. The young warriors commenced to annoy us in all manner of ways, trying to exasperate us to resent their annoyances so they could have an excuse to make an attack on us. At this time, Fred Jones and Lieutenant Heselberger, who had been up to Satanta's lodge, came to our camp and, seeing the taunts and annoyances to which we were being subjected, admonished us not to resent them, for if we did the whole party would be massacred or made prisoners and burned at the stake. Jones, the interpreter, immediately went back to Satanta and reported the situation. Satanta, at once, had a guard of old warriors thrown around us and thus saved us from further annoyances. Not that Satanta was any too good or had any love for us that he should protect us, but at that immediate period it was not policy for him to make any rash movements.

All night long the Indian drums were continually thumping and the Indians were having a big dance in their council chamber, which was always a custom, among the wild Indian tribes, when any unusual event was taking place. The next morning we were up bright and early, teams were hitched to the wagons and proceeded to the center of the Indian camp in front of the council chamber, where the goods were unloaded. The two young girls were then turned over to us by one of the chiefs. They were a pitiful looking sight. They had been traded from one chief to another for nearly a year, and had been subjected to the most cruel and degrading treatment. The eldest girl gave birth to a half-breed a short time after their rescue. One of the girls was seventeen and the other fourteen years old. They had been captured near the Texas border and had been with the Indians some time, according to the story told us. The father, a man by the name of Box, the mother, and their four children were returning to their home, when they were overtaken by a band of Indians. The Indians killed Mr. Box because he refused to surrender; the youngest child was taken by the heels and its brains beaten out against a tree; the mother and three children were taken back to the main camp. The mother and youngest child were taken to the Apache camp, an Apache chief purchasing them from the Kiowas. We felt confident that, later on, we would get possession of the mother and youngest child, for the Apaches would want to trade too, when they learned how the Kiowas had succeeded. But the articles which were traded to the Kiowas were of very poor quality. The guns were old, disused muzzle-loading rifles; the powder had but little strength, having lost its strength and a man would be quite safe, fifty feet away from it when discharged; the lead was simply small iron bars, with lead coating; but the Indians seemed to think it was all right, as they didn't do much kicking, but people who, in a trade, would take a ten-cent "shin-plaster" in preference to a twenty-dollar bill, were easy marks to deal with.

After a long, hard march, we finally arrived again on the banks of the Arkansas River, which we had had little hopes of doing. Knowing the treacherous disposition of the Indians, we expected they would lie in ambush for us, so we were continually on the alert and always went into camp at a location where we had a good view for several rods around us. It took Custer's whole Seventh United States cavalry, in the winter of '68 and '69, to get some white women from the Indians, and the way he succeeded was by getting the head chiefs to hold a treaty, then taking them prisoners and holding them until the Indians surrendered the women. Our party's going into the Indian camp, as we did, was a very hazardous undertaking, and the only reason we ever got back was that the Apaches had the other two members of the Box family, they wanted to trade for them, and they knew if they killed us the trade would be off. Such a foolhardy undertaking was not attempted again, to my knowledge, in the years I was on the plains.

When we arrived at Fort Dodge, we were given a very pleasant reception, and the young ladies received the tenderest care, but were naturally terribly distressed at their terrible sorrow and affliction. General Sherman, at this time, arrived at Fort Dodge. He had been on a tour of inspection of the frontier forts, and was then on his way to Washington. After learning what the commanding officer had done, he instructed him not to send any more details on so hazardous an undertaking, and not to trade any more goods for prisoners, as it would only have the tendency to encourage the Indians to more stealing.

As we expected, a few days after our return to Fort Dodge the sentry reported a party approaching from east of the fort. All that could be seen was the glittering, bright ornaments, dazzling in the sunlight, but shortly, the party approached close enough for it to be seen that they were Indians. They proved to be a party of Apaches, as we expected, chief Poor Bear being with them. When he was informed that the Indians were coming, Major Andrew Sheridan, who was still in command of Fort Dodge, sent the interpreter, Fred Jones, out to meet them and arrange with the head chief, Poor Bear, to come into the fort and hold a council, a customary thing in those days, when a trade was to be made.

Fort Dodge was located on the north bank of the Arkansas River, and was in the shape of a half circle.

Close to the river was a clay bank about twelve feet high, where were a number of dugouts, with port-holes all around, in which the men were quartered, so that, if the Indians ever charged and took the fort, the men could fall back and retire to the dugouts. On the east side of the fort was a large gate. The officers were quartered in sod houses, located inside the inclosure. When Poor Bear and his warriors came into the fort, Major Sheridan informed them that the great chief, meaning General Sherman, had given instructions that no more goods would be delivered to the Indian camp in trade for white women, but if the woman and daughter were brought in, a council would be held to determine what could be done. At this, the Indians left for their camp to report progress. In about two weeks, we noticed Indians by the score, crossing from the south side of the river, below the fort about a mile, near where the old dry route formed a junction with the wet route. A guard at once was instructed to notify the Indians that they must not come any nearer the fort than they were, but must camp at a place designated by the commanding officer, nearly a mile below Fort Dodge.

The Indians proved to be Apaches and the whole tribe came in, numbering about two thousand. They had brought along the white woman, Mrs. Box, and her young daughter, expecting to make a big "swap." There was no intention of giving anything for them, but there was a plot to get the Indians in, gain possession of the chiefs and head men of the Apache tribe, and hold them as hostages until they would consent to surrender the woman and child. It was a desperate and dangerous experiment, for the Indians outnumbered us greatly. I don't think, at this time, there were over one hundred and seventy-five men, altogether, at Fort Dodge, including civilians, and against these was one of the most desperate tribes on the plains. When the time arrived for the council, about a hundred of the chiefs, medicine men, and leading men of the Indians were let in through the big gate at the east side of the fort. As soon as they were inside, the gate was closed. When they were all ready for the big talk, and the customary pipe had been passed around, Major Sheridan instructed the interpreter to inform the Indians that they were prisoners, and that they would be held as hostages until Mrs. Box and her daughter were brought in and turned over to him.

The Indians jumped to their feet in an instant, threw aside their blankets, and prepared for a fight. Prior to the time the Indians were admitted into the fort inclosure, the mountain howitzers had been double-shotted with grape and canister, the guns being depressed so as to sweep the ground where the Indians were located. Some of the soldiers were marching back and forth, with guns loaded and bayonets fixed, while a number of others, with revolvers concealed under their blouses, were sitting around watching the proceedings. The main portion of the garrison was concealed in the dugouts, the men all armed and provided with one hundred rounds of ammunition per man. The Indians were all armed with tomahawks which they had carefully concealed under their blankets. When they were informed that they were prisoners, they made a dash for the soldiers in sight, as they were but few, the majority, as has been said, being hid in the dugouts; but when the men came pouring out of the dugouts and opened fire, the Indians fell back and surrendered. One of the old chiefs was taken up on the palisades of the fort and compelled to signal to his warriors in their camp. In less than thirty minutes Mrs. Box and her child were brought to the big east gate, and one of the most affecting sights I ever witnessed was that of the mother and girls as they met and embraced each other. It was a sight once seen, never to be forgotten.

Major Sheridan then told the interpreter to inform the Indians that they could go, warning them not to steal any more women or children. But the warning was of no avail, for the next two years the frontier was terribly annoyed by Indian raids and depredations.

There were but few fatalities when the soldiers opened fire on the Indians at the fort, as it was done more to intimidate than to kill. A representative of Harper's Weekly was at Fort Dodge, at the time, and took a number of photographs of the Indians and the Box family, but if there are any of the pictures in existence today, I am not aware of it, but I should like to have them if they exist. This piece of diplomacy on the part of the commanding officer of Fort Dodge cost scores of lives afterwards, for those Apaches went on the war-path and murdered every person they came across, until the Seventh United States cavalry caught up with and annihilated many of them, in the Wichita mountains, in November, 1868.

All the great expeditions against the Indians, horse thieves, and bad men were organized and fitted out at Fort Dodge or Dodge City, because, as I remark elsewhere, they were at the edge of the last great frontier or the jumping-off place, the beginning and the end—the end of civilization, and the beginning of the badness and lawlessness of the frontier. Here civilization ended and lawlessness began.

This gave rise to and the necessity for many great and notable men coming to Dodge, such as Generals Sherman, Sheridan, Hancock, Miles, Custer, Sully, and many others, even including President Hayes. Dodge was acquainted with all of these, besides dukes and lords from over the water, who came out of curiosity. We feel proud that she knew these men, and General Miles told the writer that Fort Dodge should have been made one of our largest forts, at least a ten-company post. But he did not take in the situation in time, as it was the key to all the country south of us, and, had it been made a ten-

or twelve-company post, one can easily see how the garrison could have controlled all the Indian tribes south, who were continually escaping from their agencies and going north, to visit, intrigue, and combine with the northern Indians, the northern tribes doing the same thing when they went south. The troops could have intercepted the Indians either way, and cut them off and sent them back before they were able to do any devilment. Particularly could this have been done when Dull Knife and Wild Hog made their last raid through Kansas. There were only about seventy-five warriors, besides their women and children, in this little band, but they managed to make a laughing stock and a disgrace of our troops; at least, so it appeared from the actions of the officers who were sent after them.

In September, 1868, at the Darlington Agency, there were, under the leadership of Wild Hog and Dull Knife, a small bunch of Cheyenne Indians, who had been moved from their northern agency and, for various reasons, were determined to go back, much against the wishes and orders of the United States government and also their agent, who positively forbade their going. They had secretly been making preparations for this tramp, for some time, but they had no horses, but few guns and ammunition, and very little provisions of any kind. Now, under these adverse circumstances, they stole away.

As has been said, there were only seventy-five warriors all told, outside of their women and children. Their first care was to get themselves mounts, then arms and ammunition, and provisions. Little by little, they stole horses and picked up guns and ammunition from the cattle camps and deserted homes of the frontier settlers, so, when they got within forty miles of Fort Dodge, south, they were supplied with horses, and fairly well supplied with their other wants.

On Sand Creek, they were confronted with two companies of cavalry and several parts of companies of infantry, with wagon transportation. These soldiers outnumbered the Indians nearly three to one; besides, quite a lot of settlers and some cowboys had joined the troops. To be sure, the settlers were poorly armed, but they were of assistance, in some ways, to the troops.

On their march, the Indians had scattered over a large scope of country. That is, the warriors did, while the women and children kept straight on in the general direction they wanted to go. But the warriors raided and foraged some fifteen or twenty miles on either side of the women and children, and at night they would all rendezvous together. This gave rise to the erroneous impression that the band was very much larger than it was. In fact, there were supposed to be several hundred warriors, and this reckoned greatly in their favor. The bold daring front that they assumed was another big thing in their favor, and made the troops and others believe there were many more of them than there were. When they were confronted with the troops on Sand Creek, they stopped in the bluffs and fortified, while the troops camped in the bottom to watch their movements and hold them in check. But the cowboys said that the Indians only stopped a short time, and, when night came, they broke camp and left the troops behind. The soldiers did not find this out for nearly two days, and, in this maneuver, they had nearly two days the start of the soldiers.

The Indians, next day, trailed by Belle Meade, a little settlement, where they were given a fine beef just killed. Strange to say, they disturbed no one here, except taking what arms they could find and some more "chuck." Up to this time, they had killed only two or three people. Starting off, they saw a citizen of Belle Meade, driving a span of mules and wagon, coming home.

They killed him and took his mules and harness, after scalping him. This was done in sight of the town. A few miles further on, they espied another wagon, and, after chasing it within ten miles of Dodge, the driver was killed and his mules and harness taken; and so on. They raided within a few miles of Dodge. Twelve were seen four miles west of Dodge, on an island, where they plundered and burned a squatter's house. The Dodge people had sent out and brought every one in for miles around, which is the reason, I suppose, the Indians did not kill more people close to Dodge.

I here quote largely from an enlisted man, stationed at Fort Supply, more than a month after this Indian raid through Kansas and Nebraska was over, so he had time to look calmly over the situation, and the excitement had died down. As his views and mine are so nearly alike, I give the most of his version. He says:

"Field-marshal Dull Knife outgeneraling the grand pacha of the United States army, and reaching, in safety, the goal of his anticipations, being, it is said, snugly ensconced among his old familiar haunts in Wyoming and Dakota. Without casting the least reflection upon or detracting a single thing from the ability, loyalty, or bravery of our little army, it must be said, that the escape of Dull Knife and his followers, from the Cheyenne Agency, and their ultimate success in reaching Dakota territory, is certainly a very remarkable occurrence in the annals of military movements. I have no definite means of giving the exact number of Dull Knife's force, but, from the most reliable information, it did not exceed one hundred warriors (this is about Agent Mile's estimate). Dull Knife's movements, immediately after he left the reservation, were not unknown to the military authorities. He was pursued and overtaken by two companies of cavalry, within sixty miles of the agency he had left. He there gave battle, killing three soldiers, wounding as many more, and, if reports of eye witnesses are to be believed, striking terror into the hearts of the remainder, completely routing them. All the heads of the military in the Department of the Missouri were immediately informed of the situation, and yet, Dull Knife passed speedily on, passing in close proximity to several military posts, and actually marching a portion of the route along the public highway, the old Santa Fe trail, robbing emigrant trains, murdering defenseless men, women, and children as their fancy seemed to dictate, and, at last, arriving at their destination unscathed, and is, no doubt, ere this, in conference with his friend and ally, Sitting Bull, as to the most practicable manner of subjugating the Black Hills.

"While we look the matter squarely in the face, it must be conceeded that Dull Knife has achieved one of the most extraordinary *coup d'etat* of modern times, and has made a march before which even Sherman's march to the sea pales. With a force of a hundred men, this untutored but wily savage encounters and defeats, eludes, baffles, and outgenerals ten times his number of American soldiers. At one time during his march, there were no less than twenty-four companies of cavalry and infantry in the field against him, and he marched a distance of a thousand miles, almost unmolested. Of course, most of the country he passed through was sparsely settled, but, with the number of military posts, (six), lying almost directly in his path, and the great number of cattle men, cowboys, freighters, etc., scattered over the plains, that came in contact with his band, it does seem strange that he slipped through the schemes and plans that were so well laid to entrap him. However, Dull Knife has thoroughly demonstrated the fact that a hundred desperate warriors can raid successfully through a thousand miles of territory, lying partly in Dakota, Nebraska, Kansas, and the Indian Territory, steal stock, and perpetrate outrages too vile and horrible to print;

and this in the face of ten times their number of well equipped United States troops. That some one is highly reprehensible in the matter of not capturing or annihilating Dull Knife and his entire band is believed by all, but who the culpable party is will probably never be placed on the pages of history.

"The cause that led to the outbreak is the same old story—goaded into desperartion by starvation at the hands of the Indian agents. There are no buffalo anywhere near the agency, and this same band were allowed, last fall and winter, to go from their reservation to hunt, to supply themselves with meat. They did not find a single buffalo. A portion of them killed and ate their ponies, and the remainder feasted on their dogs. An Indian never eats his dog except when served up on state occasions, and their puppies are considered a great delicacy. They only feed these to their distinguished guests, at great night feasts. They consider they are doing you a great honor when they prepare a feast of this kind for you, and they are badly hurt and mortified if you do not partake freely of same. Dull Knife appealed so persistently for aid, the commanding officer ordered a few rations to be given them (which military establishments have no authority to do). These were eagerly accepted and greedily devoured.

"After soldiering, as a private, ten years on the plains, I am convinced that a majority of the Indian raids have been caused by the vacillating policy of the government, coupled with the avaricious, and dishonest agents. I do not pretend to hold the Indian up as an object of sympathy. On the contrary, I think they are treacherous, deceitful, black hearted, murdering villians. But we should deal fair with them and set them an example for truthfulness and honesty, instead of our agents, and others in authority, being allowed to rob them. Two wrongs never made a right, and no matter

A. J. ANTHONY
One of the Seven Old Timers of Dodge City

what wrongs they have committed, we should live strictly up to our promises with them.''

I will give only a brief account of this raid through our state, from my own memory. I was on my way to Boston to sell a lot of buffalo robes we had stored there. At Kansas City I received a telegram from my firm, saying, "Indians are out; coming this way; big Indian war expected.'' I returned to Dodge at once, found everything in turmoil, and big excitement. After getting the news and advice from Colonel Lewis, commander of Fort Dodge (who was well posted, up to that time, in regard to the whereabouts of these Indians, though he had no idea of their number, supposing them to be a great many more than there were), William Tighlman, Joshua Webb, A. J. Anthony, and myself started southwest, thinking to overtake and join the troops already in the field. We made fifty miles that day, when we met a lot of farmers coming back. They said the Indians made a stand against the soldiers, in the bluffs on Sand Creek. The soldiers camped a short distance down the creek, for two days, when they made a reconnaissance and found the Indians had been gone for nearly two days, while the troops thought they were still there and were afraid to move out. But it seems the Indians broke camp the first night, and were nearly two days' march ahead of the troops, Captain Randebrook in command, trailing on behind them.

Before our little company started, Colonel Lewis requested me to report to him immediately upon our return, which I did. When he heard the story of the cowboys and settlers who were on Sand Creek with the troops, and how cowardly the officers had acted in letting the Indians escape them when there was such a fine opportunity to capture them, Colonel Lewis was utterly disgusted. I never saw a more disgusted man. He didn't swear, but he thought pretty hard, and he said: ''Wright,

I am going to take the field myself and at once, and, on my return, you will hear a different story." Poor fellow! He never returned. The troops just trailed on behind the Indians, when they crossed the Arkansas, and followed on, a short distance behind them, until Colonel Lewis joined them and took command.

And now I'll tell the story, as told to me, about the killing of Colonel Lewis, as gallant an officer as ever wore a sword. The troops, with Colonel Lewis in command, overtook the Indians this side of White Woman creek, and pressed them so closely they had to concentrate and make a stand. Lewis did the same. Late in the afternoon, he made every arrangement to attack their camp at daybreak next morning, having posted the troops and surrounded the Indians as near as possible. Colonel Lewis attended to every little detail, to make the attack next morning a success, and they were to attack from all sides at the same time, at a given signal. About the last thing he did, before going to headquarters for the night, he visited one of the furthest outposts, where a single guard was concealed. Colonel Lewis had to crawl to get to him. The guard said the Colonel was anxious to shoot an Indian who was on post and very saucy. The guard said, "Colonel, you must not raise up. These outposts and sharp shooters are just waiting for us to expose ourselves, and that fellow is acting as a blind, for others to get a chance at us." But the Colonel persisted. He said he wanted to stir them up; and, just as he rose up, before he got his gun to his shoulder, he was shot down. They had to crawl to Colonel Lewis and drag him out on their hands and knees. The surgeon in charge knew he would die, and started with him at once for Fort Wallace, but he died before reaching that post. This happened about dark, and the news soon spread throughout the camp—Colonel Lewis was killed—which had a great demoralizing effect upon the troops, as they knew he was a brave man and liked him and had great confidence in his ability. His orders were never carried out, and the attack was not made. The Indians broke camp and marched away next morning, but, from the signs they left behind, it was very evident they would not have made much of a fight. Indeed, I have been told there was a flag of truce found in their camp. This was vouched for by several, and there were evidences that they intended to surrender, and it is the opinion of the writer they intended to surrender. Anyhow, I do think, if Colonel Lewis had lived, they would have been so badly whipped they never would have got any further north, and the lives of all those people, who were killed on the Sappa and after they crossed the Missouri, Pacific railroad, would have been saved. I think they killed about forty people, after they left White Woman creek. The farmers and citizens, who were along with the soldiers, censure the two cavalry captains severely and claim they acted cowardly, several times and at several places. They, I believe, were both tried for cowardice, but were acquitted after a fair trial.

Our citizens of Dodge City, as well as his brother officers and the enlisted men under his command, held Colonel Lewis in great respect, as the following resolutions, presented by the enlisted men, assembled in a meeting for the purpose, at the time of his death, will show:

"Whereas, the sad news has been brought to us of the death, on the field of battle against hostile Indians, of our late commanding officer, Lieutenant Colonel William H. Lewis, Nineteenth United States infantry;

"Be it resolved, that his death is felt as a great calamity to the army of the United States, as well as for his family, to whom we tender our most heartfelt sympathy, and that we deplore, in his demise the loss of one of the kindest, bravest, and most impartial commanders to be found in the service;

"And be it further resolved, that these resolutions be published in the 'Army and Navy Journal,' the Washington and Leavenworth papers, the 'Ford County Globe,' and the 'Dodge City Times,' and a copy be sent to his relatives.

"THOMAS G. DENNEN,

"Ordnance Sergeant, President,

"LOUIS PAULY,

"Hospital Steward, Secretary."

The meeting then adjourned.

The old servant, who had been with Colonel Lewis for many years and was greatly attached to him, could not be comforted after his master's death. He wept and mourned as if he had lost a near relative. After the Colonel had received his mortal wound and knew that he must die, he instructed his attendants to tell the old servant to go to his mother's, where he would find a home for the balance of his days. Accordingly, after all the business at Fort Dodge had been settled, he started, with a heavy heart, for his new home. He said he knew he would have a nice hime in which to spend his last days, but that would not bring his old master back. There is nothing that speaks plainer of the true man, than the disinterested devotion of his servants.

Long years afterwards, when the veterans of the Civil War, living at Fort Dodge, organized a post of the Grand Army of the Republic, they named it the Lewis Post, in honor of the brave but unfortunate Colonel.

Referring again to the subject of General Miles' opinion that Fort Dodge should have been at least a ten-company post, it might be added that the General, with that very purpose in mind, visited the fort, several years after its abandonment. I was living there at the time, being appointed by the government to take charge of the property left there, and see to the care of the buildings.

I drove him down, and he took lunch with me. He said: "Wright, your Dodge people made a big mistake when you placed your small-pox patients in the old hospital." You see, Dodge City was visited once with small-pox, and it raged pretty strongly. A great many of our people took it, and it was so violent and virulent that it carried off not a few. Mayor Webster seized the old military hospital and had the patients quarantined in it.

The General further said: "I see Fort Dodge's great military importance, and I would like to garrison it to its full capacity and would do so; but, Wright, you know, if a single soldier died there from small-pox, even years from now, the press of the country would get up and howl, and censure me ever so severely for subjecting the army to this terrible disease. I can't afford to take such chances." General Miles was right; this is just what would have been done, if the small-pox had ever broken out.

CHAPTER VII

The Beginnings of Dodge City

It has already been said that Dodge City was established in 1872, upon the advent of the Atchison, Topeka & Santa Fe railroad. Dodge was in the very heart of the buffalo country. Hardly had the railroad reached there, long before a depot could be built (they had an office in a box car), business began; and such a business! Dozens of cars a day were loaded with hides and meat, and dozens of car-loads of grain, flour, and provisions arrived each day. The streets of Dodge were lined with wagons, bringing in hides and meat and getting supplies from early morning to late at night.

Charles Rath & Company ordered from Long Brothers, of Kansas City, two hundred cases of baking-powder at one order. They went to Colonel W. F. Askew, to whom we were shipping immense quantities of hides, and said: "These men must be crazy, or else they mean two hundred boxes instead of cases." They said there were not two hundred cases in the city. Askew wired us if we had not made a mistake. We answered, "No; double the order." Askew was out a short time after that and saw six or eight car-loads of flour stacked up in the warehouse. He said he now understood. It was to bake this flour up into bread.

I have been to several mining camps where rich strikes had been made, but I never saw any town to equal Dodge. A good hunter would make a hundred dollars a day. Everyone had money to throw at the birds. There was no article less than a quarter—a drink was a quarter, a shave was a quarter, a paper of pins a quarter, and needles the same. In fact, that was the smallest change.

PEACE COMMISSION

W. H. HARRIS, LUKE SHORT, BAT MASTERSON,

Governor St. John was in Dodge once, when he was notified that a terrible cyclone had visited a little town close to the Kansas line, in Nebraska. In two hours I raised one thousand dollars, which he wired them. Our first calaboose in Dodge City was a well fifteen feet deep, into which the drunkards were let down and allowed to remain until they were sober. Sometimes there were several in it at once. It served the purpose well for a time.

Of course everyone has heard of wicked Dodge; but a great deal has been said and written about it that is not true. Its good side has never been told, and I cannot give it space here. Many reckless, bad men came to Dodge and many brave men. These had to be met by officers equally brave and reckless. As the old saying goes, "You must fight the devil with fire." The officers gave them the south side of the railroad-track, but the north side must be kept respectable, and it was. There never was any such thing as shooting at plug hats. On the contrary, every stranger that came to Dodge City and behaved himself was treated with politeness; but woe be unto the man who came seeking a fight. He was soon accommodated in any way, shape, or form that he wished. Often have I seen chivalry extended to ladies on the streets, from these rough men, that would have done credit to the knights of old. When some man a little drunk, and perhaps unintentionally, would jostle a lady in a crowd, he was soon brought to his senses by being knocked down by one of his companions, who remarked, "Never let me see you insult a lady again."

In fact, the chivalry of Dodge toward the fair sex and strangers was proverbial. Never in the history of Dodge was a stranger mistreated, but, on the contrary, the utmost courtesy was always and under all circumstances extended to him, and never was there a frontier town whose liberality exceeded that of Dodge. But, while women, children, and strangers were never, anywhere, treated with more courtesy and respect; while such things as shooting up plug hats and making strangers dance is all bosh and moonshine, and one attempting such would have been promptly called down; let me tell you one thing—none of Dodge's well known residents would have been so rash as to dare to wear a plug hat through the streets, or put on any "dog," such as wearing a swallow-tail or evening dress, or any such thing.

The general reputation of young Dodge City is well described in an article entitled, "Reminiscences of Dodge," written in 1877, and expressing what a stranger has to say about the town. The article runs as follows:

"By virtue of the falling off in the cattle drive to Kansas for this year, and the large number of cattle driven under contract, Dodge City became the principal depot for the sale of surplus stock; buyers met drovers at this point, purchased and received purchases without unnecessary delay, thereby greatly facilitating business and enabling quick returns of both owners and hands. In the future, situated as it is upon one of the best railroads traversing the country from east to west, the Atchison, Topeka & Santa Fe, it will probably occupy an enviable position as a cattle market.

"Dodge has many characteristics which prevent its being classed as a town of strictly moral ideas and principles, notwithstanding it is supplied with a church, courthouse, and jail. Other institutions counterbalance the good works supposed to emanate from the first mentioned. Like all frontier towns of this modern day, fast men and fast women are around by the score, seeking whom they may devour, hunting for a soft snap, taking him in for cash, and many is the Texas cowboy who can testify as to their ability to follow up successfully the calling they have embraced in quest of money.

"Gambling ranges from a game of five-cent chuck-a-luck to a thousand dollar poker pot. Nothing is secret, but with open doors upon the main streets, the ball rolls on uninterruptedly. More than occasionally some dark-eyed virago or some brazen-faced blonde, with a modern sundown, will saunter in among the roughs of the gambling houses and saloons, entering with inexplicable zest into the disgusting sport, breathing the immoral atmosphere with a gusto which I defy modern writers to explain. Dance houses are ranged along the convenient distances and supplied with all the trappings and paraphernalia which go to complete institutions of that character. Here you see the greatest abandon. Men of every grade assemble to join in the dance. Nice men with white neckties, the cattle dealer with his good clothes, the sport with his well turned fingers, smooth tongue, and artistically twisted mustache, and last but not least the cowboy, booted and spurred as he comes from the trail, his hard earnings in his pocket, all join in the wild revel; and yet with all this mixture of strange human nature a remarkable degree of order is preserved. Arms are not allowed to be worn, and any noisy whisky demonstrations are promptly checked by incarceration in the lock-up. Even the mayor of the city indulges in the giddy dance with the girls, and with his cigar in one corner of his mouth and his hat tilted to one side, he makes a charming looking officer.

"Some things occur in Dodge that the world never knows of. Probably it is best so. Other things occur that leak out by degrees, notwithstanding the use of hush-money. That, too, is perhaps the best. Men learn by such means.

"Most places are satisfied with one abode of the dead. In the grave there is no distinction. The rich are known from the poor only by their tombstones, so the sods that are upon the grave fail to reflect the characters buried beneath them. And yet Dodge boasts of two burying spots, one for the tainted whose very souls were steeped in immorality, and who have generally died with their boots on. 'Boot Hill' is the somewhat singular title applied to the burial place of the class just mentioned. The other is not designated by any particular title but it is supposed to contain the bodies of those who died with a clean sheet on their beds—the soul in this case is a secondary consideration."

So much for one view of Dodge City, but, though common, this view was not quite universal. Sometimes a writer appeared who could recognize a few slightly better features in the border town, and who could look beyond its existing lawlessness and see the possibilities and beginnings of a higher state of things. In proof of this I'll quote an article, written in 1878, a year later than the last, and entiled, "The Beautiful, Bibulous Babylon of the Frontier:"

"Standing out on the extreme border of civilization, like an oasis in the desert, or like a light-house off a rocky coast, is 'The Beautiful, Bibulous Babylon of the Frontier,' Dodge City, so termed by Lewis, editor of the 'Kingsley Graphic.' Dodge City is far famed, not for its virtues, but for its wickedness; the glaring phases of its vices stand pre-eminent, and attract the attention of the visitor; and these shadows of Babylon are reproduced in the gossip's corner and—in the press. It is seldom the picture has fine embellishments; but the pen artist of the 'Graphic' put the finer touches of nature to the pen portrait of Dodge—'she is no worse than Chicago.' This, we admit, is a slight leverage in the social scale, to be placed in the catagory of Chicago's wickedness.

"Dodge City has magnetic attractions. Few people are attracted here by curiosity; every one has business, except the tramps, and they have no business here. But our visitors see it all before they leave, and they use the same circumspection here they would under their own

ANDY JOHNSON
One of the Seven Old Timers of Dodge City

vine and fig tree. Many of them are not charitable enough to tell the unvarnished truth. In vain boast and idle glory they recount the pilgrimage to Dodge as though they passed through blood, rapine, and war—fully attested their courage.

"But the 'Kingsley Graphic' pays the 'Bibulous Babylon' a high compliment, besides raising the moral standard of Dodge to that of the immaculate virtue of Chicago.

"Kansas has but one Dodge City. With a broad expanse of territory sufficiently vast for an empire, we have only room for one Dodge City. Without particular-izing at length, we were most favorably impressed gener-ally during a brief visit at our neighboring city Tuesday. Beautiful for situation, cozily nestled on the 'beach' of the turbid Arkansas, while on the north the palisades rise above the busy little city, which in the near future will be ornamented with cozy cottages, modern mansions, and happy homes. The view from the elegant brick court house, situated above the town, is grand. The panorama spread out west, south, and east, takes in a vast scope of valley scenery such as only can be found fringing our river. Seventy-five thousand head of cattle, recently driven in from the ranges south, can be seen lazily feed-ing on the nutritious native meadows, while the cowboys gallop here and there among these vast herds, displaying superior horsemanship. Five miles down the river, the old flag floats proudly over the garrison at the military post.

"The city proper is a busy beehive of bustle and busi-ness, a conglomerated aggregation of every line of business alternating with saloons. Francis Murphy don't live in Dodge. There are a few institutions of which Dodgeites are justly proud—the ever popular Dodge House, 'The Times,' the court house, the fire company, Mayor Kelley's hounds, and the 'Varieties.' Much has been said of the wickedness and unrighteousness of the city. If 'old Probe' should send a shower of fire and brimstone up there, we would not vouch for there being a sufficient number of righteous citizens to save the city; yet with all her wickedness, she is no worse today than Chicago and many other cities where the music of the chimes are daily heard. There is but one difference, however, which is a frontier characteristic; our neighbors do not pretend to hide their peculiarities. A few years hence Dodge City will be a model of morality and a city of no mean importance.

"For courtesies shown us we acknowledge our obligations to Messrs. Kline & Shine of the lively 'Times,' Judge Gryden (who deserves to be known as Prince Harry, and whose only fault is his rock-footed Democracy), Mayor Kelley, Hon. H. M. Sutton, the popular county attorney, E. F. Colburn, the modest city attorney, Samuel Marshal, the portly judge, Fringer, the postmaster, Hon. R. M. Wright, Dr. McCarty, Sheriff Masterson and his efficient lieutenant City Marshal Basset, and our old friends at the signal office."

Again, under the heading, "The Wickedest City in America," the "Kokomo, Indiana, Dispatch," of an issue in July, 1878, refers to Dodge: "Its character as a hell, out on the great plains, will be," said a local writer, "maintained in the minds of traveling newspaper writers, just so long as the city shall remain a rendezvous for the broad and immense uninhabited plains, by narrating the wildest and wickedest phases of Dodge City; but we have to commend them for complimenting Dodge on its orderly character." The "Dispatch" speaks very highly of Dodge as a commercial point, and his letter bears many complimentary features. We extract the following:

" 'My experience in Dodge was a surprise all around. I found nothing as I pictured it in my mind. I had expected, from the descriptions I had read of it, to find it a perfect bedlam, a sort of Hogathian Gin Alley, where rum ran down the street gutters and loud profanity and vile stenches contended for the mastery of the atmosphere. On the contrary, I was happily surprised to find the place in the daytime as quiet and orderly as a country village in Indiana, and at night the traffic in the wares of the fickle Goddess and human souls was conducted with a system so orderly and quiet as to actually be painful to behold. It is a most difficult task, I confess, to write up Dodge City in a manner to do impartial fairness to every interest; the place has many redeeming points, a few of which I have already mentioned. It is not nearly so awful a place as reports make it. It is not true that the stranger in the place runs a risk of being shot down in cold blood, for no offense whatever.''

In the year, 1878, the ''Topeka Times'' says, in a certain issue:

''During the year of 1873 we roughed it in the West. Our first stopping place was the famous Dodge City, at the time a perfect paradise for gamblers, cut-throats, and girls. On our first visit the buildings in the town were not buildings, with one or two exceptions, but tents and dugouts. Everyone in town, nearly, sold whisky or kept a restaurant, perhaps both. The Atchison, Topeka & Santa Fe railroad was just then working its way up the low banked Arkansas, and Dodge was the frontier town. Its growth was rapid, in a month from the time the railroad was completed to its borders, the place began to look like a city; frame houses, one story high, sprang up; Dodge became noted as the headquarters for the buffalo hunters, and the old town was one of the busiest of trading points, and they were a jolly set of boys there. They carried a pair of Colt's revolvers in their belts, wore their pants in their boots, and when they died, did so generally with their boots on. It wasn't safe, in those

times, to call a man a liar or intimate that his reputation
for honesty was none of the best, unless you were spoiling
for a fight. In those days, 'Boot Hill' was founded, and
the way it grew was astonishing to new comers and
terrifying to tenderfeet. We well remember, but now
forget the date, when a party of eastern capitalists came
out to look around with a view to locating. They were
from Boston and wore diamonds and kid gloves. The
music at one of the dance halls enticed the bald headed
sinners thither, and what with wine and women, they
became exceedingly gay. But in the midst of their sport
a shot was fired, and another, and, in a little time, the
room gleamed with flashing pistols and angry eyes. This
was enough, and the eastern capitalists hurried to the
depot, where they remained until the first train bore
them to the classic shades of Boston. But with all its
wildness, Dodge could then, as it does yet, boast of
some of the best, freest, and whitest boys in the country.
We were down there again last week, and were surprised in the change in the city. It has built up wonderfully, has a fine court house, church, good schools, large
business blocks, a good hall, first-class hotels, and two
live newspapers. The editor of the 'Times' was not in,
but we saw Honorable D. M. Frost, the editor of the
'Globe.' Dodge is coming out and is destined to be a
city of considerable size.''

Another writer of the times, defending Dodge City,
says:

''There is an evident purpose to malign and create
false impressions concerning the character of Dodge City.
It is a pretty general impression that a person here is
insecure in life, and that the citizens of Dodge are walking howitzers. This is a bad impression that should, by
all means, be corrected. Having but a short residence
in this town, it is our deliberate opinion, from a careful
observation, that Dodge is as quiet and orderly as any
town of its size in Kansas. We have been treated with

the utmost cordiality. We have observed officers prompt and efficient, in the discharge of their duties. There is an ordinance prohibiting the carrying of fire arms, which is rigidly enforced. The citizens are cordial, industrious, and display a business alacrity, characteristic of the frontier tradesman. We are surprised to note the difference of character of this town and the impression aimed to be made upon us before coming here. There is a lurking jealousy somewhere, that gives rise to false rumors, and we trust every citizen of Dodge City will correct these false impressions, as far as lies in his power. This, alone, would efface bad impressions and false rumors, but forbearance ceases to be a virtue, and we kindly protest.''

Again, the character of early Dodge was defended by Charles D. Ulmer, of the ''Sterling Bulletin,'' thus:

''On Friday, the party visited Dodge City, the rip-roaring burg of the West. As we glided into the depot, we looked anxiously along the street, expecting to see many squads of festive cowboys, rigged out with arms enough to equip a regiment, and ready to pop a shot at any plug hat that might be in the crowd, but nothing of the kind was to be observed; instead, there was a busy, hustling little city, like many others in Kansas, with, perhaps, a few extra saloons thrown in for variety. Dodge City was a surprise to us. It is beautifully located—the residence portion on the hills which command a magnificent view of the country, east, west, and south. The business portion is on the level bottom at the foot of the hills. The railroad track is a little close to the main business street for convenience.

''The party, on landing, instead of being received by a howling lot of cowboys, with six-shooters and Winchester rifles rampant, were received by a delegation of as gentlemanly and courteous men as can be found in the state. During our stay in Dodge, we had the pleasure of meeting most of the men who have been so prominently mentioned in the late trouble at that place. Instead of low-browed ruffians and cut-throats, we found them to be cultivated gentlemen, but evidently possessing plenty of nerve for any emergency. Among those we met and conversed with was Luke Short, his partner, Mr. Harris, who is vice-president of the Dodge City bank, and Mr. Webster. The late trouble originated in differences between Messrs. Short and Webster, and, we believe, after both sides get together it could and should have been settled without the hubbub made, and interference of the state authorities. Mr. Short, Mr. Harris, and others assured us that their side, at all times, was ready and willing to submit their differences to the decision of the courts. The trouble has been amicably adjusted, and no further trouble is anticipated on the old score.''

But, as has already been stated, often only the worst side of Dodge City was written up, in a way to make the most of it. In protest against this practice, a local writer of early times refers to a write-up of the sort, in this wise:

''A verdant editor of the 'Hays City Sentinel' visits our brothels and bagnios. From the tone of his article, he must have gone too deep into the dark recesses of the lascivious things he speaks of, and went away in the condition of the monkey who got his tail too near the coals. He says: 'After a long day's ride in the scorching sun, I arrived in Dodge City. Dodge is the Deadwood of Kansas. Her incorporate limits are the rendezvous of all the unemployed scallawagism in seven states. Her principal business is polygamy without the sanction of religion, her code of morals is the honor of thieves, and decency she knows not. In short, she is an exaggerated frontier town, and all her consistences are operated on the same principle. Her every day occurrences are such as would make the face of a Haysite, accustomed as he is to similar sights, color to the roots of his hair and

DODGE CITY IN 1878

draw away disgusted. Dodge is a fast town and all of her speedy proclivities exhibit to the best advantage. The employment of many citizens is gambling. Her virtue is prostitution and her beverage is whisky. She is a merry town and the only visible means of support of a great many of her citizens is jocularity. Her rowdyism has taken a most aggravated form, and was it not for the most stringent ordinances (some of which are unconstitutional), and a fair attempt to enforce them, the town would be suddenly depopulated and very much in the manner that Ireland got rid of her snakes. Seventeen saloons furnish inspiration and many people become inspired, not to say drunk. Every facility is afforded for the exercise of conviviality, and no restriction is placed on licentiousness. The town is full of prostitutes and every other place is a brothel. Dodge by day and Dodge by night are different towns;'' and, then he goes on with more abuse too vile and untruthful to mention. Our brother from Hays City must indeed have been hard hit, but must not have visited any good spot in Dodge City, but, on the contrary, must have confined himself entirely to the very lowest places and worst society in Dodge. Birds of a feather, you know, will flock together. We hope his dose was a mild one— though he does not deserve our sympathy.

Besides this generally sensational mode of writing up the town, Dodge City was the theme of many lurid stories and sulphurous jokes which tended, no less than the write-ups, to establish her position, in the public eye, as the ''Wickedest Town in America.'' The following letter is from the ''Washington, D. C., Evening Star,'' January 1st, 1878.

''Dodge City is a wicked little town. Indeed, its character is so clearly and egregiously bad that one might conclude, were the evidence in these latter times positive of its possibility, that it was marked for special Providential punishment. Here those nomads in regions remote from the restraints of moral, civil, social, and law enforcing life, the Texas cattle drovers, from the very tendencies of their situation the embodiment of waywardness and wantonness, end the journey with their herds, and here they loiter and dissipate, sometimes for months and share the boughten dalliances of fallen women Truly, the more demonstrative portion of humanity at Dodge City gives now no hopeful sign of moral improvement, no bright prospect of human exaltation; but with Dodge City itself, it will not always be as now. The hamlet of today, like Wichita and Newton farther east in the state, will antagonize with a nobler trait, at some future day, its present outlandish condition. The denizen of little Dodge City declares, with a great deal of confidence, that the region around about the place is good for nothing for agricultural purposes. He says the seasons are too dry, that the country is good for nothing but for grazing, and that all they raise around Dodge is cattle and hell. The desire of his heart is the father of the statement. He is content with just what it is, and he wants that to remain. He wants the cattle droves and his associations and surroundings to be a presence and a heritage forever.''

Referring to this article, the Ford County ''Globe,'' of January 1st, 1878, says: ''We think this correspondent had a sour stomach when he portrayed the wickedness of our city. But we must expect it unless we ourselves try to improve the present condition of things. There is not a more peaceful, well regulated, and orderly community in the western country;'' and then, as the office boy entered to say that somebody wanted to see him, he took his bowie knife between his teeth, put a Colt's new pattern six-shooter on his desk in front of him, and then said: ''Jim, get out another coffin, a plain one this time, and let the critter come in.''

About thirty miles from Dodge the train stopped at
a little station, and a cowboy got on, very drunk, and
fully equipped in chapps, spurs, six-shooter, and quirt.
The conductor, John Bender, asked him his fare and
destination. He replied, "I want to go to hell!" Bender
said, "All right; give me a dollar and get off at Dodge."

Thus Dodge City's evil reputation became established, whether deserved or undeserved. People living at
a distance and having no way of knowing where truth
ended and falsehood began, naturally gave credence to
all reports they saw published, until, in places remote,
the very name of Dodge became a synonym for all that
was wild, reckless, and violent. Strangers, approaching
the town for the first time, did so with dread, entered it
with fear and trembling, or passed through it with a sigh
of relief as its last roof was left behind. Tales of the
fate of tenderfeet in the border city struck terror to the
soul of many a new comer in the community, and the
dangers apprehended by these new arrivals on the
dreaded scene, were limited only by the amount of courage, credulity, and imagination they possessed. To illustrate, a young man, going west with a party of movers,
wrote a card to his father back east, just before reaching
Dodge City, not mailing it till after passing through.
Here is what he wrote while anticipating the entrance
into the dreaded town:

"In Camp Fifteen Miles from Dodge, May 7, 1877.
'Dear Father:—

"As I've a little time I'll drop you a card, so you
can see we are all well and headed west. Have laid over
here to wait for a larger crowd so as to be perfectly safe
going through Dodge. There are nine teams now and
will be three more in the morning, so we will be safe
anyway. There are a good many coming back from
Colorado but that don't discourage us any. That is no
sign we can't do well. Everything goes on as nice as

— 153 —

clock work among ourselves; not a word as yet and no hard feelings.

"HERBERT."

In somewhat sarcastic comment upon this postal card, the "Dodge City Times," of May 19th, 1877, says:

"The card was evidently written while awaiting reinforcements to assist in making a charge through our city, but not mailed until they had run the gauntlet and halted to take breath at a safe distance on the west side. To the father and friends who are no doubt anxiously waiting to know if our blood-thirsty denizens exterminated the caravan, we can say that they escaped us without a serious loss of life."

What made Dodge City so famous was that it was the last of the towns of the last big frontier of the United States. When this was settled, the frontier was gone, it was the passing of the frontier with the passing of the buffalo, and the Indian question was settled forever. Here congregated people from the east, people from the south, people from the north, and people from the west. People of all sorts, sizes, conditions, and nationalities; people of all colors, good, bad, and indifferent, congregated here, because it was the big door to so vast a frontier. Some came to Dodge City out of curiosity; others strictly for business; the stock man came because it was a great cattle market, and here, on the Arkansas river, was the place appointed for the cattle going north to be classed and passed on, for bargains to be closed, and new contracts made for next year; the cowboy came because it was his duty as well as delight, and here he drew his wages and spent them; the hunter came because it was the very heart of the greatest game country on earth; the freighter came because it was one of the greatest overland freight depots in the United States, and he hauled material and supplies for nearly four hundred miles, supplying three military posts, and all the frontier or that far south and west; last but not least, the gambler and the bad man came because of the wealth and excitement, for obscene birds will always gather around a carcass.

Money was plentiful and spent lavishly, and here let me say, there are different classes of men who are producers or money-makers, and misers, up to a certain amount. There were numbers of people, to my certain knowledge, who would carefully save up from two hundred to five hundred dollars, and then come to Dodge City and turn it loose, never letting up until every dollar was gone. There were others whose ambition was higher. They would save up from five hundred to two thousand dollars, come to Dodge City and spend it all. There were still others who would reach out to five thousand dollars and upwards, come to Dodge, and away it would all go, and, strange to say, these men went back to their different avocations perfectly satisfied. They had started out for a good time and had had it, and went back contented. Indeed, one man started with twenty thousand dollars for New York, struck Dodge City, spent the most of his twenty thousand, and went back to begin over again. He said: "Oh, well, I did start to have a good time in New York, but I tell you, you can make New York anywhere if you only have the money and the luxuries and attractions are there." And these all could be had for the price, in Dodge City. There were women, dance halls, music, saloons and restaurants, equipped with every luxury, while gambling in every conceivable form, and every gambling device known at that time was in full blast.

I will now say something of the business of early Dodge, which has been mentioned as being tremendous. At that time we were often asked, "What sustains your city?" "Where does your trade come from?" and many such questions, which, no doubt, will recur to the mind of the reader, at the present time. First and foremost of our industries was the cattle and stock trade, with its buying, selling, and shipping for the whole southwestern range, and which lasted till other railroads extended into this territory and cut off the trade from Dodge City. Then there was the government freight business, with Dodge the point of supply to many military posts and their garrisons, in the surrounding wilderness. This, alone, was heavy traffic, while local and general freighting, to ranches, inland settlements, and hunters' camps, was an important addition to this line of business. Again, as Dodge City was the point of supply, in all general commodities, for so vast a section of country, the mercantile business promptly assumed enormous proportions.

One of Dodge City's great industries was the bone trade. It certainly was immense. There were great stacks of bones, piled up by the railroad track—hundreds of tons of them. It was a sight to see them. They were stacked up way above the tops of the box cars, and often there were not sufficient cars to move them. Dodge excelled in bones, like she did in buffalo hides, for there were more than ten times the number of carloads shipped out of Dodge, then out of any other town in the state, and that is saying a great deal, for there was a vast amount shipped from every little town in western Kansas.

The bones were a godsend to the early settler, for they were his main stock in trade for a long, long time; and, if it had not been for the bone industry, many poor families would have suffered for the very necessaries of life. It looked like a wise dispensation of Providence. Many poor emigrants and settlers came to Kansas with nothing but an old wagon and a worse span of horses, a large family of helpless children, and a few dogs—nothing else. No money, no work of any kind whatever to be had, when, by gathering buffalo bones, they could make a living or get a start. Game was all killed off and starvation staring them in the face; bones were their only salvation, and this industry saved them. They gathered and piled them up in large piles, during the winter, and hauled them to Dodge at times when they had nothing else to do, when they always demanded a good price. This industry kept us for many years, and gave the settler a start, making it possible for him to break the ground from which he now raises such large crops of wheat, making him rich and happy. Yes, indeed! Many of our rich farmers of today, once were poor bone pickers, but if they hear this, it don't go. Certainly, this was a great business, as well as a godsend, coming at a time when the settlers most needed help. All this added to the wealth and prosperity of Dodge, and added to its fame. "Buffalo bones are legal tender in Dodge City," was the strolling paragraph in all the Kansas exchanges.

As to the magnitude of the early day mercantile business of Dodge City, the writer can speak, at any length, from his own experience, as he followed that line, there, for many years. As an introduction to the subject, I'll give a clipping from the "Ford County Globe," of 1877, entitled, "Wright, Beverly & Company's Texas Trade." Now one of the editors, Mr. Morphy, was a bitter enemy of the writer, who was head of the firm of Wright & Beverly, because he abused the writer so maliciously and scandalously and lied so outrageously about him, when the writer was running for the legislature, that the latter whipped him on the street; for which, Morphy sued the writer for ten thousand dollars. The jury awarded a damage of four dollars and a half for the plaintiff's doctor's bill, and they hung out, for a long time, against giving anything, until the judge instructed them they must render a verdict for that amount, as Mr. Morphy had clearly proven that he had paid the doctor four dollars and a half, as a result of the whipping; so you can see, he would not give the firm any too much praise, in writing them up. He says:

"Those gentlemen do an immense business and make a specialty to cater to the immense Texas trade. The jingling spur, the carved ivory-handled Colt, or the suit of velveteen, and the many, many other Texas necessaries, you here find by the gross or cord. An upstairs room, thirty by seventy-five feet, is devoted entirely to clothing and saddlery. In their warehouses and yard, it is no uncommon thing to find from sixty to eighty thousand buffalo robes and hides. This house also does a banking business for the accommodation of its customers. Mr. John Newton, the portly and benevolent *charge de affairs* of the office, will accommodate you with five dollars or five thousand dollars, as the case may be. We generally get the former amount. Mr. Samuels, who has special charge of the shooting irons and jewelry stock, will entertain you in Spanish, German, Russian, or Hebrew. The assistance of Mr. Isaacson, the clothier, is demanded for *parrle vous,* while Bob, himself, has to be called on when the dusky and dirty 'child of the setting sun' insists on spitting and spouting Cheyenne and Arapahoe and goes square back on the king's English. They employed over a dozen outside men to check off the wagons that were loading, and their sales were on an average of a thousand dollars a day, Sundays not excepted, or three hundred and fifty thousand dollars a year, and several years it was over four hundred thousand dollars.'' There was no article you could mention we did not handle. Our remittances to banks in Leavenworth were frequently as high as fifty thousand dollars. This was owing to stock men depositing their whole pile with us, and drawing against it as they needed it. We have had parties leave with us endorsed, certified checks, as high as fifty thousand dollars each, to pay for cattle or close some deal for them. Strange to say, there was but little currency in circulation, and, notwithstanding the railroad agent was instructed to turn over his receipts of greenbacks, and take our check for same, we had to have shipped to us, by express, from two thousand dollars to five thousand dollars in currency every few days.

The Santa Fe railroad was another great factor in making the wealth and splendid prosperity of Dodge City. Indeed, it was the first cause of the development of Dodge City's greatness. It was this road, you might say, that made us. It, at least, gave us a big start. Hundreds of its employees made it their home from the very beginning. Dodge was not only its terminus, for awhile, but it always has been the end of a division. The officers of the road and the people of the town have always enjoyed great harmony. They have treated us justly and kindly, favoring us whenever and in whatever way they could, and, in return and to show them gratitude, the Dodge people have worked right in with them; and never have they been at outs, or has the least thing ever arisen which would lessen the friendship between them. Even yet, (1913), the railroad company is making great improvements in buildings, grades, yardage, etc., at Dodge City.

Another great feature belonging to Dodge City, and which brought many people there at an early date, is its beautiful, health giving climate and pure air. It was, and is, a great resort for invalids afflicted with the white plague. This should be the stopping off place for all those badly afflicted with this dread disease, as the great change in altitude, from lowlands to mountains, is often too sudden. I have known many people to stop off here until they got accustomed to light air and great altitude, and then go on to the mountains, and, in time, be completely cured. Others would stop only a short time and take the consequences. Others, after a short stay here, would feel so much better they would return home, thinking they were cured, and make a grand mistake. A lovely lady, the wife of one of Missouri's greatest lawyers, stopped off here a short time, and her health improved so wonderfully that she went back to Missouri, but we heard of her death a short time afterwards. I have known several parties who would receive so great a benefit from a short stay in Dodge, they would insist, against the wishes of their doctor and friends, on going on to the mountains, and come back, in a few weeks, in a box, or return to die among their eastern friends. You see, they did not stay in Dodge long enough to get used to the great altitude of the mountains.

Dodge City was conspicuous in the sight of newspaper men, and complimentary notices of its business men were often unique. For instance, the "Walnut City Blade," says: "The gentlemen of Dodge City are whole-souled fellows and fine business men. Although our acquaintance was limited, we can say that Sutton, Whitelaw, Winnie, Gryden, Bob Wright, Shinn, Klaine, and Frost are each a whole team with a mule colt following."

As an instance of the splendid liberality of Dodge City in times of emergency, as already mentioned, its response to Governor St. John's petition for the cyclone sufferers has been given. Another instance, among any number that might be given, was the conduct of Dodge City toward the yellow fever situation, in Memphis, Tennessee, in 1878. September 10th, of that year, a mass meeting was called for the purpose of alleviating the sufferers of Memphis from the terrible yellow fever scourge. The people only had a few hours' notice of the meeting, but, in such short time, two or three hundred gathered. A few speeches were made by some of our prominent citizens, when Mr. P. L. Beaty jumped upon a stand and said: "I have been a victim of this yellow fever, and know how these people in the South suffer; here's what talks!" at the same time throwing a ten dollar bill into the hat, amidst wildest enthusiasm. Other speeches followed, while contributions flowed into the hat in splendid style, the poor bootblack dropping in his nickel, and the rich nerchant his ten dollar bill. The total amount collected vas over three hundred dollars, which was promptly forvarded to the Howard Association of Memphis. Instances f charity equal to that of Dodge City are as scarce on he records as, elsewhere, the rarity of Christian charity s plentiful. Hurrah, for little Dodge! She is still bad n war, good in peace, and has a bigger heart, for her ize, than any town in Kansas. A short time after this neeting, it was found that the terrible scourge of yellow ever still held Memphis in its grip; and at another mass neeting to relieve the suffering, Dodge City sent more han double the former amount.

This puts me in mind of a little priest, by the name f Father Swineberg, who was a little fellow with a big leart, with charity for all and malice toward none, no natter what the denomination. He was very highly eduated, could speak fluently more than a half-dozen differnt languages, and visited Fort Dodge to look after his 'lock and minister to the wants of his people, years before Dodge City was established. It was the writer's happy uck to be able to accommodate him several times, in lriving him from one post to another, looking after the leeds of the church and his ministerial duties, and, in hat way, the writer and he became warm friends.

In the course of time, he called on me at the fort, irmed with letters to the commanding officer of Fort Dodge, and instructing said officer to give Father Swineierg all the assistance in his power. His objective point vas way down in old Mexico, across the borders of that inknown region, those days, of New Mexico, Arizona, ind old Mexico, a distance from Fort Elliott, his starting ioint, of over one thousand miles. It was a desert, enirely unknown, in those days, without water, wood, or labitations, or civilization of any kind. His stock of trade vas splendid maps of the region he was to traverse, incased in an oil-cloth covered tin tube. I, being familiar vith the terrible dangers and privations he would have

— 161 —

to undergo, from lack of food and water, exposure to the elements both heat and cold, as well as the terrible storms that visited that country, and some big rivers to cross, tried to persuade him to desist. I told him it was as much as his life was worth—that he must not go. He said he had to go. I asked him, why. Shrugging his shoulders, like a Frenchman would, he said: "Because my bishop ordered me."

The commanding officer at Fort Elliott fitted out Father Swineberg and another priest, who was to be his traveling companion, with two fine horses, what grub they could conveniently carry, and blankets. They had no arms of any kind or description except knives; they said they didn't need any. Remarkable to relate, they made the trip, accomplished their object, and came back safely. Father Swineberg told me that they enjoyed the trip. That once, when they were in one of the greatest straits and lost without food or water, they ran into a very large band of Indians, who received them kindly, and several of the band understood Spanish and some understood French. They stayed with the Indians about a week, preaching alternately in French and Spanish, which a good many of the Indians seemed to understand and enjoy and appreciate.

Now comes my yellow fever episode which reminded me of this story. When the great call was made from the South to the North, for aid and nurses to subdue the terrible scourge, Father Swineberg, with twenty-odd other priests, nobly responded, well knowing they were going to their death. Very few ever returned, and Father Swineberg was among the number that went down. His was a noble life.

There was a society known as "The Orients," in Dodge City, with charitable work as its real object, and fun as a side line. A few disparaging remarks, made by a young blood who desired membership, subjected the individual to a "side degree," upon which lavish hands performed all sorts of excruciating tricks, which were absurd and ridiculous. When it came to ridicule, the old-timer was not sparing in punishment.

The greatest excitement ever caused in Dodge was the advent of an Indian, one of the principal chiefs of the Cheyennes. In the winter of 1872, W. D. Lee, of the firm of Lee & Reynolds, doing a large business at Supply as freighters, government contractors, sutlers, and Indian traders combined, brought this Indian to Dodge City to show him the wonders of the railroad and impress upon him how civilization was advancing. There happened to be several hunters in town at that time, driven in by a heavy storm and snow. No sooner did the Indian make his appearance on the street than the excitement began. Most of the hunters hated an Indian, and not a few of them had suffered more or less from their depredations. Among the latter was one Kirk Jordan, a very desperate man, whose sister, brother-in-law, and whole family had been wiped out by the savages, and their home and its contents burned and every vestige of stock stolen. This had happened in the northwest part of the state. Jordan had sworn to kill the first Indian he saw, no matter what the consequences might be. He was a leader and a favorite with the hunters, and, together with his companions, being inflated with liquor, had no trouble in getting followers. We ran the Indian into a drug-store and locked the doors. There was no egress from the rear, but two families occupied houses adjoining the drug-store, and someone quickly tore off one of the upright partition boards that separated the drug-store from the dwellings containing the families, and the Indian squeezed through. The board was quickly and neatly replaced, leaving no trace of its having been removed; so when the crowd of excited hunters burst into the store and could not find the Indian, they were as puzzled a lot as ever lost a trail upon open prairie.

That afternoon I thought things had quieted down, and I saddled one of Lee's finest horses (Lee had brought up a magnificent team), and led it around to the back door—of course the Indian had been previously instructed to mount and make for his tribe as fast as the horse would carry him; but before I rapped at the door I looked around, and from the back of the dance hall, a hundred yards distant, there were fifty buffalo guns leveled at me. I knew those fellows had nothing against me, but I was afraid some of the guns might go off by accident, and wished right there that the ground would sink down deep enough to cover me from the range of their guns. I led the horse back to the stable as quickly and quietly as possible, feeling relieved when inside. I at once dispatched a courier to the commander at the fort, with the request that he send up a company of cavalry, but he wouldn't do it. As soon as it got dark, Lee and I got in his carriage, loaded with buffalo-robes, had the Indian rushed out, robes piled on top of him, and went out of Dodge on the run. We met Captain Tupper's troop of the Sixth United States cavalry about a mile out, coming after the chief. There were no more Indians seen in Dodge except under big escort.

The following rules were posted in one of the Dodge City hotels for the guidance of guests (some say rules were stolen from Mark Twain's hotel).

HOTEL RULES.

"These are the rules and regulations of this hotel.

"This house will be considered strictly intemperate.

"None but the brave deserve the fare.

"Persons owing bills for board will be bored for bills.

"Boarders who do not wish to pay in advance are requested to advance the pay.

"Boarders are requested to wait on the colored cook for meals.

"Sheets will be nightly changed once in six months—oftener if necessary.

"Boarders are expected to pull off their boots if they can conveniently do so.

"Beds with or without bedbugs.

"All moneys and other valuables are to be left in charge of the proprietor. This is insisted upon, as he will be held responsible for no losses."

And now follows an early day market report:

DODGE CITY MARKETS

(Corrected weekly by Wright, Beverly & Company).

Dodge City, Kansas, Jan. 5th, 1878.

Flour, per 100 lbs.	$2.50	@ $ 4.00
Corn Meal, per 100 lbs.	2.00	
Oats, per bu.	.45	
Corn, per bu.	.56	
Hides, Buffalo, per lb.	.03¾ @	.04¾
Wolf	.75 @	1.25
Coyote	.30 @	.50
Skunks	.10 @	.50
Chickens, dressed, per lb.	.10	
Turkeys, per lb.	.12½	
Potatoes, per bu.	1.40	
Apples, dried, per lb.	.08 @	.10
Peaches, dried, per lb.	.12½	
Bacon, per lb.	.12½	
Hams, per lb.	.15 @	.17
Lard, per lb.	.12 @	.14
Beef, per lb.	.08 @	.10
Butter, per lb.	.30 @	.35
Eggs, per doz.	.35	
Salt, per bbl.	4.50	
Coffee, per lb.	.25 @	.26
Tea, per lb.	.80 @	1.00
Sugar, per lb.	.12 @	.14
Coal Oil, per gal.	.50	
Coal, per ton	9.00 @	10.00

I give this market report to show the difference between then, 1878, and now.

The lexicographers of today should credit Dodge City with contributions to our language, as certain significations or meanings of three words, now very much used, can be traced to our early philologists. The words are "stinker," "stiff," and "joint." These words are not considered the sweetest nor most elegant in the language, by our institutions of learning nor in the realms of culture and refinement, yet they are very expressive and are warranted by sufficient use.

The word "stinker," or rather the signification in which it is used when applied to a person in a contemptuous way, originated in this way. In the early days of this country, the buffalo or bison densely populated the plains. The killing of this noble animal for the hide was a great industry, and it was nothing uncommon for the buffalo hunter to get a stand on a herd and kill scores of them in a very short time. Such occurrences were sometimes in winter, and, before the hunter could skin all the animals, the carcasses would freeze and he would be compelled to leave many frozen on the prairies. When the weather moderated and the carcasses thawed, newcomers or "tenderfeet," as we called them, would skin them for the hides. Natural causes and decay would render such hides very inferior and almost worthless, and, as these thrifty beneficiaries of the prowess of the genuine buffalo hunter were despised by him, the name "stinker" was originated and applied to him, and the word has since supplied the vocabulary of many, when their systems were surcharged with contempt and hatred.

The word "stiff," as applied to people in a contemptuous way, originated in Dodge City. The readers of this book will gather from this record of the early history of Dodge City, the fact that the lifeless remains of people were a common sight here, in those days, and veneration and respect for the dead was somewhat stinted, unless some tie of friendship or relationship existed with the

"BAT" MASTERSON

departed. As the lifeless body of a human being soon becomes rigid, our philologists substituted the easily spoken word "stiff" for the ghostly word "corpse," in referring to the dead in which they had no special interest, and, from this, the word received an appropriate application to such people as suggest death or worthlessness, or, in other words, "dead ones."

A very common signification or meaning of the word "joint" is easily traced to Dodge City, and I here submit my proof. I quote from an edition of the Dodge City Times, dated June 2nd, 1877:

"Washington, D. C., May 17, '77.
"Editor Dodge City Times:

"I trust you will not take this, from its postmark outside, as being an appointment to a lucrative official position.

"Such is not the case. I write to the far West seeking information. I see, at times, in your sprightly paper, the use of the term or terms 'go to the joint,' or 'gone to the joint,' etc.

"Will you please inform me what it means?

"Yours,
"INQUIRER."

"We are always willing to give the people of Washington City any information they may desire on matters of public interest. In order that the president and his cabinet may get a clear idea of this grave question, we will endeavor to be explicit. Gilmore, on municipal elections, page 77, says, 'The gang got to the joint in good shape.' This is the best authority we have. As an instance more easily understood by the average Washingtonian, suppose Hayes and Morton should get on a bender and put their jewelry in soak for booze, then it would be appropriate to say they 'got to the joint' by this means. For further particulars, address,

"L. McGLUE."

I remember well the first child born in Dodge. Early in the morning, a young doctor came into the only drug store in Dodge, with a look of thorough disgust on his countenance, saying, "My God! I did something last night that I never thought is possible to fall to my lot, and I am so ashamed that I never will again practice in Dodge. I delivered an illegitimate child from a notorious woman, in a house of prostitution." The druggist and I both laughed at him and told him he must not think of leaving the profession for such a little thing as that; he must keep right on and fortune would sure follow, as it was a great field for his profession, and we knew he was fully capable; and so he did, and has become one of the most prominent, as well as skillful physicians, not only of Dodge City, but the whole state of Kansas.

This was in the fall of 1872. Soon after, followed the birth of Claude, son of Dr. T. L. and Sallie McCarty; and close after him, Jesse Rath was born, son of Charles and Carrie Rath, who died in infancy. So Claude McCarty can well claim the distinction of being the first legitimate child born in the town, and the eldest native.

CHAPTER VIII

Populating Boot Hill

The first man killed in Dodge City was a big, tall, black negro by the name of Tex, and who, though a little fresh, was inoffensive. He was killed by a gambler named Denver. Mr. Kelly had a raised platform in front of his house, and the darkey was standing in front and below, in the street, during some excitement. There was a crowd gathered, and some shots were fired over the heads of the crowds, when this gambler fired at Texas and he fell dead. No one knew who fired the shot and they all thought it was an accident, but years afterwards the gambler bragged about it. Some say it was one of the most unprovoked murders ever committed, and that Denver had not the slightest cause to kill, but did it out of pure cussedness, when no one was looking. Others say the men had an altercation of some kind, and Denver shot him for fear Tex would get the drop on him. Anyhow, no one knew who killed him, until Denver bragged about it, a long time afterwards, and a long way from Dodge City, and said he shot him in the top of the head just to see him kick.

The first big killing was down in Tom Sherman's dance hall, some time afterwards, between gamblers and soldiers from the fort, in which row, I think, three or four were killed and several wounded. One of the wounded crawled off into the weeds where he was found next day, and, strange to say, he got well, although he was shot all to pieces. There was not much said about this fight, I think because a soldier by the name of Hennessey was killed. He was a bad man and the bully of the company, and I expect they thought he was a good riddance.

Before this fight, there was "a man for breakfast," to use a common expression, every once in a while, and this was kept up all through the winter of 1872. It was a common occurrence; in fact, so numerous were the killings that it is impossible to remember them all, and I shall only note some of them. A man by the name of Brooks, acting assistant-marshal, shot Browney, the yard-master, through the head—over a girl, of course, by the name of Captain Drew. Browney was removed to an old deserted room at the Dodge House, and his girl, Captain Drew, waited on him, and indeed she was a faithful nurse. The ball entered the back of his head, and one could plainly see the brains and bloody matter oozing out of the wound, until it mattered over. One of the finest surgeons in the United States army attended him. About the second day after the shooting, I went with this surgeon to see him. He and his girl were both crying; he was crying for something to eat; she was crying because she could not give it to him. She said: "Doctor, he wants fat bacon and cabbage and potatoes and fat greasy beef, and says he's starving." The doctor said to her: "Oh, well, let him have whatever he wants. It is only a question of time, and short time, for him on earth, but it is astonishing how strong he keeps. You see, the ball is in his head, and if I probe for it, it will kill him instantly." Now there was no ball in his head. The ball entered one side of his head and came out the other, just breaking one of the brain or cell pans at the back of his head, and this only was broken. The third day and the fourth day he was alive, and the fifth day they took him east to a hospital. As soon as the old blood and matter was washed off, they saw what was the matter, and he soon got well and was back at his old job in a few months.

A hunter by the name of Kirk Jordan, (previously mentioned), and Brooks had a shooting scrape, on the street. Kirk Jordan had his big buffalo gun and would have killed Brooks, but the latter jumped behind a barrel of water. The ball, they say, went through the barrel,

THE OLD BRIDGE

This bridge was replaced, several years ago, by a magnificent steel bridge.

water and all, and came out on the other side, but it had lost its force. We hid Brooks under a bed, in a livery stable, until night, when I took him to the fort, and he made the fort siding next day, and took the train for the East. I think these lessons were enough for him, as he never came back. Good riddance for everybody.

These barrels of water were placed along the principal streets for protection from fire, but they were big protection in several shooting scrapes. These shooting scrapes, the first year, ended in the death of twenty-five. and perhaps more than double that number wounded. All those killed died with their boots on and were buried on Boot Hill, but few of the number in coffins, on account of the high price of lumber caused by the high freight rates. Boot Hill is the highest and about the most prominent hill in Dodge City, and is near the center of the town. It derived its name from the fact that it was the burying ground, in early days, of those who died with their boots on. There were about thirty persons buried there, all with their boots on and without coffins.

Now, to protect ourselves and property, we were compelled to organize a Vigilance Committee. Our very best citizens promptly enrolled themselves, and, for a while, it fulfilled its mission to the letter and acted like a charm, and we were congratulating ourselves on our success. The committee only had to resort to extreme measures a few times, and gave the hard characters warning to leave town, which they promptly did.

But what I was afraid would happen did happen. I had pleaded and argued against the organization for this reason, namely: hard, bad men kept creeping in and joining until they outnumbered the men who had joined it for the public good—until they greatly outnumbered the good members, and when they felt themselves in power, they proceeded to use that power to avenge their grievances and for their own selfish purposes, until it was a farce as well as an outrage on common decency. They got so notoriously bad and committed so many crimes, that the good members deserted them, and the people arose in their might and put a stop to their doings. They had gone too far, and saw their mistake after it was too late. The last straw was the cold blooded, brutal murder of a polite, inoffensive, industrious negro named Taylor, who drove a hack between the fort and Dodge City. Whilst Taylor was in a store, making purchases, a lot of drunken fellows got into his wagon and was driving it off. When Taylor ran out and tried to stop them, they say a man, by the name of Scotty, shot him, and, after Taylor fell, several of them kept pumping lead into him. This created a big row, as the negro had been a servant for Colonel Richard I. Dodge, commander of the fort, who took up his cause and sent some of them to the penitentiary. Scotty got away and was never heard of afterwards.

When railroads and other companies wanted fighting men (or gunmen, as they are now called), to protect their interests, they came to Dodge City after them, and here they could sure be found. Large sums of money were paid out to them, and here they came back to spend it. This all added to Dodge's notoriety, and many a bunch of gunmen went from Dodge. Besides these men being good shots, they did not know what fear was—they had been too well trained by experience and hardships. The buffalo hunters lived on the prairie or out in the open, enduring all kinds of weather, and living on wild game, often without bread, and scarcely ever did they have vegetables of any description. Strong, black coffee was their drink, as water was scarce and hardly ever pure, and they were often out for six months without seeing inside of a house. The cowboys were about as hardy and wild, as they, too, were in the open for months without coming in contact with civilization, and when they reached Dodge City, they made Rome howl. The freighters were about the same kind of animals, perfectly fearless. Most of these men were naturally brave, and their manner of living made them more so. Indeed, they did not know fear, or any such thing as sickness—poorly fed and poorer clad; but they enjoyed good pay for the privations they endured, and when these three elements got together, with a few drinks of red liquor under their belts, you could reckon there was something doing. They feared neither God, man, nor the devil, and so reckless they would pit themselves, like Ajax, against lightning, if they ran into it.

It had always been the cowboy's boast as well as delight to intimidate the officers of every town on the trail, run the officers out of town, and run the town themselves, shooting up buildings, through doors and windows, and even at innocent persons on the street, just for amusement, but not so in Dodge. They only tried it a few times, and they got such a dose, they never attempted it again. You see, here the cowboys were up against a tougher crowd than themselves and equally as brave and reckless, and they were the hunters and freighters—"bull-whackers" and "mule-skinners," they were called. The good citizens of Dodge were wise enough to choose officers who were equal to the emergency. The high officials of the Santa Fe railroad wrote me several times not to choose such rough officers—to get nice, gentlemanly, young fellows to look after the welfare of Dodge and enforce its laws. I promptly answered them back that you must fight the devil with fire, and, if we put in a tenderfoot for marshal, they would run him out of town. We had to put in men who were good shots and would sure go to the front when they were called on, and these desperadoes knew it.

The last time the cowboys attempted to run the town, they had chosen their time well. Along late in the afternoon was the quiet time in Dodge; the marshal took his rest then, for this reason. So the cowboys tanked up pretty well, jumped their horses, and rode recklessly up and down Front Street, shooting their guns and firing through doors and windows, and then making a dash for camp. But before they got to the bridge, Jack Bridges, our marshal, was out with a big buffalo gun, and he dropped one of them, his horse went on, and so did the others. It was a long shot and probably a chance one, as Jack was several hundred yards distant.

There was big excitement over this. I said: "Put me on the jury and I will be elected foreman and settle this question forever." I said to the jury: "We must bring in a verdict of justifiable homicide. We are bound to do this to protect our officers and save further killings. It is the best thing we can do for both sides." Some argued that these men had stopped their lawlessness, were trying to get back to camp, were nearly out of the town limits, and the officer ought to have let them go; and if we returned such a verdict, the stock men would boycott me, and, instead of my store being headquarters for the stock men and selling them more than twice the amount of goods that all the other stores sold together, they would quit me entirely and I would sell them nothing. I said: "I will risk all that. They may be angry at first, but when they reflect that if we had condemned the officer for shooting the cowboy, it would give them encouragement, and they would come over and shoot up the town, regardless of consequences, and in the end there would be a dozen killed." I was satisfied the part we took would stop it forever; and so it did. As soon as the stock men got over their anger, they came to me and congratulated me on the stand I took, and said they could see it now in the light I presented it.

There was no more shooting up the town. Strict orders were given by the marshal, when cowboys rode in, to take their guns out of the holsters, and bring them across to Wright & Beverley's store, where a receipt was given for them. And, my! what piles there were of them. At times they were piled up by the hundred. This order was strictly obeyed and proved to be a grand success, because many of the cowboys would proceed at once to tank up, and many would have been the killings if they could have got their guns when they were drunk; but they were never given back unless the owners were perfectly sober.

In the spring of 1878, there was a big fight between the Atchison, Topeka & Santa Fe railroad and the Denver & Rio Grande, to get possession of and hold the Grand Canyon of the Arkansas River where it comes out of the mountains just above Canon City, Colorado. Of course, the Atchison, Topeka & Santa Fe folks came to Dodge City for fighters and gunmen. It was natural for them to do so, for where in the whole universe were there to be found fitter men for a desperate encounter of this kind. Dodge City bred such bold, reckless men, and it was their pride and delight to be called upon to do such work. They were quick and accurate on the trigger, and these little encounters kept them in good training. They were called to arms by the railroad agent, Mr. J. H. Phillips. Twenty of the brave boys promptly responded, among whom might be numbered some of Dodge's most accomplished sluggers and bruisers and dead shots, headed by the gallant Captain Webb. They put down their names with a firm resolve to get to the joint in creditable style, in case of danger. The Dodge City Times remarks:

"Towering like a giant among smaller men, was one of Erin's bravest sons whose name is Kinch Riley. Jerry Converse, a Scotchman, descendant from a warlike clan, joined the ranks of war. There were other braves who joined the ranks, but we are unable to get a list of their names. We will bet a ten-cent note they clear the track of every obstruction." Which they did in creditable style.

Shooting all along the line, and only one man hurt! This does seem marvelous, for the number of shots fired, yet the record is true of the story I am about to relate. This was one of the most daring and dangerous shooting scrapes that Dodge City has ever experienced, and God knows, she has had many of them.

It seems that Peacock and James Masterson, a second brother of Bat, ran a dance hall together. For some reason, Masterson wanted to discharge their bar-keeper, Al Updegraph, a brother-in-law of Peacock, which Peacock refused to do, over which they had serious difficulty; and James Masterson telegraphed his brother, Bat, to come and help him out of his difficulties. I expect he made his story big, for he was in great danger, if the threats had been carried out. Bat thought so, at least, for he came at once, with a friend.

Soon after his arrival, he saw Peacock and Updegraph going toward the depot. Bat holloed to them to stop, which I expect they thought a challenge, and each made for the corner of the little calaboose across the street. Bat dropped behind a railroad cut, and the ball opened; and it was hot and heavy, for about ten minutes, when parties from each side the street took a hand. One side was firing across at the other, and vice versa, the combatants being in the center. When Updegraph was supposed to be mortally wounded and his ammunition exhausted, he turned and ran to his side of the street, and, after a little, so did Peacock, when Bat walked back to the opposite side and gave himself up to the officers. The houses were riddled on each side of the street. Some had three or four balls in them; and no one seemed to know who did the shooting, outside the parties directly concerned. It caused great excitement, at first, but the cooler heads thought discretion was the better part of valor, and, as both parties were to blame, they settled the difficulties amicably, and Bat took his brother away with him. Both parties displayed great courage. They stood up and shot at each other until their ammunition was exhausted.

Though all did not contribute directly to the population of Boot Hill, there were many deeds of violence committed in Dodge City's first ten years of life, that paralleled any which added a subject for interrment in that primitive burying ground. Such a case was the shooting of Dora Hand, a celebrated actress.

The killing of Dora Hand was an accident; still, it was intended for a cold blooded murder, so was accidental only in the victim that suffered. It seems that Mayor James Kelly and a very rich cattleman's son, who had marketed many thousand head of cattle in Dodge, during the summer, had a drunken altercation. It did not amount to much, at the time, but, to do the subject justice, they say that Kelly did treat Kennedy badly. Anyhow, Kennedy got the worst of it. This aroused his half-breed nature. He quietly went to Kansas City, bought him the best horse that money could secure, and brought him back to Dodge. In the meantime, Mr. Kelly had left his place of abode, on account of sickness, and Miss Dora Hand was occupying his residence and bed. Kennedy, of course, was not aware of this. During the night of his return, or about four o'clock next morning, he ordered his horse and went to Kelly's residence and fired two shots through the door, without dismounting, and rode away. The ball struck Miss Hand in the right side under the arm, killing her instantly. She never woke up.

Kennedy took a direction just opposite to his ranch. The officers had reason to believe who did the killing, but did not start in pursuit until the afternoon. The officers in pursuit were Sheriff Masterson, Wyat Erb, Charles Bassett, Duffy, and William Tighlman, as intrepid a posse as ever pulled a trigger. They went as far as Meade City, where they knew their quarry had to pass and went into camp in a very careless manner. In fact, they arranged so as to completely throw Kennedy off his guard, and he rode right into them, when he was ordered three times to throw up his hands. Instead of doing so, he struck his horse with his quirt, when several shots were fired by the officers, one shot taking effect in his left shoulder, making a dangerous wound. Three shots struck the horse, killing him instantly. The horse fell partly on Kennedy, and Sheriff Masterson said, in pulling him out, he had hold of the wounded arm and could hear the bones craunch. Not a groan did Kennedy let out of him, although the pain must have been fearful. And all he said was, "You sons of b—, I will get even with you for this."

Under the skillful operation of Drs. McCarty and Tremaine, Kennedy recovered, after a long sickness. They took four inches of the bone out, near the elbow. Of course, the arm was useless, but he used the other well enough to kill several people afterwards, but finally met his death by someone a little quicker on the trigger than himself. Miss Dora Hand was a celebrated actress and would have made her mark should she have lived.

One Sunday night in October, 1883, there was a fatal encounter between two negroes, Henry Hilton and Nigger Bill, two as brave and desperate characters as ever belonged to the colored race. Some said they were both struck on the same girl and this was the cause.

Henry was under bonds for murder, of which the following is the circumstances. Negro Henry was the owner of a ranch and a little bunch of cattle. Coming in with a lot of white cowboys, they began joshing Henry, and one of them attempted to throw a rope over him. Henry warned them he would not stand any such rough treatment, if he was a nigger. He did this in a dignified and determined manner. When one rode up and lassoed him, almost jerking him from his horse, Henry pulled his gun and killed him. About half of the cowboys said he was

CHUCK WAGONS ON A ROUND-UP IN SOUTHWEST KANSAS

justifiable in killing his man; it was self defense, for if he had not killed him, he would have jerked him from his horse and probably killed Henry.

Negro Bill Smith was equally brave, and had been tried more than once. They were both found, locked in each other's arms (you might say), the next morning, lying on the floor in front of the bar, their empty six-shooters lying by the side of each one. The affair must have occurred some time after midnight, but no one was on hand to see the fight, and they died without a witness.

T. C. Nixon, assistant city marshal, was murdered by Dave Mathers, known as "Mysterious Dave," on the evening of July 21st, 1884. The cause of the shooting was on account of a shooting altercation between the two on the Friday evening previous. In this instance, it is alleged, Nixon had fired on Mathers, the shot taking no effect. On the following Monday evening, Mathers called to Nixon, and fired the fatal shot. This circumstance is mentioned as one of the cold blooded deeds, frequently taking place in frontier days. And, as usual, to use the French proverb for the cause, "Search the woman."

A wild tale of the plains is an account of a horrible crime committed in Nebraska, and the story seems almost incredible. A young Englishman, violating the confidence of his friend, a ranchman, is found in bed with the latter's wife. This continues for some months until, in the latter part of May, 1884, one of the cowboys, who had a grievance against Burbank, surprised him and Mrs. Wilson in a compromising situation and reported it to the woman's husband, whose jealousy had already been aroused. At night, Burbank was captured while asleep in bed, by Wilson and three of his men, and bound before he had any show to make resistance. After mutilating him in a shocking manner, Burbank had been stripped of every bit of clothing and bound on the back of a wild broncho, which was started off by a vigorous lashing. Before morning, Burbank became unconscious, and was, therefore, unable to tell anything about his terrible trip. He thinks the outrage was committed on the night of May 27th, and he was rescued on the morning of June 3rd, which would make seven days that he had been traveling about the plains on the horse's back, without food or drink, and exposed to the sun and wind. Wilson's ranch is two hundred miles from the spot where Burbank was found, but it is hardly probable that the broncho took a direct course, and, therefore must have covered many more miles in his wild journey. When fully restored to health, Burbank proposed to make a visit of retaliation on Wilson, but it is unknown what took place.

The young man was unconscious when found, and his recovery was slow. The details, in full, of the story, would lend credence to the tale; but this modern Mazeppa suffered a greater ordeal than the orthodox Mazeppa. This story is vouched for as true, and it is printed in these pages as an example of plains' civilization.

"Odd characters" would hardly express the meaning of the term, "bad men"—the gun shooters of the frontier days; and many of these men had a habitation in Dodge City. There was Wild Bill, who was gentle in manner; Buffalo Bill, who was a typical plains gentleman; Cherokee Bill, with too many Indian characteristics to be designated otherwise; Prairie Dog Dave, uncompromising and turbulent; Mysterious Dave, who stealthily employed his time; Fat Jack, a jolly fellow and wore good clothes; Cock-Eyed Frank, credited with drowning a man at Dodge City; Dutch Henry, a man of passive nature, but a slick one in horses and murders; and many others too numerous to mention; and many of them, no doubt, have paid the penalty of their crimes.

Several times, in these pages, the "dead line" is mentioned. The term had two meanings, in early Dodge phraseology. One was used in connection with the cattle trade; the other referred to the deeds of violence which were so frequent in the border town, and was an imaginary line, running east and west, south of the railroad track in Dodge City, having particular reference to the danger of passing this line after nine o'clock of an evening, owing to the vicious character of certain citizens who haunted the south side. If a tenderfoot crossed this "dead" line after the hour named, he was likely to become a "creature of circumstances;" and yet, there were men who did not heed the warning, and took their lives in their own hands.

"Wicked Dodge" was frequently done up in prose and verse, and its deeds atoned for in extenuating circumstances; but in every phase of betterment the well being was given newspaper mention, for it is stated: "Dodge City is not the town it used to be. That is, it is not so bad a place in the eyes of the people who do not sanction outlawry and lewdness." But Dodge City progressed in morality and goodness until it became a city of excellent character.

Even the memory of the wild, wicked days will soon be effaced, but, as yet, when one recounts their wild stories and looks upon the scenes of that wildness and wickedness, one can almost fancy the shades of defunct bad men still walking up and down their old haunts and glaring savagely at the insipidity of their present civilized aspect. The "Denver Republican" expresses a similar thought in a certain short poem, thus:

THE TWO GUN MAN

The Two Gun Man walked through the town,
  And found the sidewalk clear;
He looked around, with ugly frown,
  But not a soul was near.
The streets were silent. Loud and shrill,
  No cowboy raised a shout;
Like panther bent upon the kill,
  The Two Gun Man walked out.

The Two Gun Man was small and quick;
  His eyes were narrow slits;
He didn't hail from Bitter Creek,
  Nor shoot the town to bits;
He drank, alone, deep draughts of sin,
  Then pushed away his glass,
And silenced was each dance hall's din,
  When by the door he'd pass.

One day, rode forth this man of wrath,
  Upon the distant plain,
And ne'er did he retrace his path,
  Nor was he seen again;
The cow town fell into decay;
  No spurred heels pressed its walks;
But, through its grass grown ways, they say,
  The Two Gun Man still stalks.

"CHALK" BEESON

CHAPTER-IX

The Administration of Justice on the Frontier

The story of Justice Joyce, in a previous chapter, sufficiently proves that the interpretation of law and the proceedings of courts of justice, were, to say the least, irregular, in their infant days on the Kansas plains. That Joyce was not alone in his peculiar legal practices, is verified by authentic accounts of similar practices in other places, not the least of which was Dodge City.

A cattleman by the name of Peppard was one whom the officers disliked to see come to Dodge. Invariably rows began then, and he was in all of them. While driving up a bunch of beeves to Dodge, so the story goes, Peppard's boss killed the negro cook. It has been said that the boss and Peppard were great friends and chums, and the boss killed the cook because Peppard wanted him killed. Anyway, a short time after they arrived at Dodge, Peppard and his boss fell out. The next morning Peppard saw him behind a bar in one of the saloons, and straightway procured a shot-gun loaded with buck, and turned it loose at the boss, who dodged behind the ice-chest, which was riddled. A very narrow escape for the boss it was. Peppard then took a man and dug up the dead negro, chopped off his head with an ax, brought it in a sack to within thirty miles of Dodge, when nightfall overtook them and they had to lay out. The negro had been dead two weeks, and it was very warm weather. Wolves were attracted by the scent, and made a most terrible racket around the camp-fire, and it was decidedly unpleasant for the two men. Peppard's man weakened first and said they must remove the head or the camp. Inasmuch as the head was the easier to remove, they took it a mile or two away. Then the wolves took it and the sack several miles further, and they had much difficulty in finding it. At last it was produced in court with the bullet-hole in the skull, and the perplexing question was sprung on the court as to its jurisdiction to hold an inquest when only a fractional part of the remains was produced in court. The case was ably argued, pro and con. Those in favor of holding the inquest maintained that the production of the head in court included the other necessary parts of the anatomy, and was the best evidence on earth of his demise, and that the bullet-hole was a silent witness of his taking-off. The opposition argued that if the court had jurisdiction to hold an inquest on the head, there was no reason why the courts of Comanche county and other localities could not do the same on any other fractional part of the anatomy which might be found scattered over their bailiwick. The court, after mature deliberation, decided to give continuance until such time as the rest of the remains could be produced in court. Peppard left the town disgusted with the decision, and, for all I know to the contrary, the case is still docketed for continuance.

Here is an early day account of a proceeding in the Dodge City Police Court:

" 'The marshal will preserve strict order,' said the judge. 'Any person caught throwing turnips, cigar stumps, beets, or old quids of tobacco, at this court, will be immediately arraigned before this bar of justice.'' Then Joe looked savagely at the mob in attendance, hitched his ivory handle a little to the left, and adjusted his mustache. 'Trot out the wicked and unfortunate, and let the cotillion commence,' said the judge.

" 'City vs. James Martin'—but just then, a complaint not on file had to be attended to, and 'Reverant' John Walsh, of Las Animas, took the throne of justice, while the judge stepped over to Hoover's, for a drink of old rye to brace him up for the ordeal to come.

" 'You are here for horse stealing,' says Walsh. 'I can clean out the d—d court,' says Martin, and the city attorney was banged into a pigeon-hole in the desk, the table upset, the windows kicked out, and the railing broke down. When order was restored, Joe's thumb was 'some chawed,' Assistant Marshal Masterson's nose sliced a trifle, and the rantankerous originator of all this trouble, James Martin, Esquire, was bleeding from a half dozen cuts on the head, inflicted by Masterson's revolver. Then Walsh was deposed and Judge Frost took his seat, chewing burnt coffee for his complexion.

"The evidence was brief and to the point. 'Again,' said the judge, as he rested his alabaster brow on his left paw, 'do you appear within this sacred realm, of which I, and I only, am high muck-i-muck. You have disturbed the quiet of our lovely village. Why, instead of letting the demon of passion fever your brain into this fray, did you not shake hands and call it all a mistake. Then the lion and the lamb would have lain down together, and white-robed Peace would have fanned you with her silvery wings, and elevated your thoughts to the good and pure by her smiles of approbation. But, no! You went to chawing and clawing and pulling hair. It's ten dollars and costs, Mr. Martin.'

" 'Make way for the witnesses,' says Joe, as he winks at the two coons that come to the front, and plants one on each side of Mr. Morphy who appears for the defendant. 'A thorn between two roses.'

"It was the City vs. Monroe Henderson, all being 'niggas' except the city attorney and Mr. Morphy. The prosecuting witness, Miss Carrie, looked 'the last rose of summer all faded and gone.' Her best heart's blood (pumped from her nose) was freely bespattering the light folds which but feebly hid her palpitating bosom. Her star-board eye was closed, and a lump like a burnt biscuit ornamented her forehead. The evidence showed that the

— 185 —

idol of her affections, a certain moke named Harris, had first busted her eye, loosened her ribs, and kicked the stuffing generally out of Miss Carrie. Carrie then got on the warpath, procured a hollow-ground razor, flung tin cans at the defendant, and used such naughty language as made the judge breathe a silent prayer, and caused Walsh to take to the open air in horror. But the fact still remained that the defendant had 'pasted' her one on the nose. The city attorney dwelt upon the heinousness of a strong giant man smiting a frail woman. Mr. Morphy, for the defendant, told two or three good stories, bragged on the court, winked at the witnesses, and thought he had a good case; but the marble jaws of justice snapped with firmness, and it was five dollars and costs, and the court stood adjourned.

Joe Waters tells a humorous story which is a fair specimen of the rough verbal joking, common to early day conversation. It was issued in 1881, is entitled, "The Attorney for Jesus," and runs as follows, the location being the Ford county court at Dodge City, of course; and Waters the prosecuting attorney. The case appeared on the docket entitled, "The State of Kansas vs. Jesus Perea," was solemnly called by the judge, and the proceedings are in this wise, by Waters:

" 'The State vs. Jesus Perea,' the court now calls;
'I appear for Jesus,' Gryden bawls;
'His last name you will please to state,
Or, Harry, I will fine you, sure as fate.'

" 'Perea,' says Gryden, so low the court could hardly hear,
'He is the man for whom I appear;'
Says the court, sotto voce, 'When the savior employs such as him,
Our chances for heaven are getting quite slim.' "

The wit or humor of attorney and court was not confined to bench and bar, but the following is a terse argument by a lay woman:

— 186 —

"A good story is told of a Dodge City divorce suit. The jury refused to grant the lady a divorce, and, when the court inquired if she would like to 'poll the jury,' she said: 'That is just what I would delight to do if your honor will give me a pole;' and the glance she gave the jury made the cold chills run up and down their spinal columns."

Dodge City had some unique characters in the judicial harness. Bill Nye, the humorist of the Larimie, Wyoming, "Boomerang," has a story about "McIntosh on Fees," a justice of the peace named McIntosh furnishing the humorist with his droll account. On one occasion, in a case before Justice McIntosh, the jury rendered a verdict for the plaintiff who was unable to pay the fees; so the justice promptly reversed the judgment in favor of the defendant, who made good. The plaintiff appealed the case, but was killed one morning before breakfast, prior to the session of the circuit court which was to dispose of the case.

"McIntosh on Fees" didn't know the difference between *quo warranto* and the erysipelas, but he had more dignity than the chief justice of the supreme court of the United States. Once, however, his dignity was seriously ruffled, when old Spangler brought to him the exhumed head of a deceased darkey in a gunny-sack, for the inquest mentioned at the beginning of this chapter. The gruesome find, with an aperature on the side of the head, so mortified the dignity of the justice that he resigned his office and left the country.

The subject of the administration of justice on the frontier would hardly be duly considered without some reference to lynchings. But, in speaking of lynching, in the early days of Dodge City, there was not much of this kind of work carried on. When certain party or parties got too obnoxious to the decent part of the community, they would be notified to leave town, and, if they did not go, the vigilants or respectable citizens would raise up in their might and shoot them to death. There were only two lynchings or hangings. One occurred in the west part of town, for horse stealing. One night, long after sundown, a small party of men rode into town, stopped at the store, bought a piece of rope, and quietly mounted and rode away. The next day, report reached Dodge that three men were hanging to a big cottonwood tree—a large lone tree, in the center of a nice little bottom near the crossing of Saw Log Creek, about twelve miles northeast of Dodge.

One of the three was a young man, about twenty-one, Calahan by name, who had been brought up in the right way. His father was a good Christian gentleman, and a minister of the gospel, and it nearly broke his heart, as well as the mother's. His uncle, Dr. Calahan, was the leading dentist of Topeka, and stood at the head of his profession throughout the state. Of course, they took his remains to Topeka for decent burial. The young man had no idea what he was getting into when he came to Dodge a stranger, looking for work, and hired out to herd horses for a noted horse thief, Owens by name, residing in Dodge. But Calahan gradually drifted in with them, and, I suppose, found the employment so fascinating and exciting that he became one of them. But this broke up the Owens gang here, and Owens emigrated north, where his business was more flourishing, and soon after, his son was hung for the same crime.

CHAPTER X

The Passing of the Buffalo

From the nature and habits of the buffalo hunter as already described, and from the fact of his having figured so extensively in all these stories of frontier life, it will readily be seen that the buffalo hunter was closely identified with every phase of existence, of that period and locality. Indeed, for many years, the great herds of buffalo was the pivot around which swung the greater part of the thrilling activities of the plains in early days. When the railroad appeared the shipping of buffalo hides and meat had much to do with the immense trade that immediately sprang up in frontier towns like Dodge City. With the removal of the buffaloes from the range, room was made for the cattleman who immediately followed with his wide-stretching and important industry. And, again, the passing of the buffalo herds, at the hands of the white men, was one of the prime causes of Indian hostility, and the keynote of their principal grievance against the whites, and its resulting atrocities and bloodshed.

In a former chapter, I endeavored to give an idea of the size of the buffalo herds of early days. I here give a clipping from the Dodge City Times, of August 18th, 1877, in support of my estimate of the great number of buffaloes on the plains at that time:

TERRIBLE SLAUGHTER OF BUFFALO.

"Dickinson County has a buffalo hunter by the name of Mr. Warnock, who has killed as high as 658 in one winter.—Edwards County Leader.

"O, dear, what a mighty hunter! Ford County has twenty men who each have killed five times that many in one winter. The best on record, however, is that of Tom

Nickson, who killed 120 at one stand in forty minutes, and who, from the 15th of September to the 20th of October, killed 2,173 buffaloes. Come on with some more big hunters if you have any.''

This slaughter, of course, was resented by the Indians and the conflicts between them and the hunters were fierce and frequent. In fact, the hunters were among the most intrepid and determined of Indian fighters, and were known as such. In John R. Cook's remarkable book, ''The Border and the Buffalo,'' remarkable not only for its wonderful stories of Indian fights and terrible suffering from thirst, but remarkable also for its honest truthfulness, he says: ''That noble band of buffalo hunters who stood shoulder to shoulder and fought Kiowas, Comanches, and Staked Plains Apaches, during the summer of 1877, on the Llano Estacado, or the Staked Plains of Texas.''

This refers to a body of men, largely from Dodge City, and Charles Rath and myself among the latter, who previously located in that country. On our arrival, we camped on a surface lake whose waters were from a June water-spout or cloud burst, and now covered a surface of about five acres of ground, Lieutenant Cooper's measurement. In the center of the basin it showed a depth of thirty-three inches. Here we witnessed a remarkable sight. At one time, during the day, could be seen horses, mules, buffaloes, antelope, coyotes, wolves, a sand hill crane, negro soldiers, white men, our part Cherokee Indian guide, and the Mexican guide, all drinking and bathing, at one and the same time, from this lake. Nearly all these men were from Dodge City; that is why I mention them, and you will hear of their heroic deeds of bravery and suffering further along.

Outside of a tented circus, that mentioned was one of the greatest aggregations of the animal kingdom, on so small a space of land and water. One can imagine what kind of water this must have been when taking into account that nearly a month previous it had suddenly fallen from the clouds, upon a dry, sun parched soil with a hard-pan bottom, being exposed to a broiling hot sun about sixteen hours of every twenty-four, while the thermometer was far above one hundred degrees Fahrenheit, and an occasional herd of buffaloes standing or walowing in it, not to mention the ever coming and going antelope, wild horse, wolves, the snipe, curlew, cranes and other wild fowl and animals, all of which frequented this place for many miles around. And yet, we mixed bread, made coffee, and filled our canteens as well as our bellies with it. And yet again, there were men in our party who, in six more days would, like Esau, have sold their birthright for the privilege of drinking and bathing in this same decoction. This was on the Staked Plains—Llano Estacado.

The spring of 1877, the Indians had got very bold. They raided the Texas frontier for hundreds of miles, not only stealing their stock but burning the settlers' homes and killing the women and children, or carrying them into captivity which was worse than death. Captain Lee, of the Tenth cavalry, a gallant, brave officer and Indian fighter, had rendered splendid service by breaking up and literally distroying a band of Staked Plains Indians, bringing into Fort Griffin all the women and children and a number of curiosities. As these Indians got all their supplies through half breed Mexicans, strange to say, all these supplies came from way down on the Gulf of California, hundreds of miles overland. And I will interpolate here, that these Indian women and children never saw a white man before they were captured.

Captain Lee, at one time, commanded Fort Dodge, and was stationed there a long time. While he was a brave and daring officer and did great service, it resulted in stirring up these Indians, making them more revengeful, villainous, and blood thirsty than ever. They now began to depredate on the hunters, killing several of the best and most influential of them, and running off their stock. This the hunters could not stand, so they got together at 'Charles Rath's store (a place they named "Rath," and, as I said before, most of these hunters had followed Rath down from Dodge City), and organized. There were not more than fifty of them, but my, what men! Each was a host within himself. They feared nothing and would go anywhere, against anything wearing a breech-clout, no matter how great the number. I do not give the names of these brave men because I remember but a few of their names and, therefore, mention them collectively.

This little band of brave men were treated liberally by the stock men, those who had lost horses by the Indian raids. They were given mounts, and these stock men also gave the hunters bills of sale to any horses of their brand they might capture. They knew to encourage these men and lend them assistance was protecting their frontier.

The hunters chose Mr. Jim Harvey, I think, for their captain, and they chose wisely and well. They organized thoroughly and then started for the Indians. They had a few skirmishes and lost a few men, and also went through great hardships on account of hunger, thirst, cold and exposure, but they kept steadily on the trail. You see, these hardy men had all the endurance of the Indian, could stand as much punishment in the way of hunger, thirst, and cold, were good riders, good shots, and superior in every way to the Indians.

Finally, they discovered about where the main camp of the Indians was, about the middle of March, 1877. The trail got warm, and they knew they were in close proximity to the main camp at some water-holes on the Staked Plains. This country was new to the hunters and they knew they were up against a big band of Indians. Nevertheless, they were determined to fight them, no matter at what odds.

In the afternoon they discovered an Indian scout. Of course, they had to kill him; if he escaped he would warn the camp. Now then, after this happened, the hunters were obliged to use due diligence in attacking the camp because when the Indian scout did not turn up in a certain time, the Indians' suspicions would be aroused. The hunters expected to discover the camp and attack just before day, but they had difficulty in finding the camp in the night. Long after midnight, however, the hunters' scouts got on to it, but by the time the scouts got back to the boys and reported, notwithstanding they made great haste, it was after sunrise before the hunters got to it. This frustrated all their plans, but the hunters attacked them gallantly and rode into sure range and opened fire. Unfortunately, nearly the first volley from the Indians one of the hunters was shot from his horse and another had his horse killed under him and in falling broke his wrist, while their main guide, Hosea, was shot through the shoulder. Thus handicapped with three badly wounded men from their little band, one having to be carried back on a stretcher which required three or four men, all under a murderous fire, no wonder they had to retreat back to the hills, but fighting every step of the way. And, if I remember rightly, the Indians afterwards acknowledged to Captain Lee, that they lost over thirty men killed outright, and a much larger number wounded, and they abandoned everything to get away with their women and children. They abandoned, on their trail, several hundred head of horses.

Now these forty hunters were fighting three hundred warriors. It was a most wonderful fight and broke the backbone of the Indian depredations. There were only a few raids made after this, and I quote from Cook who says:

"There was a bill up in the Texas legislature, to protect the buffalo from the hunters, when General Sheridan went before that body and said: 'Instead of stopping the hunters, you ought to give them a hearty, unanimous vote of thanks, and give each hunter a medal of bronze with a dead buffalo on one side and discouraged Indian on the other. These men have done more in the last two years, and will do more in the next year to settle the vexed Indian question, than the regular army has done in the last thirty. They are destroying the Indians' commissary, and it is a well known fact that an army, losing its base of supplies, is placed at a great disadvantage. Send them powder and lead, if you will, but, for the sake of peace, let them kill, skin, and sell until the buffalo are exterminated. Then your prairies can be covered with cattle and the cowboy, who follows the hunter as a second forerunner of an advanced civilization.' "

How literally true his prediction has become!

Naturally, the affairs and movements of the hunters was the foundation for much of the news of the day, at this period. The following is a common newspaper item in 1878:

"Messrs. T. B. Van Voorhis, J. A. Minor, H. L. Thompson, Ira Pettys, George W. Taylor, Frank Van Voorhis, Frank Harder, and D. C. Macks, all residents of the eastern portion of Ford County, arrived in the city last Tuesday after an absence of seven weeks on a hunting expedition through the southern country. While hunting on the Salt Fork of Red River the party found a span of mules that had been stolen from Van Voorhis last July. They were in possession of Milton Burr who had purchased them of Chummy Jones who is now in hell, if there is such a place. Mr. Burr, upon hearing the evidence of the claimant promptly turned the mules over to the owner who brought them home with him. One of

SOULE COLLEGE

IN THE EARLY DAYS OF THE HIDE TRADE AT DODGE CITY.
OLD DANCE HALL AT RIGHT.

the party informed us that he saw a couple of animals that were stolen from Mr. Hathaway but when he went to identify them they could not be found.

"Some of the party called at Mr. Dubb's camp and found him and Mr. Stealy doing well. They were camped on Oakes Creek, eight miles this side of Red River and have killed about 1,500 buffaloes. They have a nice lot of meat and hides. Mr. Dubbs asked the party to remember him to his friends in Dodge City."

Another newspaper item very much to the point, since it gives an excellent description of the mode of killing and preparing the buffalo for market, is entitled, "Slaughtering the Buffalo," and is from a "Shackelford County (Texas) Letter to the Galveston News." It follows verbatim:

"The town of Griffin is supported by buffalo hunters and is their general rendezvous in this section. The number of hunters on the ranges this season is estimated at 1,500. We saw at Griffin a plat of ground of about four acres covered with buffalo hides spread out to dry, besides a large quantity piled up for shipment. These hides are worth in this place from $1.00 to $1.60 each. The generally accepted idea of the exciting chase in buffalo hunting is not the plan pursued by the men who make it a regular business. They use the needle gun with telescope, buy powder by the keg, their lead in bulk and the shells and make their own cartridges. The guns in a party of hunters are used by only one or two men, who say they usually kill a drove of thirty or forty buffaloes on one or two acres of ground. As soon as one is killed the whole herd, smelling the blood, collect around the dead body, snuffing and pawing up the ground and uttering a singular noise. The hunter continues to shoot them down as long as he can remain concealed or until the last animal 'bites the dust.' The buffalo pays no attention to the report of the gun, and flees only at the sight or scent of his enemy. The others of the party then occupy themselves in 'peeling.' Some of these have become so skillful they offer to bet they can skin a five or six-year-old bull in five minutes. The meat is also saved and sent to market and commands a good price.''

We mention this special article because these hunters were all from Dodge City, formerly, and they drifted south along with the buffalo.

The Llano Estacado, or Staked Plains, in Texas, which has been mentioned as the scene of a particularly fierce battle between Dodge City hunters and Indians, was a great range for buffalo; and perhaps a description of it, at that time, would be in order. A writer in a Texas paper, in 1881, treats the subject in an interesting way:

''There is something romantic about these canyons and surrounding plains, familiarly known as the 'Llano Estacado.' One would imagine a boundless stretch of prairie, limited, in all directions, by the horizon, a monotonous, dreary waste, the Great American Desert, offering but little to invite settlement or attract interest. My observation, from two months' surveying and prospecting in this 'terra incognita,' has convinced me of the error of any previous opinions I may have formed of this section of the state. The canyons, hemmed in by the plains, the latter rising some two hundred feet above the bed of the streams in the former, are as fair and picturesque as the famous Valley of the Shenandoah, or the most favored sections, in this respect, in California, affording perennial springs of pure, sweet, and mineral waters, gypsum, salt, iron, lime, and sulphur; also, nutritious grasses, green all winter, capable of sustaining sufficient cattle to supply a nation.

''The breaks of the plains, corresponding to second valley prairie, incrusted with pure white gypsum and mica, assuming many dazzling shapes, remind one of the battlements of an old fort or castle, or the profile of a large city with its cathedral walls and varied habitations of the humble and princely of a huge metropolis. Romance lingers on the summit of these horizontal, fancifully-shaped bluffs of the Llano Estacado, so called, and the dreamer or romancer would never exhaust his genius in painting vivid pictures of the imagination.

"This portion of the state, having little protection from the incursions of the Indians, has not yet been a favorite field for settlement, and only within the past three or four years a few hardy, fearless stockmen have brought out their flocks, from the overcrowded ranges of the interior, to enjoy the rich pasturage afforded here. These pioneers, for such they are and deserve to be regarded as stockmen, are traduced and misrepresented, and live in the most primitive style imaginable. A cave in the ground, in many instances, covered only with poles and earth, affords them shelter from the snow and blood-freezing northers, which come often with the force and intensity of a sirocco, from the timberless plains.

"Agriculture has not been tried here, but the soil in this and many of the surrounding counties, a red chocolate loam, in some instances a mold, must yield abundantly to the efforts of the husbandman. The immense amount of snow (we have it on the ground now five inches deep), falling during the fall months, it seems would prepare the soil for early spring crops of cereals; and the volunteer plum thickets and currants indicate that many of the fruits would do well here. The rainfall, so I am informed by the settlers, has averaged well for many years past, even upon the plains; and, with the exception of a few arid sand wastes and salt deposits, it is fair to predict that, in time, the Great American Desert will have followed the red man, or proved as veritable a myth as the Wandering Jew.

"The tall sedge grass upon the plains has been burning for a week or more past, only ceasing with the recent snow-falls, and the canyons are lit up as by the intensity of a Syrian sun or electric light. These annual burnings are really an advantage, fertilizing and adding strength to the spring grasses."

Notwithstanding the possibilities of the Llano Estacado and other sections of the great plains, one can imagine what the lives of the buffalo hunters must have been amid such wild and comfortless surroundings. For all that, many of the hunters seemed happy in the life, and occasionally one even waxed eloquent, not to say poetical, upon the subject. The following lines bear witness to this fact, being composed in the very midst of buffalo hunting days, by as unlikely an aspirant to efforts at poesy as one can well imagine. The lines are not classical, but, considering their author, they are as wonderful production of the pen as the perfect verses of scholarly Milton. Whatever their faults as literature, they at least give a concise and telling picture of the buffalo hunter's life.

THE BUFFALO HUNTER.

"Of all the lives beneath the sun,
The buffalo hunter's is the jolliest one!
His wants are few, simple, and easily supplied,
A wagon, team, gun, and a horse to ride.
He chases the buffalo o'er the plains;
A shot at smaller game he disdains.
Bison hides are his bills of exchange,
And all are his that come within range;
From the wintry blast they shield his form,
And afford him shelter during the storm.
A steak from the hump is a feast for a king;
Brains, you know, are good, and tongue a delicious thing.
When the day's hunt is over, and all have had their
      dinners,

DODGE CITY IN THE EARLY 70's

In Order from Left to Right: Barber Shop, Restaurant, Bill
Playford's Saloon, Dance Hall, and M. V. Cutler's Store

The hunter lights his pipe, to entertain the skinners;
He tells of the big bull that bravely met his fate;
Of the splendid line shot that settled his mate;
Of the cow, shot too low, of another, too high;
And of all the shots that missed he tells the reason why;
How the spike stood his ground, when all but him had fled,
And refused to give it up till he filled him with lead;
How he trailed up the herd for five miles or more,
Leaving, over forty victims weltering in their gore;
All about the blasted calves that put the main herd to
    flight,
And kept them on the run until they disappeared from
    sight.
When weary of incidents relating to the chase,
They discuss other topics, each one in its place;
Law, politics, religion, and the weather,
And the probable price of the buffalo leather.
A tender-footed hunter is a great greenhorn,
And the poor old granger an object of scorn;
But the worst deal of all is reserved for hide buyers,
Who are swindlers and robbers and professional liars.
The hunter thinks, sometimes in the future, of a change in
    his life,
And indulges in dreams of a home and a wife,
Who will sit by his side and listen to his story of the boys
    and the past,
And echo his hopes of reunion in the happy hunting
    grounds at last.''

My old time friend and former partner, Charles Rath,
was a great buffalo hunter and freighter. No one handled
as many hides and robes as he, and few men killed more
buffaloes. He was honest, true, and brave. He bought
and sold more than a million of buffalo hides, and tens
of thousands of buffalo robes, and hundreds of cars of
buffalo meat, both dried and fresh, besides several car
loads of buffalo tongues. He could speak the Cheyenne

and Arapahoe languages, and was one of the best sign
men. He lived right among the Indians for many years
and acquired their habits; but he never gained great
confidence in them, and no man used greater precaution
to guard against their attacks.

Nearly all of the buffalo hunters, bull-whackers, cowboys, and bad men had a popular nickname or peculiar
title of some kind bestowed upon them, supposed to be
more or less descriptive of some peculiarity in their
make-up, and which was often in such common use as to
almost obscure the fact that the individual possessed any
other or more conventional name. Prairie Dog Dave,
Blue Pete, Mysterious Dave, and others are mentioned
elsewhere in these pages. In addition, might be named,
many others, some very significant and appropriate; such
as, Dirty Face Charley, The Off Wheeler, The Near
Wheeler, Eat 'Em Up Jake, Shoot 'Em Up Mike, Stink
Finger Jim, The Hoo-Doo Kid, Frosty, The Whitey Kid,
Light Fingered Jack, The Stuttering Kid, Dog Kelley,
Black Kelley, Shot Gun Collins, Bull Whack Joe, Bar
Keep Joe, Conch Jones, Black Warrior, Hurricane Bill,
and Shoot His Eye Out Jack. Women were also often nick-
named, those of unsavory character generally taking a
title of the same sort; and the married sharing the honors
of their husbands title, as Hurricane Bill and Hurricane
Minnie; Rowdy Joe and Rowdy Kate.

Prairie Dog Dave is distinguished as being the hunter
who killed the famous white buffalo, which he sold to
the writer for one thousand dollars, in the early days
of Dodge City. So far as early settlers know, only one
white buffalo has been known. Of the thousands upon
thousands shot by the plainsmen, in buffalo hunting days,
none were ever white. Naturally, Dave's specimen, which
I had mounted and shipped to Kansas City, forty years
ago, attracted wide attention, not only in Kansas City,
but throughout the West. It was exhibited at fairs and
expositions, and Indians and plainsmen traveled for miles

ɔ get a look at it. The specimen was loaned to the State
f Kansas, and, until nine years ago, was on exhibition
ı the state capitol at Topeka.

I would feel that these sketches were incomplete
id I not give at least a brief account of the "battle of
he adobe wall," in which the handful of brave men who
ought so valiantly against the Indians were all Kansans.

Long years ago, before General Sam Houston led the
'exans on to victory, before their independence was
chieved, while the immense territory southwest of the
ιouisiana purchase was still the property of Mexico, a
arty of traders from Santa Fe wandered up into north-
vestern Texas and constructed a rude fort. Its walls,
ιke those of many Mexican dwellings of the present day,
vere formed of a peculiar clay, hard baked by the sun.
ιt that time the Indians of the plains were numerous and
varlike, and white men who ventured far into their
ountry found it necessary to be prepared to defend
hemselves in case of attacks. Doubtless the fortress
erved the purpose of its builders long and well. If the
ld adobe wall had been endowed with speech, what
tories might it not have told of desperate warfare, of
avage treachery, and the noble deeds of brave men.
Iowever, in the '70's, all that remained to even suggest
hese missing leaves of the early history of the plains
vere the outlines of the earthen fortifications.

In 1874 a number of buffalo hunters from Dodge
Jity took up headquarters at the ruins. The place was
ιelected, not only because of its location in the very
ιenter of the buffalo country, but also because of its
ιumerous other advantages, and the proximity of a
ιtream of crystal, clear water which flowed into the
Janadian River a short distance below. After becoming
ιettled at the trading post, and erecting two large
ιouses of sod, which were used as store buildings, the
nen turned their attention to building a stockade, which

was never completed. As spring advanced and the weather became warm, the work lagged and the hunters became careless, frequently leaving the doors open at night to admit the free passage of air, and sleeping out-of-doors and late in the morning, until the sun was high.

Among the Indians of the plains was a medicine man, shrewd and watchful, who still cherished the hope that his people might eventually be able to overcome the white race and check the progress of civilization. After brooding over the matter for some time, he evolved a scheme, in which not only his own nation, but the Arapahoes, Comanches, and Apaches were interested. A federation was formed, and the Indians proceeded against the settlements of northwestern Texas and southwestern Kansas. Minimic, the medicine man, having observed that the old Mexican fort was again inhabited, and being fully informed with regard to the habits of the white men, led the warriors to attack the buffalo station, promising them certain victory, without a battle. He had prepared his medicine carefully, and in consequence the doors of the houses would be open and the braves would enter in the early morning, while their victims were asleep, under the influence of his wonderful charm. They would kill and scalp every occupant of the place without danger to themselves, for his medicine was strong, and their war paint would render them invisible.

On the morning of the fight, some of the hunters who were going out that day were compelled to rise early. A man starting to the stream for water suddenly discovered the presence of Indians. He ran back and aroused his comrades; then rushed outside to awaken two men who were sleeping in wagons. Before this could be accomplished, the savages were swarming around them. The three men met a horrible death at the hands of the yelling and capering demons, who now surrounded the sod buildings. The roofs were covered with dirt, making it mpossible to set fire to them, and there were great double doors with heavy bars. There were loopholes in the building, through which those within could shoot at the enemy.

The Indians, sure of triumph, were unusually daring, and again and again they dashed up to the entrances, three abreast, then suddenly wheeling their horses, packed against the doors with all possible force. The pressure was counteracted by barricading with sacks of flour. The doors were pushed in by the weight of the horses, until there was a small crevice through which they would hurl their lances, shoot their arrows, and fire their guns as they dashed by. Now they would renew their attack more vigorously than ever, and dash up to the port holes by the hundreds, regardless of the hunters' deadly aim. Saddle after saddle would be empty after each charge, and the loose horses rushed madly around, adding to the deadly strife and noise of battle going on. At one time there was a lull in the fight; there was a young warrior, more daring and desperate than his fellows, mounted on a magnificent pony, decorated with a gaudy war bonnet, and his other apparel equally as brilliant, who wanted, perhaps, to gain distinction for his bravery and become a great chief of his tribe, made a bold dash from among his comrades toward the buildings. He rode with the speed of an eagle, and as straight as an arrow, for the side of the building where the port holes were most numerous and danger greatest, succeeded in reaching them, and, leaping from his horse, pushed his six-shooter through a port hole and emptied it, filling the room with smoke. He then attempted a retreat, but in a moment he was shot down; he staggered to his feet, but was again shot down, and, whilst lying on the ground, he deliberately drew another pistol from his belt and blew out his brains.

There were only fourteen guns all told with the hunters, and certainly there were over five hundred

Indians, by their own admission afterwards. The ground around, after the fight, was strewn with dead horses and Indians. Twenty-seven of the latter lay dead, besides a number of them had been carried off by their comrades. How many wounded there were we never knew, and they (the Indians) would never tell, perhaps, because they were so chagrined at their terrible defeat. After the ammunition had been exhausted, some of the men melted lead and molded bullets, while the remainder kept up the firing, which continued throughout the entire day. Minimic rode from place to place with an air of braggadocio encouraging his followers and making himself generally conspicuous. A sharp-shooter aimed at him, in the distance, possibly a mile, and succeeded in killing the gaily painted pony of the prophet. When the pony went down, Minimic explained to his followers that it was because the bullet had struck where there was no painted place. In the midst of the excitement, while bullets were flying thick and fast, a mortally wounded savage fell almost on the threshold of one of the stores. Billy Tyler, moved with pity, attempted to open the door in order to draw him inside, but was instantly killed. The struggle lasted until dark, when the Indians, defeated by fourteen brave men, fell back, with many dead and wounded. The hunters had lost four of their number, but within a few days two hundred men collected within the fortifications, and the allies did not venture to renew the conflict. Old settlers agree that the "battle of adobe wall" was one of the fiercest fought on the plains.

Such is a brief account, founded on the author's personal knowledge, of the "adobe wall fight," in the Panhandle of Texas, just due south of Dodge, all who were engaged in it being formerly citizens of Dodge. In addition I herewith give the story of one of the participants:

"Just before sunrise on the morning of June 27th, 1874, we were attacked by some five hundred Indians. The walls were defended by only fourteen guns. There were twenty-one whites at the walls, but the other seven were non-combatants and had no guns. It was a thrilling episode, more wonderful than any ever pictured in a dime novel, and has the advantage over the average Indian story in being true, as several of the leading men of Dodge City can testify, who were present at the fight, among them being Mr. W. B. Masterson, sheriff of our county.

"About three o'clock in the morning of the fight, several parties sleeping in the saloon of Mr. James Hanerhan were awakened by the falling in of part of the roof which had given way. The men awakened by the crash jumped up, thinking they had been attacked by Indians, but, discovering what was the matter, proceeded to make the necessary repairs. It was about daylight when through, and Billy Ogg went out to get the horses which were picketed a short distance from the house. He discovered the Indians, charging down from the hills, and immediately gave the alarm and started for the building. The Indians charged down upon the little garrison in solid mass, every man having time to get to shelter except the two Sheidler brothers and a Mexican bullwhacker, who were sleeping in their wagons a short distance from the walls, and who were killed and their bodies horribly mutilated. They were just about to start for Dodge City, loaded with hides for Charles Rath & Company.

"The red devils charged right down to the doors and port holes of the stockade, but were met with such a galling fire they were forced to retire. So close were they that, as the brave defenders of the walls shot out of their port-holes, they planted the muzzles of their guns in the very faces and breasts of the savages, who rained a perfect storm of bullets down upon them. For two terrible hours did the Indians, who displayed a bravery and recklessness never before surpassed and seldom equalled, make successive charges upon the walls, each time being driven

back by the grim and determined men behind, who fired
with a rapidity and decision which laid many a brave
upon the ground. But two men were killed in the stockade, Billy Tyler, who was trying to draw in a wounded
Indian, mortally wounded and lying groaning against the
door, which, when Tyler opened it, he was shot. The
Indian who gave Tyler his death wound was scarcely
fifteen feet from him at the time. A man, by the name of
Olds, was coming down the ladder from the lookout post,
with his gun carelessly in front of him, and the hammer
caught on something, the ball entering his chin and coming out the top of his head.

"After two hours' hard fighting, the Indians with-
drew to the hills but kept up a bombardment on the stockade for some time afterwards. In the afternoon, while
the bullets were coming down on them like hailstones,
Masterson, Bermuda, and Andy Johnson came out and
found ten Indians and a negro dead; but when the savages
were driven in by General Miles, they acknowledged to
seventy being killed, and God knows how many were
wounded.

"The Comanches, in the adobe wall fight, were led
by Big Bow; the Kiowas by Lone Wolf; and the Cheyennes by Minimic, Red Moon, and Gray Beard. The
Indians, shortly afterwards, were completely subdued by
that indefatigable Indian trailer and fighter, the gallant
General Miles. The Miles expedition started from Dodge
on the 6th of August, and on the 30th fought the redskins
on Red River. Masterson, who participated in the adobe
wall fight, went out with the expedition as a scout under
Lieutenant Baldwin, of the gallant old Fifth Infantry,
and was with Baldwin at the time of the capture of the
Germain children."

As an example of fighting of a different sort, I must
here relate the story of a little fight between the Indians
and hunters. Charles Rath & Company loaded a small
mule train, belonging to the hunters, with ammunition

ind guns for their hunters' store at adobe walls. When about half way, on the old Jones and Plummer trail, they were suddenly rushed by a band of Indians five times their number. The hunters hastily ran their wagons into corral shape, and turned loose on them. The Indians were only too glad to skedaddle, leaving several dead horses behind. The hunters pulled into the trail and went on, without losing a moment's time. The Indians killed a favorite buffalo pony, which was the only injury the hunters sustained, and they saw no more of Mr. Redskin.

While much of the history connected with the buffalo is nothing but a record of hardships, fighting, and slaughter of various sorts, there is a brighter tinge to it, now and then, and sometimes its incidents are even laughable, as the story of Harris' ring performance with the bull buffalo, in another chapter, can testify. In many ways, the buffalo was much like domestic cattle in their nature. They could be tamed, handled, and trusted to the same extent. At one time, in Dodge City's early days, Mr. Reynolds had two very tame, two-year-old buffaloes. They were so exceedingly tame and docile that they came right into the back yards, and poked their noses into the kitchen doors, for bread and other eatables.

There came a large troupe to Dodge City, to play a week's engagement at our nice little opera house, just built. They had a big flashy band of about twenty-four pieces, their dress was very gaudy, indeed—like Jacob's coat, made up of many colors—and their instruments, as well as their uniforms, were very brilliant; so much so that they attracted great attention, and I presume their flashy appearance also attracted the attention of the two tame buffaloes, who took exceptions to the noise and appearance, and they took their time and opportunity to resent it.

The band leader was a great tall man, and he had a big bear-skin cap, a baton, and all the shiny regalia they generally wear. Now, as this big band was strung out, coming down Bridge Street, playing for all that was out, those two buffaloes were listening in their back yard, and began to snort and show other signs of restlessness. The band leader stepped out of the ranks, shook his baton, and flourished it right in the buffaloes' faces. This was too much— or more than the buffaloes could stand, and they made a vicious charge at the fellow. With heads lowered, they made for him, and of course he ran right into his band, the buffaloes following, with nostrils distended and blood in their eyes. The waterworks had the street all torn up, a big ditch full of water in the middle of the street, and a picket fence on each side. On charged the buffaloes, horning and plunging into everything in sight. The big bass drum was thrown up into the air, and, as it came down, the buffaloes went for it, as well as for the members of the band, and such a scatterment you never saw. Some took the fence; some took the ditch; all threw away their instruments; some had the seats of their pants town out; the drum major lost his big hat; and there were those who took the fence, roosting there on the pickets, holloing like good fellows to be rescued.

Now this might have been the last of it; but that night, when the buffalo charge had been forgotten, and the band was drawn up in the street, playing in front of the opera house before the performance, some mischievous persons led the two buffaloes down, and turned them loose in the rear of that band, with a big send off, driving them right into the thickest of the band. This was enough. They not only threw away their instruments, but took to their heels, shouting and holloing, almost paralyzed with fear.

CHAPTER XI

Joking With Powder and Ball

As has been said, the well behaved stranger, visiting Dodge City in the old days, was always treated courteously and never molested; on the other hand, however, the stranger entering town in quarrelsome, patronizing, critical, or any other boldly flaunted mood, distasteful to the resident citizens, was quite likely to receive a swift and severe check to his propensities, by being made the butt of some prank, designed to cure him forever of his offensive quality. In like manner, if one of the resident citizens chanced to assume undue airs or otherwise conduct himself in a way not strictly in accordance with the popular idea of what was comely, he was a certain candidate for some practical joke which would speedily show him the error of his ways, and even punish him for it. That such pranks and jokes were neither gentle nor considerate of the feelings of the victims, need not be said. Indeed, the humor of those wild days was often almost as startling and nerve-testing, as its warfare was desperate and its adventures were thrilling.

Our boys were in possession of a great many Indian trophies which they had captured at the adobe wall fight. Among them were war bonnets, shields, bows and arrows, and quivers; and when twenty or more of them would don these costumes and mount their horses, also decorated with Indian fixings, at a short distance they appeared like the Simon-pure stuff.

If a young man came to Dodge, bragging that he would like to participate in an Indian fight, he would surely get it. Once a young man, who is now a merchant in Kansas City, arrived, and expressed himself as eager to meet hostile Indians. The boys invited him to an antelope hunt. Antelope were plentiful then. Young men in Indian costume quietly slipped out ahead. A dozen or more went along with the visitor. After proceeding ten or twelve miles his companions commenced to brace the stranger up by saying: "We had better keep a sharp lookout. Indians have been in this vicinity lately, and they say they are the 'dog soldiers,' the worst on the plains." Then they told him a few blood-curdling stories about horrible atrocities, just to keep up his courage. At this juncture from out of the arroyo came the most unearthly yells, and at the same time the twenty men dashed out. The boaster fled precipitately, coming into town on the dead run, yelling to every one he saw to get his gun; the town would soon be attacked by a thousand Indians; all the other boys were killed and he had a narrow escape; to send at once to the fort for the Gatling gun and the soldiers to defend the town, as he was sure they would take it if they didn't get assistance. This young man was easily scared; but one time they got the wrong rooster. When they ran up close to him and com-menced firing at short range, (and this man Pappard, of whom I spoke before, was one of those who did it), he found his horse could not outrun the others and stopped and commenced firing back. Peppard said he heard one bullet whiz right by his head, and had enough and quit. After Peppard got in, he said it was a put-up job to get him killed, and wanted to murder the whole outfit.

Above Dodge, and nearly adjoining thereto, was a large marsh grown up with brush and high grass. Many times was the unsuspecting stranger and the young unso-phisticated traveling man invited to a snipe hunt, and with sack and lantern trudged away with bounding hopes and a stomach fairly yearning for the delicious feast awaiting him next morning at breakfast, instead of the tough buffalo meat. When they got to the swamp, they would place the traveling man on a path leading into the swamp, tell him to spread his sack open with a hoop, and have his lantern at the mouth of the sack. The snipe would see the light and run right into the sack; and as soon as the sack was full, it was to be closed. In the meantime, they would go up and beat all around the swamp and drive the snipe down to his trap. Of course, they would come home and leave the traveling man holding the sack. Some of the hunters would find their way back that same night; others came in in the morning.

Along in the early years of Dodge City's existence, a doctor from the east, a specialist in venereal and private diseases, wrote persistently to our postmaster and others, to know if it was not a good field for his practice. Some of the gang got hold of his letters and wrote him that the town was overrun with disease, that even our ministers were not free, and that more than half the people were suffering. Anyhow, they made out a frightful condition our people were in and that it had got beyond our physicians, and to come at once if he wanted to make a fortune. They signed one letter, "Sim Dip, Ed Slump;" and another, "Blue Pete."

Now, if the man had had any gumption, he would have known these were fictitious names, but he took the bait and away he came. On his arrival he hunted up Sim Dip and Blue Pete. Of course he was introduced to these gentlemen. They came to me for the key and the loan of the Lady Gay Theater, a large old building. At first I refused, but they promised to do no harm, or only to scare the fellow and have some fun. They printed and put out their notices and in the afternoon started two boys with bells to ring up the town, which they did effectually, judging by the crowd assembled that night. The house was crammed and jammed from the door to the stage. Bat Masterson was on one side of the doctor and Wyat Erb on the other, with Jack Bridges and other gun men sitting around on the stage in chairs.

The doctor had only got on a little way in his lecture when some one in the audience called him a liar. He stopped and said to Bat, "What is that? I don't understand." Bat got up, pulled his gun in front, and said: "I will kill the first man that interrupts this gentleman again." The lecturer had not gone much farther when some one again called him a vile name. Bat and Wyat both got up and said: "This gentleman is a friend of ours, you want to understand that, and the next time he is interrupted we will begin shooting and we will shoot to kill." He had not gone much further in his talk when some one in the audience said, "You lie, you s— of a b—!"

Bat, Wyat, and Bridges all arose and began shooting at the same time. First they shot out the lights and my! what a stampede began. The people not only fell over each other, but they tumbled over each other, and rolled over, and trampled each other under foot. Some reached the doors, others took the windows, sash and all, and it was only a short time till darkness and quiet reigned in the Lady Gay. Only the smell of powder and a dense smoke was to be seen, coming out the windows and doors.

There was a broken down, tin-horn gambler by the name of Dalton, a total wreck from morphine and whisky, whose avocation was a sure-thing game, and his specialty was robbing the stiffs (as the dead bodies were called), and he was an expert at this. Dalton happened to be asleep when this occurred, in a room back of the stage, but the noise and shooting awakened him. He located the place at once from the pistol smoke coming through the windows, and was sure there must be stiffs in the building after so much shooting.

I must interpolate here, there was scarcely any one of that big audience who were wise to the lecture, but nearly all thought everything was straight and, when the shooting began, thought, as a matter of course, it was a genuine shooting scrape, and they could not get away from the scene of action fast enough or far enough, but kept on running in the opposite direction and never looking back. Now this lecturer thought as the audience did and, as soon as the firing began, he ducked down under a table in front of the platform and there he lay, as still as a mouse, for fear someone would find him and kill him yet.

Mr. Dalton crawled along the floor on his belly, hunting the stiffs. When he came to the table, of course he felt the stiff underneath and proceeded to divest him of his wealth. But the lecturer gave one mighty spring, threw Dalton over to one side, and jumped up and ran for dear life holloing, "Murder! Thieves!" and everything else, as loud as he could bawl. Dalton, equally scared to have a stiff come to life and pitch him off, just as he was about to rob him, took to his heels the other way. That was the last seen of the lecturer that night; he sneaked off and hid out.

The next morning Sim Dip and Blue Pete waited on him and told him a fine story—how sorry they were, but if he would stay over that night, they would assure him a fine audience and ample protection to his meeting, and he, never dreaming but what it was all on the square, stayed.

The gang wanted to know of me if ten pounds of powder would hurt him. I told them a pound would kill him if it was rightly confined. This put me on my guard and, just before dark, I found out they were going to place a big lot of powder under the box on which he was going to lecture, and I knew it would blow him up and maybe kill him. So I sent to him privately and said: "My friend, you don't know what you are up against. Get on the local freight, which leaves here inside an hour, and never stop until you get back to your own Illinois, because you are not fit to be so far away from home without a guardian." When the gang was certain he was gone, they touched a match to the fuse they had connected with the powder under the box, and blew it to kingdom come. It went way up in the air and came down a mass of kindling wood. When the boys saw the result, they were glad they did not carry the joke any further.

Soon after the little town of Jetmore, the county seat of Hodgman County, twenty-five miles north of Dodge City, was started, a man who resided in that neighborhood walked to Dodge. He said he came to see the sights, the rows, and ructions, which he had heard of, that were a daily occurrence in Dodge.

After "histing" in a few big drinks that the boys had treated him to, he was full of Dutch courage, said he was wild and wooly and hard to curry, that he could whip his weight in wildcats, and the gang could not start anything too rough for him, and the sooner he got action the better it would suit him. He was a tall, lank, slab-sided galoot—one of those overgrown, loose jointed specimens of humanity, without muscle, brawn, or brains, all blow and bluster, and a weak coward one could see by his looks.

The gang saw at once there was more chance for fun than a fight, and they took him in hand and treated him accordingly. He was very poorly dressed, his pants stuck down in his old boots, an old, flap-down, dirty white hat, and a long, dirty, drab duster for a coat. This duster had once been white, but was now so ragged and dirty you could scarce tell what color it had been. Well, it was not worth two bits, and his old woolen shirt was no better. The boys soon found him a freak from way back, and, as usual, the gang was flush, and you never struck a more liberal crowd when they had money. It was, "Come on boys! brace up to the bar and name your poison," and it was their especial delight to entertain strangers.

The man from Jetmore was no exception. As fast as one would treat him another would step to the front, but it was just like pouring water down a rat hole; and,

THIRD WARD SCHOOL ON FAMOUS BOOT HILL.

while he was drinking, someone would set his duster on fire, and I expect a dozen times they came near burning him up, until the old duster was completely used up. Of course, the man would rave and swear and go on at a terrible rate, threatening the ones who set the fire with all kinds of punishment, if he only knew who they were. They then bought him a new duster, but he took it so hard and raised such a row that this duster shared the same fate as the old one, until they had bought him three or four. Besides burning his duster, they had all sorts of fun with him—had gun plays with blank cartridges, but of course the man didn't know they were blank, and they frightened him nearly to death.

When they found there was no fight in him at all, they persuaded him to have these parties arrested, and, sure enough, they made several arrests for the man, appointed a sheriff, empaneled a jury, and held court that night in one of the principal saloons. There were several bright young lawyers in Dodge, and they were anxious for the play, and let me say right here, there was much wit and argument and repartee displayed on both sides. It was really a great treat to hear the witty arguments that each side put up, as well as the eloquence that flowed spontaneously from these lawyers over nothing. The twelve jurors were selected with all the decorum a regular court would exact. They were seated in chairs on a raised platform, they erected a rostrum for the judge, a box for the prisoner, and a seat for the witness. Whenever a good point was made by either side, someone proposed a drink for all hands; judge, jury, prisoner, and witness, as well as the general crowd, all planted their stomachs up to the bar and were helped.

Soon, with the constant drinking, the crowd began to get hilarious, and began to pelt the witness, the prisoner, the sheriff, and the jury with eggs. They were fresh, (they could get no bad ones), and they kept that crowd dodging. First one and then another, and then the sheriff, the witness, and the jury would get it all together. I tell you, the eggs fell around there as thick as hail, and no one would seem to be hit who was looking; they were always taken by surprise. The judge sat there on his platform and just shook with laughter until the tears came out of his eyes. I never did see a more tickled man. He just enjoyed that fun more than anyone in the crowd. He was nicely dressed and well gotten up for the occasion, very slow and dignified, except when he gave way to laughter.

When the egging had been going on some time, I took several of the boys outside and said: "This is too good for the judge; why not give him some of the chicken pie? We're not giving him a fair deal. It is a shame to neglect him; he might feel offended. He ought to have his share of the hen fruit." The idea caught and they went back loaded. The judge was giving in his wise opinion on a point when, whang! an egg took him in the forehead and then another came. He took out his fine, large, white silk handkerchief and said: "This may be real funny to you, but d—d if I see any fun in it. You all think yourselves mighty smart!" This was too much and they just showered him, pelted him from head to foot. He got down, put on his hat, and walked out as mad as a bull, and never more was seen down town after night. It cured him completely of playing his jokes. He had been, up to that time, one of the greatest jokers Dodge City ever had, but, while he delighted in playing them on others, it made him hot to have jokes played on him. He was one of those who couldn't stand a joke. He caught the writer asleep one day, and succeeded in handcuffing him, and I had to get the services of a blacksmith. Still, he was an all around good fellow, God bless his soul! and was beloved by every one who knew him.

Among the first signal officers sent to Dodge was Sergeant W. W. Wimberg, an innocent, nice, polite gentleman, but what a greenhorn! and he richly deserved the name—as green as a gourd. The gang soon got on to this, and what pranks they did play on him!

He was taking a young lady, on whom he was much struck, home from a dance one night, to the west part of the town, when the boys jumped out of a hollow and began firing their guns. The young lady, I think, was wise to the job, but Wimberg never bade that young lady goodnight; he stood not on the question of going, but, without looking to the east or west, he turned tail and just flew.

Mr. A. B. Webster took it upon himself to avenge the insult to the lady, said his conduct was unbecoming an officer and a gentleman, and next day challenged the sergeant. He—the sergeant—took the matter up before the commanding officer at Fort Dodge, who was onto the joke and in with the boys. He promptly told Wimberg he must accept the challenge and fight Webster. He said the dignity of the army must be maintained at all hazards, but referred him to General Pope, the Commander of the Department of the Missouri, at Fort Leavenworth, saying he must consult the general by wire. The gang had the operator fixed, so when Wimberg telegraphed General Pope, of course the message never went, but General Pope's answer was prompt and to the point: "You must fight, by all means. The dignity of the army must be maintained, or resign at once." Of course, the poor fellow was in a great dilemma, and of the two evils he chose the least and wrote out his resignation, when mutual friends interfered and stopped the duel.

They had charades at Dodge, and the sergeant was generally head man. They got him to deliver a darkey speech, and of course he had to black up for the occasion, so they put shellac or some kind of substance into the blacking, which, when dried, could not be rubbed off nor washed off, and this poor fellow had to keep his room until the blacking wore off his face.

Once they were moving a house, just outside the back door of which there was a large sink hole, filled with vile filth, and this sink was lightly covered up to stop the smell. An idea struck the gang, and they got Wimberg next to this door, while right across the street opposite the back door they started to shooting. Some one threw open the back door, exclaiming, "There is murder going on!" Wimberg was very excited, and this was enough for him. He made a big jump and landed in that vile filth, up to his neck, and he could not get out without assistance. He always was neatly dressed, but this day, I think he had on a white suit. He was so hounded by these rough jokes that he asked to be changed, and the boys lost their game, much to their sorrow.

Once upon a time, a long while ago, when Dodge was young and very wicked, there came a man to town, an itinerant preacher. In the present age you would call him an evangelist. Well, anyway, he possessed a wonderful magnetic power, he was marvelously gifted that way; he would cast his spell over the people, and draw crowds that no one ever dreamed of doing before, in fact he captured some of the toughest of the toughs of wicked Dodge, and from the very first he set his heart on the capture of one Dave Mathews—alias, Mysterious Dave— who was city marshal at the time, said to be a very wicked man, a killer of killers. And it was and is an undoubted fact that Dave had more dead men to his credit, at that time, than any other man in the west. Seven by actual count in one night, in one house, and all at one sitting. Indeed he was more remarkable in his way than the preacher was in his.

Well, as I said, he set his heart on Dave, and he went after him regularly every morning, much to the disgust of Dave. Indeed he was so persistent, that Dave began to hate him. In the meantime, the people began to feel the power of the preacher, for he had about him an unexplainable something that they could not resist, and

Just After the Round-up

the one little lone church was so crowded they had to get another building, and this soon would not hold half the audience. Finally they got a large hall known as the "Lady Gay Dance Hall" and fitted it up with boards laid across empty boxes for seats. There was a small stage at the rear of the building, and on this was placed a goods box for a pulpit for the preacher. Now whether or not Dave had become infected by the general complaint that seized the people, or whether the earnest persistence of the preacher had captured him I know not. Anyhow, certain it was, he promised the preacher to attend the meeting that night, and certain it was, Dave would not break his word. He was never known to do that. If he promised a man he would kill him, Dave was sure to do it.

It was soon noised around by the old "he pillars" of the church, and the "she pillars" too that Dave was captured at last, and what a crowd turned out that night to see the wonderful work of God brought about through the agency of the preacher—the capture of Mysterious Dave.

Soon the hall was filled to its utmost capacity, and Dave, true to his promise, was seen to enter. He was at once conducted to the front, and given the seat of honor reserved for him in front of the preacher, and Oh! how that preacher preached straight at him. He told how wonderful was the ways of Providence in softening the heart of wicked Dave Mathews, and what rejoicing there would be in heaven over the conversion of such a man. Then he appealed to the faithful ones the old "he pillars" of the church, and said to them, now he was ready to die. He had accomplished the one grand object of his life. He had converted the wickedest man in the country, and was willing now and at once to die, for he knew he would go right straight to heaven. Then he called upon the faithful ones to arise and give in their experience, which they did, each one singly, and said, they too, like the preacher, were willing to die right now and here, for they knew that they too would go right straight to heaven for helping to carry out this great work. In fact, most of them said, like the preacher, that they wanted to die right now so they could all go to heaven rejoicing together. Dave sat there silent with bowed head. He told me afterwards, he never in all his scrapes was in such a hot box in his life. He said he would much rather to have been in a hot all around fight with a dozen fellows popping at him all at once, than to have been there. He said he would have been more at ease, and felt more at home, and I expect he told the truth.

Finally he raised to his feet and acknowledged he had been hard hit and the bullet had struck a vital spot, and at last religion had been poured into him; that he felt it tingling from his toes through his whole body, even to his finger tips, and he knew he had religion now sure, and if he died now would surely go to heaven, and pulling both of his six shooters in front of him, he said further, for fear that some of the brothers here tonight might backslide and thereby lose their chance of heaven he thought they had better all die tonight together as they had so expressed themselves, and the best plan he said would be for him to kill them all, and then kill himself. Suddenly jerking out a pistol in each hand, he said to the preacher, "I will send you first," firing over the preacher's head. Wheeling quickly he fired several shots into the air, in the direction of the faithful ones.

The much frightened preacher fell flat behind the dry goods box, as also did the faithful ones who ducked down as low as they could. Then Dave proceeded to shoot out the lights, remarking as he walked towards the door, "You are all a set of liars and frauds, you don't want to go to heaven with me at all." This broke up the meeting, and destroyed the usefulness of that preacher in this vicinity. His power was gone, and he departed for new fields, and I am sorry to relate, the people went back to their backsliding and wickedness.

Notwithstanding the general tone of these stories, all the joking of early days did not revolve around the six shooter and cartridge belt. Sometimes a widely different instrument of administration was choosen, though the methods of administrating never varied; it was ever direct, vigorous, and practically merciless.

In the first years of Dodge City a merchant in the town had a government hay contract. He was also sutler at the fort. There was also a saloon keeper who kept the best billiard hall in the town, an Irishman, and a clever fellow, whom the officers preferred to patronize, by the name of Moses Waters. Now, this Waters was full of jokes, and a fighter from away back. The officers made his saloon their headquarters when they came to Dodge, but, as a general thing, upon their arrival, they sent for the sutler and had him go the rounds with them—a chaperon they deemed essential, lest they might get into difficulties, and the sutler was as eager to have their company as they were to have him along. One evening about dark the post sutler came into Dodge from his hay camp to purchase a suit of clothes suitable for camp service. Waters, in passing along Front street, saw the sutler trying on the suit, and an idea struck him. He went immediately to his saloon, wrote a note to the sutler, as he had often seen the officers do, presenting his compliments, and requesting his presence at once at his saloon. The buildings on Front street were all low, frame shanties with porches. On the corners of the porch roofs were placed barrels of water in case of fire, and the sutler had to pass under these porches to get to Water's saloon. As soon as he was properly rigged out in his new outfit, he hurried to Water's saloon to meet his officer friends, as he supposed, not suspecting any danger, of course. But no sooner had he passed under one of these porches on the corner, than a barrel of water was dashed over him, nearly knocking him down, wetting him to the skin, and nearly drowning him. He knew as soon as he had recovered his breath, and as he heard the parties running over the roof to the rear of the building and jumping to the ground, what had happened and what was up.

When he reached Water's saloon there was a crowd, looking as innocent as could be, and saying, "Come in and wet your new clothes," which was a common custom. "Yes," the sutler said, "I will wet them. Barkeep, set up the drinks. It is all right, and I am going to get even." There were, of course, no officers in sight.

Some time previous to this, Waters, who had a lot of horses, and some fine ones by the way, had built him a large barn and painted it blood red. He took great pride in this barn, more on account of its color than anything else. He had cut out in front of each stall a place large enough for a horse to get his head through, to give the horse air and light. Waters had an Englishman, a very fine hostler, to attend his horses. One day, soon after the incident mentioned above, a tall, finely built young Missourian came to the sutler, as was frequently the case, and asked for work. The sutler said, "Yes, I can give you work. Can you whitewash?" He said, "I can beat the man who invented whitewashing." The sutler got two old-fashioned cedar buckets, holding about three gallons each, and two whitewashing brushes, a short and a long-handled one. "Now," said the sutler, "I want you to mix these buckets full and thick, and go down to that red stable (showing him the stable), and plaster it thick with whitewash. I painted it red, but everyone seems to dislike the color, and I want it changed. But, say, there is a crazy Irishman, by the name of Waters, who imagines he owns the stable. He may come around and try to give you some trouble. If he does, don't give him any gentle treatment. Use him as rough as you can. Smash him with your whitewash brush, and if you can put a whitewash bucket over his head and nearly drown him, I will pay you two dollars extra. Try and do this anyway, and I will pay you more for it than for doing the job of whitewashing.''

Soon after the talk, off went the big Missourian with his whitewash buckets and brushes. There was a strong west wind blowing, so he commenced on the east side of the barn. He went at it like he was mauling rails, and was doing a fine job. The Englishman was shut up inside, giving the horses their morning scrubbing. At last he was attracted by the continual knocking of the brush against the stable. In the meantime quite a crowd had gathered, looking on at the curious spectacle of the big Missourian whitewashing the stable. At last the Englishman poked out his head, demanding of the Missourian: ''What the bloody 'ell are you doing, anyway?'' Down comes the Missourian's brush on the face and head of the Englishman, while at the same time he said that the man who gave him the job told him that an ignorant Irishman would try to stop him. This was too much for the Englishman, who went across the street to Water's room, dripping all over with whitewash.

Waters being a saloonkeeper and compelled to be up late at night, slept late in the morning, and was still in bed. Waters could hardly believe the Englishman's story, that anyone would dare whitewash his beautiful red barn. But he put on his pants, slippers, and hat, and went over to see. Waters was a fighter—in fact, he was something of a prize-fighter, and was a powerful and heavy-set man, and did not think he could be whipped. The reason the Missourian got such an advantage of him, Waters told me afterwards, was because he was trying to get up to him as close as possible so that he could give him a knock-out blow. But the Missourian was too quick for him. Waters approached the Missourian very slowly and deliberately, talking to him all the while in a very mild and persuasive way, but when he was almost within striking distance the

Missourian put the bucket of whitewash over his head. It almost strangled Waters, and he had to buck and back and squirm to shake the bucket off. When he did, and had shaken the whitewash out of his eyes, nose, and mouth, what a fight began. The young Missourian was a giant, but Waters was more skilled by training. Still they had it, rough and tumble, for a long time, first Waters on top and then the Missourian. Finally, the Missourian found that Waters was getting the best of it, and, with a desperate effort, threw Waters to one side, tore loose, and made for the government reservation, only a few hundred yards distant, followed closely by Waters, amid great cheering by the crowd. It was indeed laughable, the Missourian in the lead, beating the ground with his big feet and long legs, with all the vim and energy he possessed, and as if his life depended on the race (and perhaps it did), followed by the low, squatty figure of Waters in his shirt sleeves and slippers, minus hat and coat with the whitewash dripping from him at every point, and tearing down with equal energy, as if his life, too, depended upon the race. The race of the two men presented a most laughable scene, too ludicrous for anything. They both seemed determined on the issue, but the long legs of the Missourian were evidently too much for Water's short ones, and he finally abandoned the chase.

There is nothing further to the story, except that the sutler had to hide out for a few days, until mutual friends could bring in a white flag and agree upon terms of peace.

I have related enough to show that the spirit of practical joking and raillery was very prevalent in southwestern, frontier days. Most of it was good natured and meant to be harmless; but I must confess that there was scarcely anything too sacred to be made the butt of a joke, if the trend of inclination turned that way. Even love, instead of being a serious matter, was often treated as a joke and laughed into materialization or renunciation, as the case might be. The following love letter of the times, might have been written en route on the Texas drive, or by the camp fire in a buffalo hunter's camp:

"Dearest:—

"My love is stronger than the smell of coffee, patent butter, or the kick of a young cow. Sensations of exquisite joy go through me like chlorite of ant through an army cracker, and caper over my heart like young goats on a stable roof. I feel as if I could lift myself by my boot straps to the height of a church steeple, or like an old stage horse in a green pasture. As the mean purp hankers after sweet milk, so do I hanker after your presence. And as the goslin' swimmeth in the mud puddle, so do I swim in a sea of delightfulness when you are near me. My heart flops up and down like cellar doors in a country town; and if my love is not reciprocated, I will pine away and die like a poisoned bed-bug, and you can come and catch cold on my grave."

CHAPTER XII

When Conviviality was the Fashion and the Rule

Those were days of hard drinking as well as hard riding and hard fighting. The man who did not drink in some degree, was regarded as something of a freak, and as lacking the social spirit. Stories innumerable, tragic, pathetic, humorous, may be told of Dodge City and her people, showing the place that intoxicants filled in the life of the time and place, and with their plots centering around the glass and the bar of the frontier saloon.

In the early days of Dodge, the town was often visited by a traveling man whom we will call Thomas Smith, who is now a very wealthy Christian gentleman, worth a million, and now making amends for his early debauches by charitable work, teaching poor boys the way they should go. This salesman would always put up at the Dodge House, and when he had finished his rounds among his customers and finished his work, he would proceed to get on his usual drunk. His firm would wire Mr. Cox, proprietor of the hotel, to take care of him until he recovered from his spree and send them his bill. Of course he had hosts of friends, as he was a fine fellow as well as salesman, when sober.

The hotel was built clear through to the other street and, in building back, the floor at the rear was below the surface of the ground, as it was a little up-hill from the front of the house, and this placed the windows of the back part level with the ground. Now, Tom was in one of these rooms with the window level with the ground, and of course the window was exposed. Tom was getting a little over his spree. He had been seeing snakes.

Mr. Kelly had a large black bear, a tremendous fellow. He had broken his chain in the night, and crawled into Tom's window and gotten under the bed. Tom had been given an opiate the night before, and of course he was dead to all noises until the effects of the drug wore off. But about breakfast time, Mr. Bear turned over and groaned. This raised Tom up in the bed and, at the same time, the bear's chain rattled. Tom said to himself, "My God! have I got 'em again?" But Mr. Bear made another move which lifted Tom up again. This was too much. He jumped out of bed, hastily lifted the bed clothes, and there was Mr. Bear, staring him in the face, yawning, and rattling his chain. Tom gave one tremendous scream and rushed for the dining room.

Breakfast was in full blast at the time, the room crowded with guests, and with six girl waitresses. When Tom rushed in in his night gown, he tripped and fell over one of the girls, with a waiter full of dishes. Of course they both went down together, and of all the screaming and holloing, and rushing out of that dining room, was a caution.

Another time Tom got on one of his sprees at Caldwell, Kansas, another wild and wooly cattle town like Dodge, and the boys hired a trained monkey, from an organ grinder, and put it in his room one morning before day. Tom was convalescing and they thought a big scare would do him good and maybe break him of his sprees. Tom was awakened about breakfast time, with the monkey sitting right over him at the head of his bed, where the boys had placed him, chattering away and cutting up all kinds of monkey tricks. Tom said he was sure he had them again. But recollecting his six-shooter, he went to his suitcase, got it out, and said: "Old fellow, if you ain't a monkey, I am in a bad fix; but if you are a monkey, you sure are in a h—l of a fix." Then he took good aim and fired. Down came Mr. Monkey, and the boys lost a hundred dollars and the joke was on them.

Bobby Gill was one of the most notorious characters and was the best all-around "sure thing" man that ever struck Dodge City. He was up-to-date in all the tricks of the trade, and was capable of working all the various devices known to the brotherhood, from the opening of a spring match safe to the gold brick proposition. He had the brains to use them all, but whisky was what caused his downfall. He could not keep away from it. At one time, he abstained from drinking for a week. He came across the "dead line," where he had been staying to keep from drinking, and was very "blue," down-hearted, and nervous. When he reached the precincts of the "gang," he was subjected to the ridicule, "kidding," and taunts of the fellows. It was a cold snowy morning, and the river was out of its banks and full of immense cakes of floating ice and a quarter of a mile wide. Bobby said to the "jokesmiths," "Kid as much as you please, but it takes more nerve to stop drinking when in the condition in which I have been, than it does to go down to the river now, strip, and swim across to the other bank." I believed him. I can sympathize with such a man because I have been in the same condition myself. He was right and I knew he told the truth.

One of the many times he was before the police court was due to hard luck. He was clear down and out of pocket and friends. One could discover a kindly feeling for him, for, as a general thing, when a man plays in such hard luck, no matter what his antecedents, one can't help pitying him. One's heart goes out to him, and so it was in this case. The sentence was twenty dollars and costs. The marshal said, "Well, so far as I am concerned, I am willing to throw off my costs;" the clerk said, "I will do the same;" and the judge said, "So will I. Mr. Gill, what have you got to say for yourself?" He promptly jumped up and, quick as a flash, and said, "Your Honor, I never was yet out-done in generosity, and I will not be in this case; I will throw off the fine." It is needless to say that he never paid any fine.

One day Bobby was in the Long Branch saloon sleeping off a big drunk. There was a ledge of wood all around the room about three and a half feet from the floor. Bobby had his chair tilted back and his head resting on this ledge, with a broad-brimmed Stetson hat half over his face. We put a line of powder along on this ledge, from the door to where Bobby was sleeping (which was quite a distance from the door), and near his head we placed a full quarter of a pound of the powder, pulled his hat well over his face to thoroughly protect it, and stationed several men in the saloon with six-shooters, and the large tin pan, used for making large quantities of "Tom and Jerry," was so placed that the most noise possible could be made when it was hit with a club by a man. The signal was given and the powder touched off, the six-shooters were fired, and the clubbing of the tin pan began while the bar and tables were hammered with billiard cues. Imagine the noise and confusion.

The smoke from the burned powder was so dense that one could scarcely see. Bobby made a dive for the door and cleared the way before him. There were some men sitting around the big stove; Bobby ran right over them and, when he encountered a chair, he just threw it over his shoulder and continued his flight. He said afterwards he had been dreaming about fire and, when the racket began, he imagined that he was in a burning building, from which all but himself had escaped, and he could see the burning rafters falling down upon him. He never opened his eyes but once, and never stopped running until he was home, on the other side of the railroad track. This was one good treatment for him and his complaint, and he was not over on the north side again for a month. He was afraid we would kill him and he actually believed so.

Bobby himself was a great practical joker. Once he secured a large queensware crate that would just comfortably fill a wagon box, and standing some four feet high. In this crate, with the assistance of Kinch Riley, he placed Jim Dalton, a notorious booze fiend, who was in a helpless state of intoxication. They covered this crate with an ample tarpaulin, entirely concealing the contents from view. Attaching a team of mules to the wagon, they drove up Main Street, stopping in front of each saloon for exhibition purposes.

Bobby acted as crier and opened the proceedings by shouting: "Come, everybody! this is the golden opportunity. We have here on exhibition, concealed under this tarpaulin, the greatest living curiosity—the only living specimen of man and brute combined, captured in the wilds of the Ozark mountains in infancy, and reared to his present physical state on the bottle, which has been the only nourishment he was ever known to take. For countless centuries, scientists have searched in vain for a living specimen of this lost link. Gentlemen, it has been the good fortune of my scientific co-worker, Professor Riley, to discover, hidden in the sand hills, this long sought specimen. We have a living proof of the Dar-winian theory of the origin of man, and it is my pleasure, gentlemen and ladies (if you are ladies), to be in a position to prove to you, by ocular demonstrations, the truthfulness of my assertions, for the small sum of one iron dollar—four quarters, two halves, or ten dimes turn the trick, and, while I pass the hat around, Professor Riley will take the pole and stir up this monstrosity."

Kinch would then stagger around to the off-side and proceed to stir up the living specimen by vigorously prodding him, in the mid-section, with a broom stick. The sports would "chip in," and soon the necessary dollar was raised, the tarpaulin would be removed, and the fun would begin. Bobby would order a "whisky sour" for himself and Kinch, and they would slowly sip the nectar, in plain view of poor parched Dalton, who would plead for just a taste.

After going through this program at several of the booze resorts, Dalton became frantic with thirst—as crazy

H. L. SITLER
One of the Seven Old Timers of Dodge City

as a loon. Bobby was deaf to his pleadings for a long while; in fact, he didn't relent until the last saloon had been worked. Then, in a maudlin tone, he ordered Kinch to feed the specimen. Kinch had an empty tobacco bucket handy, and a small force pump with hose attached. Turning this on poor Dalton, he soused him with several buckets of water.

The performance then closed, and Bobby and Kinch mounted the wagon and started over the "dead line" with their living curiosity. Their frequent libations of "lemon sours" had all but knocked them out, and they were much worse off than Dalton, who, through their heroic treatment, was now in a fairly sober condition. In crossing the railroad track, Dalton worked a bottom board loose and dropped to the road, the wheels miraculously missed him, and he got up none the worse for the drop. Bobby and Kinch were slowly plodding along, ignorant of Dalton's escape, when, suddenly, they were brought to a realization of the situation by a bombardment of rocks, at short range, from Dalton. In dodging the missles so ruthlessly hurled at them, they lost their balance, and both fell off the wagon, and the mules proceeded leisurely on their way to their barn.

Bobby had thoughtfully provided himself with a bottle of whisky, from the proceeds of the show, and, instantly regaining his feet, he produced the bottle and called for an armistice. Holding the bottle aloof, he served notice on Dalton that, if hostilities did not cease immediately, he would place the bottle in range of the flying missles, and there would be a wanton waste of valuable property; but if Dalton would call off the attack, they would adjourn to the Green Front and properly appropriate the contents of the bottle in their usual good old convivial way. It is needless to say that hostilities ceased at once, and a happy reconciliation was effected among the three.

Of a somewhat different nature from the treatment accorded Dalton, but equally heroic, was a "Dodge City Keeley Cure," administered to one of the convivial citizens.

In the bright, halcyon days of Dodge City, there dwelt a lawyer in our midst ,who was quite badly crippled, but he had a bright mind and was a good lawyer. He, unfortunately, was addicted to the liquor habit, and his earnings were spent for whisky. He neglected his wife and children, and his conduct was such as to become a disgrace to the civilization of Dodge City, so the boys concluded to put a stop to it.

One bright summer morning, this lawyer was drinking heavily, in one of the principal and most public saloons in the town, on Front Street, where everyone could see inside, as they passed, as there was a door on each street, the saloon being on the corner of two streets.

The fellows that decided to administer this dose of the "Dodge City Keeley Cure" to the lawyer, waited until he was surcharged with booze, which they knew would soon be accomplished. He attempted to leave the bar, but fell in a drunken stupor. The boys then procured a coffin, attired him in a conventional shroud, prepared him as carefully as though they were preparing him for the long sleep, except embalming him, powdered his features to give him the ghastly appearance of death, tied his jaws together, and then placed him in the coffin and placed the coffin on a table between the two doors, where he lay "in state," and in view of passersby.

Many persons thought he was really dead and placarded him with these emotional and reverential lines:

"Judge Burns is dead, that good old soul,
We ne'er shall see him more,
We never more shall see his face,
Nor hear his gentle roar (in police court), saying,
'Guilty, your Honor!' "

He remained in the coffin, in full view, for several hours before he awakened. He was a hideous sight, and, after looking in the mirror, he went home completely disgusted with himself, sobered up, and was never known to take a drink in Dodge City afterwards. He became one of our most respected citizens, and held several offices of honor and trust. This was a profitable lesson to him, and proved very beneficial to his family and the community.

While the above is highly recommended to those needing the Keeley cure, it is not guaranteed to cure all cases. It depends on the mental and physical make-up of the individual. We tried the same treatment on a prominent hotel man, the best landlord Dodge City ever had, but it was not successful in his case. When he recovered, he jumped out of his coffin, shook off his winding sheet, and proceeded to the bar, with an invitation to all the boys to have a drink.

Truth is stranger than fiction, and, to illustrate, the following story of early days in Dodge is related. Every word of this is positively true.

In the last palmy days of Dodge, when the end of her magnificent career of wealth, gambling, dance halls, gilded houses of ill fame, fascinating music, and the quick, sharp bark of the six-shooter were about over, there still clung to her a shadow of her past greatness. Mr. Charles Heins was one of the leaders, and what a great caterer he was, to the palates of those who had wealth and were willing to purchase. There was nothing too good or too rich for his larder, and he found customers, lots of them, at outrageous prices for the goods, of course. Among other things of the past, he still kept up his bar and magnificent stock of liquors, although to do so was almost certain imprisonment. He hid his bar, from the officers of the law, in every conceivable place, and the ingenuity he displayed in keeping out of their clutches was wonderful. At last he placed his bar in a dark cellar, but he had exhausted his supply of bar keepers, so he had to resort to most anyone, until he got a Frenchman who could speak no English.

The gang soon got on to the ignorance of the bar keeper, and played many a prank on him, and they finally got to passing counterfeit dollars, some a good imitation made of lead. Now Skinner and Kelly had opened up an opposition joint, around the corner, a few doors below Heins' place. Heins had a natural hatred for Skinner, and when he opened up in opposition, Heins' hatred was much greater.

By the way, Skinner set a fine "Dutch lunch," every day, from eleven o'clock to two p. m. This proceeding Heins hated cordially. Once in awhile I would go down to Skinner and Kelly's for my lunch and a glass of beer, instead of going home for my dinner. One rainy, cold day, I started for my Dutch lunch and glass of beer about one o'clock, and saw Heins standing in his door, tossing up a counterfeit silver dollar. I said to Heins: "Give me that, and I will go down celler and pass it on your Frenchman." "Not on your life," he said, "The Frenchman has had lots of them passed on him, and this is one of his take-ins." "Well," I said, "I will take it down and pass it on Bill Skinner." "My God!" he said, "if you will do that, come back and I will set up the drinks for the whole house."

Kelly had been tending bar while Skinner went to dinner, and, just as I got in, Kelly was shifting his bar apron and handing it to Skinner to put on, preparatory for Skinner to go on duty behind the bar. I noticed that all the Dutch lunch was gone, and I said: "What has become of your lunch?" Kelly spoke up and said, "Why, old John Shults came in, wet and almost frozen to death, said he had beat his way from Garden City to Dodge in a leaky box car, and was as wet as a drowned rat. He got a few glasses of beer, and ate everything in sight, but still said he was hungry, and inquired for a restaurant. I don't suppose he had eaten anything since he left here last night.''

I invited the house up, and they all took beer, and I handed Skinner the counterfeit. He served the beer, and, without looking at the dollar, threw it on the back bar with the day's receipts, and gave me the change. I sat and talked with them for awhile, and invited the crowd to drink again, then went back to Heins who was tickled to death about it, and we went below and got our beer. Just before starting back up, however, the bell boy came after Heins, saying there was a Dutchman upstairs who insisted on seeing him on particular business. Heins said, ''Stay, and I will be back soon.''

Now it seemed the night before, a short time before the passenger went west, John Shults came in pretty full of booze, as was his normal condition when in Dodge City, and asked Charley Heins to change a five dollar bill. Heins had four good silver dollars and this same counterfeit dollar. Heins said to Shults, ''I can't do it—haven't got the change.'' ''Oh, yes, you have,'' said Shults, ''I see five dollars in your drawer.'' ''Yes, but,'' Heins said, ''one of those is counterfeit.'' Of course, Shults thought he was joking, and said, ''Heinsy, I know you would not give me a counterfeit.'' Heins replied, ''No, that is the reason I can't change your bill.'' Shults said, ''Give it to me anyway; now I know you would not cheat me.'' Heins said, ''Well, if you insist on it, here goes,'' and gave him the four good dollars and the counterfeit. You see, Shults had made several trips to Garden, having business with the land office there, and he had learned to work the conductor. The fare to Garden was one dollar and a half, and Shults would give the conductor a dollar and swear that was all the money he had, and he was such an ''onery'' looking cuss, the conductor would believe him

— 235 —

and take him on. This was the reason Shults was so anxious to get the bill changed; he would save half a dollar.

Heins came back laughing and tickled to death. He said to the bar keeper, "Set them up to the house again, for this is too good; I have heard from the counterfeit already." When he went up, John Shults was there, holding the same old counterfeit in his hand, and he said: "Hensy, you know last night you gave me a counterfeit, didn't you?" Heins said, "Yes, but John, a little after you gave me the bill to change, you came back, and I took back the counterfeit and gave you a good dollar in its place, didn't I?" "Yes, but Heinsy, how the h— did I get dot?" showing the counterfeit in his hand. "Heinsy, there could not have been two of them, could there?" "No, John, only one, only one." "Well, Heinsy, you couldn't give me a good one for this now, could you?" "No, John, I could not." "Well, Heins, what's de madder wid it, anyhow? I know you gave me dis dollar." "Yes, I did, but I gave you a good one in place of it." And Heins said he begged so hard to have one that he had to leave him, or he was afraid he would give him a good dollar.

It seems, after Heins changed the bill for Shults, the night before, Shults went down to Skinner's joint and ordered a glass of beer, offering this same counterfeit dollar in payment. Skinner was very angry, because he had been a victim of counterfeit dollars himself, and he took his knife and put a private mark on the dollar, and gave it back to Shults, with a big cussing, and warned him not to try to pass one on him again or he would beat him to death.

Kelly had been tending bar while Skinner went to dinner, as I said before, and, when I left, Skinner began to look over the receipts of the day, on the back of the bar, and discovered this counterfeit. He at once blamed Kelly, and said: "Here, Kelly, you have taken in a bad

— 236 —

dollar." "Yes," said Kelly, "that is so. I am not fit to do business any more in here; I make a failure of everything." "Who was in here?" said Skinner. "Why," Kelly said, "No one; it is a very bad day, and there has been no trade." "Why," Skinner said, "who ate up all that lunch?" Kelly said, "By the hokey, old John Shults, and he gave me a silver dollar." Skinner said, "Where did he go? I want to get at him. He is the drunken bloat who tried to pass it on me last night. It is the same dollar; see where I marked it? And I told him then I would beat him to death, if ever he attempted to pass it on us again. Where did you say he went?" "Over to your brother's restaurant upstairs," replied Kelly.

Skinner rushed out without coat or hat, and caught Shults just as he was about to get down from one of those very high chairs, they have for counter lunches. He caught him by the back of the collar and hurled him violently against the floor. Before the man could get up, Skinner was on him, kicking and stomping him with both feet. Shults was helpless, and so completely taken by surprise it paralyzed him, but this did not stop Skinner, who kicked, stomped, and beat until he was worn out. The beating he got would have killed a common man, but old John was as tough as a pine knot and soon got over it. They say it was amusing to hear John holler and plead. "Ho (lam)! Ho (lam)!" he said: "You got the wrong man! I do nottings to you! Why you do dot? Ho (lam)! Ho (lam)! Stop it! I quit you; stop it! I tell you, I quit you!" Skinner would answer, "You see that dollar?" "Yes, I see; I know where you get him." "You know where I get him?" and he would go after him again, and, when he was completely worn out, he handed Shults the dollar and called for a good one, which request Shults was too glad to comply with, for fear of another beating. As a matter of fact, if Shults had only had the courage and had known it, he could have turned in and beat Skinner just as hard, as Skinner acknowledged afterwards that he had completely worn himself out.

These stories, in connection with other passages in this book, will give some idea of the position strong drink occupied in the early life of southwestern Kansas, and the almost universal popularity which the social glass enjoyed. Eventually, it was my fortune to become representative of this section in the state legislature, in which I was serving when the prohibition bill was introduced, in 1881. I must say that I think that prohibition has proved a good thing for the state, but, at that time, with such constituents behind me, I could not consistently support the temperance bill. I soon saw, however, that it was going through and that it was useless to fight it, so I contented myself with having the consoling "last word," on the subject, my short speech being the last made before the bill was put to vote. My remarks were not intended as argument, but merely as a mildly satirical fling at the opposing faction, and put a flavor of the burlesque upon the situation. But the threat to secede, while not meant seriously, was not without point, as the territory in sympathy with that I represented, forming one section for judicial purposes, comprised thirty-eight of our present counties. The "Topeka Daily Commonwealth," of February 16th, 1881, says, "Honorable R. M. Wright delivered the following witty speech on the temperance bill in the House yesterday," and reports it thus:

"Mr. Chairman and Gentlemen of the Committee:

"I feel that I would be doing my constituents a grave injustice were I to remain silent at this most portentous juncture in the history of our legislation. I cannot refrain, therefore, from raising my feeble voice in protest against this monstrous measure. I do not oppose this bill because of my own love for the distilled nectar of the cornfield, nor yet for the purple ambrosia of the vineyard. I admit that I like a glass of either now and then,

G. M. Hoover
Banker and One of the Seven Old Timers of Dodge City

but I am not a slave to the demon of the cup, and I can look upon the wine when it is red without necessarily being bitten by the adder which is alleged to be lurking at the bottom of the said utensil. In fact, Mr. Chairman, so great is my virtue in this direction, that I have gone three, aye four days, without my whisky, and I am proud to relate without any special disturbing effects upon my physiological structure, but it is a dangerous experiment, and should not be tried too often. Sir, I have been a resident of this great state for seventeen years and I have learned to know it, and to know it is to love it. I know no other home. I love its broad prairies, its rich soil, its pure air, its beautiful streams, and last, but not least, its liberal people. But alas, sir, if this bill becomes a law, I am afraid I shall cease to be one of the citizens of this proud commonwealth, as the county which I have the honor to represent on this floor threatens to secede and take with it all the unorganized counties attached to it for judicial purposes. Now, sir, under the peculiar circumstances of their situation, have they not a just and equitable cause for their professed action? Sir, this committee well knows, or if there are any of its members who do not I deplore their ignorance, that the section of the country in which I live is essentially the habitation of that most poisonous of all reptiles of the genus Crotalus, or in common parlance, as he is familiarly known to the cowboys—the rattlesnake. This insect, gentlemen of the committee, is not the phantasmagorial creature, if I may use the term, which perhaps many of you have seen when you have ''histed' too much rock and rye on board, but a genuine tangible nomad of the prairie, whose ponderous jaws, when once fastened on the calf of your leg, you will realize is no creature of the disordered brain. This octopod, this old man of the prairie, if you will permit me to indulge in a metaphor, has all his life obeyed the spiritual injunction (I am sorry I have not my little pocket Bible here to prove this, as many of the members of this committee have done in discussing this question) to increase and multiply, and accordingly he multiplyeth extraordinarily, and he doeth this without irrigation either, and in fact every farmer has an abundant crop without the trouble of cultivation. Now, sir, the only known preventive, the only known antidote to the venom of this venomous beast, is pure unadulterated corn juice, vulgarly called whisky. Aye, sir, men who have imbibed freely of the corn juice have been bitten, and the snake has always been known to die instead of the man, so you see it is not only a sure cure for the bite but is a speedy means of getting rid of the snake also.

"Ponder, oh, gentlemen of the committee, and hesitate before you take away from us that which saves life. Are you aware of what you are about to do? Do you propose in this arbitrary manner not only to deprive us of a source of solace but even to take our very lives? My people, sir, will never submit, never (No Pinafore here.) [This was in the days of Pinafore.]

"Now, sir, the only way out of this labyrinth of proposed injustice is to exclude Dodge City as well as all that region west of the one-hundredth meridian from the provisions of this bill. If you do this it will not only be an act of justice guaranteed by the constitution upon stern necessity, but will receive the rightous judgment of all the citizens of Dodge; harmony will again prevail upon the border, the scouts will be called in, and future generations of cowboys will arise and call you blessed."

In the spring of 1885, preparations were made for the enforcement of the Prohibitory Liquor Law in Dodge City, and the sale of eighty barrels of four-year-old whisky, besides other liquors and bar fixtures was announced by Henry Sturm, the well known purveyor of the city. The prohibition law put a different character on liquor sales, many of the saloons being transformed into "drug stores."

COL. BRICK BOND
One of the Seven Old Timers of Dodge City

CHAPTER XIII

Resorts Other Than Saloons, and Pastimes
Other Than Drinking

Under the heading, "A Bloody Prize Fight in Dodge City," the Dodge City Times of June 16th, 1877, gives a characteristic account of the thrilling encounter as follows:

"On last Tuesday morning the champion prize fight of Dodge City was indulged in by Messrs. Nelson Whitman and the noted Red Hanley, familiarly known as 'the Red Bird from the South.' An indefinite rumor had been circulated in sporting circles that a fight was to take place, but the time and place was known only to a select few. The sport took place in front of the Saratoga saloon at the silent hour of 4:39 a. m., when the city police were retiring after the dance hall revelry had subsided and the belles who are in there were off duty. Promptly at the appointed time, the two candidates for championship were at the joint. Colonel Norton acted as rounder-up and whipper-in for both fighters while Bobby Gill ably performed the arduous task of healing and handling and sponging off. Norton called time and the ball opened with some fine hits from the shoulder. Whitman was the favorite in the pools but Red made a brilliant effort to win the champion belt.

"During the forty-second round Red Hanley implored Norton to take Nelson off for a little while till he could have time to put his right eye back where it belonged, set his jawbone and have the ragged edge trimmed off his ears where they had been chewed the worst. This was against the rules of the ring so Norton declined, encouraging him to bear it as well as he could and squeal when he got enough. About the sixty-fifth round Red squealed unmistakably and Whitman was declared winner. The only injury sustained by the loser in this fight were two ears chewed off, one eye busted and the other disabled, right cheek bone caved in, bridge of the nose broken, seven teeth knocked out, one jaw-bone mashed, one side of the tongue bit off, and several other unimportant fractures and bruises. Red retires from the ring in disgust.''

A shade worse than the prize fight was a bout at lap-jacket, as described in the ''Dodge City Times,'' of May 12th, 1877.

''We, yesterday, witnessed an exhibition of the African national game of lap-jacket, in front of Shulz' harness shop. The game is played by two colored men, who each toe a mark and whip each other with bull whips. In the contest yesterday, Henry Rogers, called Eph, for short, contended with another darkey for the championship and fifty cents prize money. They took heavy new whips, from the harness shop, and poured in the strokes pretty lively. Blood flowed and dust flew and the crowd cheered until Policeman Joe Mason came along and suspended the cheerful exercise. In Africa, where this pleasant pastime is indulged in to perfection, the contestants strip to the skin, and frequently cut each other's flesh open to the bone.''

Dodge City is especially distinguished as the only town in the state, or the whole United States, for that matter, that ever conducted a bull fight. To use the vernacular of the time, Dodge City ''pulled off'' a genuine bull fight, according to Mexican rules and regulations, under the auspices of the Driving Park and Fair Association, on the fourth and fifth of July, 1884. The bull fighters were full-bloods of Mexico, and the ''Globe'' mentioned them as ''some of the best citizens of the City of Chihuahua, Mexico, and as intelligent a party of men as any person would wish to meet. Their redeeming trait is that they cannot be forced to drink a drop of strong liquor.''

To give local zest and character to the occasion, the bulls, which were of local origin—untamed animals of these plains—were given names purely provincial, the local cognomens of several Dodge citizens being evident. For instance, Ringtailed Snorter, Cowboy Killer, Iron Gall, Lone Star, Long Branch, Opera, Klu Klux, Sheriff, Doc, Rustler, Jim, and Eat-em Richard, were the twelve male bovines to snort at the red flag and other means of provoking anger.

An apology or explanation is given of the bull fight, previous to the occurrence, by the manager in charge of the "distinguished party," so-called, which he says is "largely misconstrued and misunderstood. Instead of being a cruel and barbarous proceeding, it is quite the reverse. While the animal is provoked and tantalized to fury, no cruelty to the animal is indulged in; and when the animal is to be dispatched, it is instantly done, and in less cruel and tortuous manner than if a butcher had slaughtered one for the block. The term, 'bull fighting,' is wrongly interpreted."

The manner of the bull fight is given, but the reader is interested in the event as it signalled Dodge City's superiority in entertainment. There were five matadors, four on foot and one on horseback, each dressed in gaudy costume. The weapons used were "bandarillos," or tastefully ornamented darts, which were placed on the animal's neck and shoulders, as he would charge upon the matadors. The attractive garbs of the bull fighters incensed the bulls, and the fight was earnest, each bull being dispatched in order. The account closes the scene with the statement that the excitement was now at its height. An infuriated bull and a slightly injured matador, whose blood was up to fever heat, made short work of the closing exercises. With much parleying, the animal was dealt a fatal blow.

During the excitement just before our great bull fight, the only one, as has been said, ever to take place in the United States, the boys were cutting out and trying the bulls, to find which would be the most vicious and the best fighters. A gentleman, whom we will call Brown, said it was all nonsense about shaking a red rag in a bull's face; that he knew it would not make him fight because he had tried it. A gentleman, overhearing the remark, said: "Brown, I will bet you a fifty dollar suit of clothes you can't shake a red rag in a bull's face without his fighting, and you have the privilege of selecting the most docile bull in this lot of fighters."

The bet was soon made, and Brown got a red shirt and climbed down into the corral. The bull was looking as calm as a summer morning, and Brown went towards the animal, keeping the red shirt well behind him. As he came close to the brute, he suddenly produced the shirt and flirted it in the bull's face. The beast jumped back in astonishment and kept his eye on Brown, while Brown waved the old vermilion garment vigorously. Then the bull shook his head several times, as if he declined to have anything to do with that business, and Brown turned towards us and put his thumb to his nose and made a sign of victory.

Just then an idea seemed to strike that bull. He put his head down and moved swiftly forward. Brown, at first, thought there had been an earthquake. Upon his descent, he thought he would try to run, but the old long horn was inserted in the seat of his trousers, and again he went up, high enough to take a bird's-eye view of the surrounding country. On the twenty-fifth descent, he fell on the other side of the corral, and we picked him up. His mouth was full of grass and sand. We asked him if his views about bulls had undergone any change; but he walked silently along. We wanted to know how he enjoyed the scenery, the last time he went up; but he would not say. He merely went into the cook-house, filled up both barrels of his gun with old nails and screws and scrap iron, and then he went to interview that bull.

Hokey-pokey (or in scientific phrase, Bisulphite of Carbon), was the means of great sport among the gang in early days. If the stuff was applied to any animal with hair, it had a wonderful effect. For the time being, the animal just went crazy, and it seemed the more sleepy and good for nothing the horse was, the better he would perform under the effects of this medicine. All you had to do was to drop a few drops on the horse, any place, and almost instantly it would take effect.

One of our most prominent lawyers used to drive, to a fine buggy, one of the most dilapidated pieces of horseflesh. The boys would josh this lawyer about driving such a woe-begone, sleepy animal. They thought they would give him a lesson, and maybe he would take the hint and get a good horse. The old horse's name was Dick. Mr. Lawyer hitched Dick in front of his office one day, and the boys were ready. They said: "Colonel, what is the matter with Dick? He acts so funny—looks like he is going mad. Has he been exposed to the bite of a mad dog?" Just then the circus began. Old Dick went up in the air, came down, kicking first one foot, then both, then all together, and away he would go, Mr. Lawyer hold of his bridle, holloing, "Whoa, Dick! Whoa Dick! What is the matter with you, Dick?" But Dick paid no heed. He just kept at it all the harder until he had kicked himself out of the shafts, and then kicked the harness all to pieces, and cut all sorts of shines and capers. He would lift the lawyer right off his feet, until he had to let go the bridle and give old Dick full sway, and I think he was one of the most astonished men I ever saw. But he never got on to their racket until the gang presented him with a new set of harness and told him the joke.

I have seen cowboys, who prided themselves on their horsemanship, ride into town, and the boys would dope a horse. The rider would stay with him a long time, but, at last, he had to go. Never yet did I see a man who could retain his seat on a doped horse.

A poor little traveling preacher rode into town, one Sunday, and rode up to a crowd that had gathered on the street, on account of some excitement. Some little urchin· got to him with the hokey-pokey, and away went that little preacher. The horse bolted right into the crowd, scattering it right and left, and kicking and squalling and bawling. First, the preacher's stove pipe hat went up into the air; next, his saddle-bags; and then, the poor fellow himself went sprawling over the pony's head. He got up and brushed the dust off, saying, "Some ungodly person has done something to my horse!"

One day a real, typical horseman rode into town, on one of the finest saddlers I ever saw. The man on this horse was a perfect picture of a centaur. He rode up to where a horse auction was in progress and said: "Mr. Auctioneer, I am going east and have no use for this horse, or I would not part with him. He is all that he appears to be, has all the gaits of a saddler, is sound as a dollar, and gentle as a dog. He never ran away, will stand without hitching, and was never known to buck, plunge, or kick." He rode up and down the street a time or two, and came back, and then they doped the horse. Now, of all the running and bucking and pitching and kicking you ever saw, that horse did it, right there. The man stayed with him a long time, and the gang began to think, "Well, here is a man that a horse can't throw." But just then, off he went, and a little further on the horse stood still. The man caught him, led him back, and apologized to the crowd. He said: "Gentlemen, I beg your pardon. I lied to you, but upon my word I never saw this horse act badly before, in any way. I withdraw him from market. The horse is not for sale." I don't think this man ever did know what ailed the horse.

There was an old man who picked bones and hauled them to Dodge. He had two very old, bony horses. They did not seem to have any life whatever, and the gang

THE OLD SANTA FE DEPOT
The first one was a box car

thought they would have fun out of the old man, so they asked him if his horses were for sale. Well, he would sell the horse but didn't want to sell the mare. They asked him if they had ever been locoed or would eat the loco weed. "No, indeed, sir! my horses were never known to touch it." "You have no objection to our trying them?" "No, indeed, sir; try them all you want to." So they took the horse out of the wagon, and some one held a bunch of loco weed to the horse's head while another applied the hokey-pokey. Now that old horse, like all the balance, just went crazy, and some one got around and applied the medicine to the mare, also, who was still hitched to the wagon. She took wagon, harness, and everything along with her, kicked out the front end of the wagon, and they liked never to have got her stopped, the way she turned that wagon around. The gang gave the old fellow a ten dollar bill, and he collected his scattered pieces of wagon and went after more bones, wondering what could have ailed the horses and made him lose a good sale.

The gang surely had great sport, until things got so bad there was an ordinance passed, prohibiting the sale of hokey-pokey.

One day two dagoes came to town, leading a very large bear. The bear sure was a good one, and performed many cute tricks. For such a tremendous animal, he was very active. When the gang had seen all they wanted of the bear's tricks, they hokey-pokied him, and we thought he was active before but we hadn't seen any of his activity. That bear rolled and ran and squalled just like a human, and he cut up all manner of didoes. The Italians tried their best, at first, to soothe down his pain by petting him, but the bear would have none of it and carried on so outrageously that the Italians got afraid of him and retreated to a safe distance. Every once in awhile that bear would spy them and rush towards them, seeking relief, I suppose, but when the dagoes would see him coming with his mouth wide open and his eyes rolling, they would turn tail and fly. They were afraid of his company, thinking he had gone mad. Well, when the effects wore off, Mr. Bear looked pretty sheepish, and the dagoes caught him by the chain and led him off out of sight into a cut, got a railroad tie, and the way they rubbed that bear's stomach, one on each side, until the sweat poured down their faces! I don't suppose they ever worked so hard before. You see, they thought the bear had eaten something that did not agree with him and he had the stomachache. When they got tired rubbing, they brought him back, but Mr. Bear, as soon as he saw the crowd, jerked away and climbed a telegraph pole and sat there among the wires until the crowd dispersed. He had more sense than his owners—he would not be hokey-pokied again.

Among the many favorite amusements, pastimes, and fun of the gang was to scare a greenhorn with a big stuffed bull snake. A party who kept a large establishment to entertain the thirsty and gratify the sports with billiards, cards, dice, and, in fact, it was a great and favorite resort for the lovers of fun; also, in his back yard he had a large wire cage, filled with big rattlesnakes. More than a dozen of these venomous reptiles occupied the cage and lived in peace and harmony, up to the fatal day which I shall tell about farther on.

Now then, it was the duty of some loafer or hanger-on around the saloon to go out and hunt up a greenhorn, invite him to a drink, then tell him about the big den of rattlers, and take him out and show him the snakes, relating an interesting history of this big rattler and that rattler, how they had bitten a man who died. When he had his auditor absorbed in the story, with his eyes bulged out, and attending to nothing else but the story of the big snakes, the story teller would suddenly say: "Bend your neck and look down there at that monster;"

and when his man would bend his head and stoop over, someone would place the enormous stuffed snake on his neck, its tail and its head almost touching the ground from either side. Mr. Man, feeling the snake and, at the same time, seeing it, would give an ungodly whoop, bend his head, and keep jumping up and down, trying to shake it off over his head, instead of straightening up, as he ought to have done, when the snake would have dropped off his back. Then there would be a seance. The crowd would whoop and hollo, and the poor fellow would join them from fear and keep jumping up and down, until, finally, he would get rid of the terrible snake—it would drop off.

Now negroes fear snakes worse than any race of people on earth, and no sooner would the darkey get over his fright (when the victim chanced to be a darkey), than he would go out into the street and bring in another darkey to go through the same performance as himself. This was his mode of revenge.

One day an old fellow came along, traveling back east to his wife's folks, and he proved to be an easy victim of the gang, but in the end, it was an expense to them. After going through the same performance as the negro, they found he had a prairie dog in his wagon, which the boys persuaded him to let them put into the cage with the snakes, and they told the old man the dog would whip the snakes. They had no idea he would, but the little fellow made a gallant fight, I tell you. He made the attack and began the fight himself, as soon as he was placed with them, and, my! how he did fight. He just went for those snakes like a little tiger, would grab one in his teeth, lift it almost off the floor, and shake it savagely; and he just kept on until he got all those snakes so riled up, he set them crazy, and they all got to fighting and biting each other. The little dog would get so tired he would rush up the side of the cage and hold on for a little while, until he regained his wind, and then he would jump down and at 'em again, harder then ever. He did make a gallant fight and a long one. It surprised us all that he could last so long, but, finally, the little fellow began to weaken, and the old man declared the fight off. The prairie dog died soon after they took him out of the cage, but he got his revenge; next day there was not one of those dozen big rattlers alive. They must have poisoned each other in the fight. Anyhow, they were all dead—not one left alive to tell of the fight; the little prairie dog took them all with him to the happy hunting grounds. It was a fit ending for such a gallant fight as the little fellow made.

CHAPTER XIV

Where the Swindler Flourished and Grew Fat

With its cosmopolitan crowds and free and easy life, with the broad frontier for refuge close at hand, it was natural that Dodge City, in its early days, should be a fruitful field for the street fraud and professional swindler of every description. Probably, there was not a confidence game nor a fake proposition known, at that time, that was not worked to the full on the streets of Dodge City, and even the open-hearted kindness and liberality which so characterized the town in cases of distress and need, was often made material for dishonest manipulation, and the foundation for ill-gotten gains, by unprincipled individuals.

So proverbial had the liberality of the citizens of Dodge City become that it was known for miles up and down the old Santa Fe trail. Unprincipled immigrants and strangers took advantage of it. For instance, a strong, hearty, middle-aged man, bronzed from exposure to the weather, and having other appearances of an honest, hard working, industrious man who was taking Horace Greeley's advice and moving west to better his condition, came into Dodge, one afternoon, hitched in harness by the side of a poor, old raw-boned horse, drawing a wagon in which was the younger portion of his family. The others were barefooted and walking. He claimed that his other horse got alkalied and died some distance down the river, which was a likely story, as there were lots of alkali pools in the river bottom. Some sympathetic persons went around with a hat in their hands and his hard luck story on their tongues, and soon enough money was raised to buy him a good span of horses, grub for his family, and to pay his expenses for some time. He went on his way, saying in his heart,

"What fools these people be! They have much more generosity than sense," for he had sent his hired man around north of town with two good horses, and we heard he was fairly well to do.

Another time, a poor family, with a dilapidated wagon and horses to match, the wagon full of children, rolled into Dodge and exhibited a dead baby and a sick mother. No money, no clothes, no food, and, as a Mexican says, "no nather." This was a piteous sight to behold, and soon the generous feeling, always slumbering in the hearts of the good people of Dodge, was aroused, and they raised a subscription for a coffin and buried the little one, and gave the mother quite a snug little sum of money, and bought groceries for the family. That night they dug up the corpse and took it and coffin to the next town, after filling up the grave. You see, it was a wax baby—a good imitation. We heard of them playing the same trick on other towns.

One morning in the early days of Dodge City, two gentlemen, elegantly dressed and groomed, made their appearance at the Long Branch saloon. One could see at a glance they were educated and refined, and both men had lovely manners and exceedingly great persuasive powers. They were quiet and unassuming, both were liberal spenders as well as drinkers, but they never were under the influence of liquor. It was only a short time until they had captivated a lot of friends, and I among the number. They were admirable story tellers. One we will call Doc Holiday, the other Creek. They had traveled all over Europe, spoke several languages, and the doctor had diplomas from several colleges in Europe, having finished his education in Heidelburg.

They and I soon became very intimate. Of course, before our friendship ripened, I took them to be what I thought them, elegant gentlemen; but, to my surprise, under a promise from me not to betray them, they told me they were big crooks and gold brick men. The first year of the great boom at Leadville, they gold-bricked an Ohio banker. The banker came to Leadville with scads of ready money, hunting soft snaps. Their stool pigeons soon discovered him and brought them together. The gold brick men claimed they were the last of a gang of mountain bandits who robbed the Deadwood stage. Most of these gold bricks, they said, belonged to the government and were being shipped to the mint at Denver when they were captured. The government had a record of the number of the bricks and the actual weight of each brick, so they could be identified, which was the reason they were making such a sacrifice, for they, themselves could not possibly dispose of the bricks, to get anywhere near their value.

The price was soon fixed at about twenty thousand dollars, but then came the test. The old banker thought he was very cunning. They brought a brick and had the banker file it at the ends, center, and middle, took the filings to an isolated spot in a fine, white silk handkerchief, and applied the acid. The filings stood the test because they had exchanged handkerchiefs, substituting genuine gold filings for the base metal. The banker then demanded to see all the bricks. They had them sunk in a little lake in the mountains, with a gravelly bottom. They dove down and brought up a brick which the banker filed the same as the other, and took the filings, that night after dark, to an old log cabin on the outskirts of the town. When they were about to make the acid test again, someone knocked. They blew out the light and made the grand change again, and told the banker to take the filings himself to a jeweler, and apply the acid. Of course, the test was approved by the jeweler and the banker, because the dust was genuine gold dust.

Now then, Creek stayed with the banker, at his request, as far as Chicago. This was playing into their hands, of course. The banker was anxious to have Creek at the final test in Chicago, but Creek had no such notion.

Of course, these men were disguised, and had their own plans, and were in constant communication with each other. At some large city east of the Missouri River, an officer came on board, put his hand on the banker's shoulder, and said: "I arrest you as an accomplice in a theft of government gold, which I have reason to believe you have with you, and, if you promise to behave, I won't put the handcuffs on you." The officer who made the arrest said to his deputy who stood behind him, "Look out for this man and his partner, too (meaning Creek); while I go out and get us some lunch, as I don't intend they shall leave this train until it pulls into Chicago." As soon as the officer was gone, Creek said to the deputy, "Please go with me to the closet." When they returned, Creek said to the banker, "The deputy wants to talk to you privately." The deputy said, "Why not buy off this United States marshal? You will not only lose your bricks, but you will be disgraced forever, and may go to the penitentiary for a long term. Try him when he gets back." Of course, at first, the United States marshal was very indignant, but finally said he would turn the banker loose on the payment of fifteen thousand dollars, and he got the money soon after reaching Chicago. It is needless to say the United States marshal was no one else but Doc Holiday.

The last I saw of the two, they were starting south, overland, in a buckboard, with tent, cooking utensils, and camp equipage of all kinds. They had along a race horse, a prize fighter, a fighting bull dog, and two prize winning game cocks. They were sports, every inch of them, if they were crooks, and both were dead shots with the six-shooter. These men were in Dodge City under cover, and stayed all summer, or until the hunt for them had been abandoned. Dodge was the hiding place for a great many crooks of every description. They even say Jesse James was here, for a short time, under cover, and Bob Ford, his murderer, was also.

On one occasion, word reached Dodge City several days in advance, of the arrival of a large band of Gypsies, headed for Dodge City. Large bodies move slowly, and so it was with this band, so the "gang" had plenty of time to prepare a proper reception for them. This band was the most filthy set of vagabonds imaginable, and their animals and outfit were worse, if such a thing could be.

They anticipated a rich harvest here, as they had heard of the liberality and generosity of our people and expected large returns from fortune telling, horse racing, horse trading, begging, and all the tricks in which they are proficient. They began business with horse racing, but the gang "hokey-pokied" their horses, and the result was the throwing of the riders over the horses' heads, and the bucking, kicking, and pitching of the animals, until they got to camp. The second day, the women brought in their chimpanzees, and they had some monsters, but they were mangy, skinny, and repulsive, and their monkeys, bears, parrots, and other animals were in the same condition. They were a scabby looking lot.

For shelter, the Gypsies had a hundred little low dog tents, black with smoke, dirt, and filth, and their wagons were dilapidated, wabbly, and of all sizes and descriptions, from a wheelbarrow and dog cart to a two-horse wagon.

Their chimpanzees were intelligent and well trained and understood their business, but they did not understand their trouble when they received a liberal application of "hokey-pokey" from the gang, and it made them vicious and crazy. They had sense enough, however, to know who applied it to them, and they went after the fellows and very nearly caught some of them. What a fight and struggle the women had to control these animals, and it certainly was an interesting and amusing diversion to see them.

There was a large, smooth piece of ground, just outside the town limits, where they camped, expecting to stay a long time. They had one very large, ferocious bear, and twenty or thirty dogs of all kinds and varieties, with which they would give their big show or "principal attraction." This attraction they would not put on unless they got their price. Their big performance was to tie a rope, several hundred feet long, to this big, half-starved bear, give him a large beef bone, then turn in the whole pack of half-starved dogs with him. Now this was a fight, as they say here, "for your whiskers." They announced their first exhibition for Saturday evening, it was soon advertised all over town, and another exhibition was announced for the following morning.

It was a beautiful summer morning, and I do not think that many went to church that day, judging from the crowd on the grounds. The boys were posted from the exhibition of the evening before, and were ready to make a slight change in the program. Just as the bear was turned out, with the rope attached, he received an application of the "hokey-pokey" and he was doped plentifully. At the same time, every cage containing a wolf, coyote, bear, monkey, or chimpanzee, which had been previously assigned to some member of the gang for attention, was carefully attended to, and all of the animals were doped. The work was perfectly done, and the results were highly satisfactory. The bear just simply went crazy, and he struck the dogs right and left, as they came to him, and every lick sent a dog some distance in some direction. The dogs were just as determined and industrious as the bear, and would come at him more fiercely than ever, but they made no impression on him. He wanted to get away from something, he did not know what. He would run the whole length of the rope, when the men at the other end of the rope would check him. He would then take a swing in some other direction, and the people would fall all over each other and in every direction. The bear had the right of way and used it. Our marshal, Low Warren, was busy, trying to keep the people out of the way of the bear and danger, and to restore order, but, notwithstanding he was perhaps the largest man in the county, he might as well have tried to stop the flow of the Arkansas river. In an attempt ·to get some women and children out of the way, he went sprawling down and took several more with him.

As here related, all the animals were doped at the same time, and the effect was the same on all, and at the same time. The howling, screaming, moaning, and acrobatic performances of people and animals were certainly worth the price of admission, and such confusion I never saw. When the Gypsies could come to a realization of what had happened, the women made a charge on the gang, armed with sticks, stones, and everything that would serve as a weapon of offensive warfare. The disregard for polite language was very noticeable, and the confusion of tongues was bewildering.

As a fitting climax to this unique entertainment, a young fellow named Gibson, rode up to the outskirts of the camp, on a fiery young colt, and was viewing the results of the performance, when some member of the fraternity slipped up behind the colt and doped him. Gibson and the colt parted company immediately, and the colt took his departure, giving an excellent exhibition of pitching and bucking through the camp, scattering the women and children of the Gypsies, and adding fuel to their already consuming passions and rage. They concluded that Dodge City was certainly the capital of all the demons in existence, and, the next day, they folded their tents and departed for more congenial parts. Dodge City was too much for them.

A unique but decidedly significant warning to the swindlers and crooks infesting Dodge City, was made by a newly elected mayor, A. B. Webster, who, upon assuming office, issued the following proclamation:

"To all whom it may concern: All thieves, thugs, confidence men, and persons without visible means of support, will take notice that the ordinances, enacted for their special benefit, will be rigorously enforced after April 7th, 1881."

CHAPTER XV

The Cattle Business and the Texas Drive

For a few of Dodge City's earliest years, the great herds of buffalo were the source from which sprung a large share of the business activity and prosperity of the place. As has been virtually stated, buffalo hunting was a regular vocation, and traffic in buffalo hides and meat a business of vast proportions. But after a time, the source of this business began to fail, and something to take its place was necessary if a gap were not to be left in Dodge City's industrial world. A substitute, in the form of a new industry, was not wanting, however, for immediately in the wake of the buffalo hunter came the cowboy, and following the buffalo came the long-horned steer. As the herds of the former receded and vanished, the herds of the latter advanced and multiplied, until countless numbers of buffaloes were wholly supplanted by countless numbers of cattle, and Dodge City was surrounded with new-fashioned herds in quite the old-fashioned way. Being the border railroad town, Dodge also became at once the cattle market for the whole southwestern frontier, and, very shortly, the cattle business became enormous, being practically all of that connected with western Kansas, eastern Colorado, New Mexico, Indian Territory (now Oklahoma), and Texas. Cattle were driven to Dodge, at intervals, from all these points, for sale and transportation, but the regular yearly drive from the ranges of Texas was so much greater in numbers and importance than the others, that they were quite obscured by it, while the Texas drive became famous for its immensity.

The "Kansas City Indicator," and other reliable papers and estimates, place the drive north from Texas, from 1866 to 1878, at 3,413,513 head. The "San Antonio

Express'' says of the enormous number: "Place a low average receipt of seven dollars per head, yet we have the great sum of $24,004,591.00. Not more than half of this vast amount of money finds its way back to the state, but much the larger portion is frittered away by the reckless owner and more reckless cowboy.'' Of this money, a contemporary writer says: "Of course Dodge receives her portion which adds greatly to the prosperity of the town and helps build up our city. The buyers pay on an average of eight dollars per head for yearling steers and seven dollars for heifers. They place these yearling steers on ranches, both north and south of us, and market them in two years, when they net in Kansas City, Chicago, and other markets at twenty-five dollars, making the net profit of two hundred per cent on their investments or doubling their capital twice over, as their losses are not more than two or three per cent, and the cost of running them for two years are very light.''

They paid no taxes; they paid no rent for their ranches; and their ranges were free. The cost of living was very light, and all they were out were the men's wages. You can readily see how all those engaged in the stock business quickly made fortunes, and the business was the cleanest, healthiest on earth.

The cattle drive to Dodge City first began in 1875-1876, when there were nearly two hundred and fifty thousand head driven to this point. In 1877, there were over three hundred thousand, and the number each year continued to increase until the drive reached nearly a half million. We held the trade for ten years, until 1886, when the dead line was moved to the state line. There were more cattle driven to Dodge, any and every year that Dodge held it, than to any other town in the state, and Dodge held it three times longer than any other town, and, for about ten years, Dodge was the greatest cattle market in the world. Yes, all the towns that enjoyed the trade of the Texas Drive, Dodge exceeded greatly in number, and held it much longer.

In corroboration of this assertion, I give a quotation from the "Kansas City Times," of that period, thus: "Dodge City has become the great bovine market of the world, the number of buyers from afar being unprecedentedly large this year (   ), giving an impetus to the cattle trade that cannot but speedily show its fruits. The wonderfully rank growth of grasses and an abundance of water this season has brought the condition of the stock to the very highest standard, the ruling prices showing a corresponding improvement. There are now upwards of one hundred thousand head of cattle in the immediate vicinity of Dodge City, and some of the herds run high into the thousands. There is a single herd numbering forty thousand, another of seventeen thousand, another of twenty-one thousand, and several of five thousand or thereabouts. On Saturday, no less than twenty-five thousand were sold. The Texas drive to Dodge this year will run close to two hundred thousand head."

A "Kansas City Times" correspondent, in a letter headed, "Dodge City, Kansas, May 28th, 1877," writes up the subject as follows:

"Abilene, Ellsworth, and Hays City on the Kansas Pacific railroad, then Newton and Wichita, and now Dodge City on the Atchison, Topeka & Santa Fe road, have all, in their turn, enjoyed the 'boil and bubble, toil trouble' of the Texas cattle trade.

"Three hundred and sixty-seven miles west from Kansas City we step off at Dodge, slumbering as yet (8:30 a. m.) in the tranquil stillness of a May morning. In this respect Dodge is peculiar. She awakes from her slumbers about eleven, a. m., takes her sugar and lemon at twelve m., a square meal at one p. m., commences biz at two o'clock, gets lively at four, and at ten it is hip-hip-hurrah! till five in the morning.

"Not being a full-fledged Dodgeite, we breakfasted with Deacon Cox, of the Dodge House, at nine o'clock, and meandered around until we found ourselves on top of the new and handsome court house. A lovely prairie landscape was here spread out before us. Five miles to the southeast nestled Fort Dodge, coyly hiding, one would think, in the brawny arm of the Arkansas. Then, as far as the eye could reach, for miles up the river and past the city, the bright green velvety carpet was dotted by thousands of long-horns which have, in the last few days, arrived, after months of travel, some of them from beyond the Rio Grande and which may, in a few more months, give the Bashi Bazouks fresh courage for chopping up the Christians and carrying out the dictates of their Koran. But we are too far off. We have invaded Turkey with Texas beef, and, though a long-horned subject, must be somewhat contracted here.

"Dodge City has now about twelve hundred inhabitants—residents we mean, for there is a daily population of twice that many; six or seven large general stores, the largest of which, Rath & Wright, does a quarter of a million retail trade in a year; and the usual complement of drug stores, bakers, butchers, blacksmiths, etc.; and last, but not by any means the least, nineteen saloons—no little ten-by-twelves, but seventy-five to one hundred feet long, glittering with paint and mirrors, and some of them paying one hundred dollars per month rent for the naked room.

"Dodge, we find, is in the track of the San Juanist, numbers of which stop here to outfit, on their way to the silvery hills.

"We had the good luck to interview Judge Beverly of Texas, who is the acknowledged oracle of the cattle trade. He estimates the drive at two hundred and eighty-

JOHN RINEY
One of the Seven Old Timers of Dodge City

five thousand, probably amounting to three hundred thousand, including calves. Three-quarters of all will probably stop at Dodge and be manipulated over the Atchison, Topeka & Santa Fe, by that prince of railroad agents, J. H. Phillips, Esq. Herbert, as he is familiarly called, is a graduate of Tammany Hall and is understood to wear in his shirt front the identical solitaire once worn by Boss Tweed. It is hinted that Herbert will buy every hoof destined for the Kansas Pacific road, at four times its value, rather than see them go that way. He would long, long ago have been a white-winged angel, playing on the harp of a thousand strings, were it not for the baneful associations of Frazer, Sheedy, Cook, et al. You can hear more about 'cutting out,' 'rounding up,' etc., in Dodge, in fifteen minutes, than you can hear in small towns like Chicago and St. Louis in a life time.''

In the same year, another newspaper representative, G. C. Noble, who visited Dodge, describes his impressions as follows:

"At Dodge City we found everything and everybody busy as they could comfortably be. This being my first visit to the metropolis of the West, we were very pleasantly surprised, after the cock and bull stories that lunatic correspondents had given the public. Not a man was swinging from a telegraph pole; not a pistol was fired; no disturbance of any kind was noted. Instead of being called on to disgorge the few ducats in our possession, we were hospitably treated by all. It might be unpleasant for one or two old time correspondents to be seen here, but they deserve all that would be meted out to them. The Texas cattlemen and cowboys, instead of being armed to the teeth, with blood in their eye, conduct themselves with propriety, many of them being thorough gentlemen.

"Dodge City is supported principally by the immense cattle trade that is carried on here. During the season that has just now fairly opened, not less than two hundred thousand head will find a market here, and there are nearly a hundred purchasers who make their headquarters here during the season. Mr. A. H. Johnson, the gentlemanly stock agent of the Atchison, Topeka & Santa Fe Company, informs us that the drive to this point, during the season, will be larger than ever before.

"From our window in the Dodge House, which, by the way, is one of the best and most commodious in the west, can be seen five herds, ranging from one thousand to ten thousand each, that are awaiting transportation. The stock yards here are the largest west of St. Louis, and just now are well filled.

"Charles Rath & Company have a yard in which are about fifty thousand green and dried buffalo hides.

"F. C. Zimmerman, an old patron of the 'Champion,' runs a general outfitting store, and flourishes financially and physically. Many other friends of the leading journal are doing business, and are awaiting patiently the opening up of the country to agricultural purposes.

"In the long run, Dodge is destined to become the metropolis of western Kansas and only awaits the development of its vast resources."

One more brief extract from a visitor's account of his visit "among the long-horns," and the extent and importance of Dodge City's early cattle trade will have been sufficiently established to permit my proceeding to some of the peculiar phases of that trade and the life of the stockmen and cowboys. This visitor sees the facetious side of the Dodge cattle traffic:

"This is May, 1877, Dodge City boiling over with buyers and drivers. 'Dodge City!' called the brakeman, and, with about thirty other sinners, we strung out to the Dodge House to command the register with our autographs, deposit our grip-sacks with Deacon Cox, and breakfast. But what a crowd is this we have elbowed our reportorial nose into? and bless your soul, what a sight! It just looks like all Texas was here. We now learn that everybody not at the Dodge House is at the Alamo. The Alamo is presided over by a reformed Quaker from New York, and it is hinted that the manner in which he concocts a toddy (every genuine cattleman drinks toddy) increases the value of a Texas steer two dollars and seventy-five cents. There is about seventy-five thousand head around town. Everybody is. buying and selling. Everything you hear is about beeves and steers and cows and toddies and cocktails. The grass is remarkably fine; the water is plenty; two drinks for a quarter, and no grangers. These facts make Dodge City the cattle point."

Notwithstanding the regularity of the great drives into Dodge, their magnitude, and the general popularity of the cattle trade as a business, the life of the cowboys and drovers was, by no means, an easy one. It was beset on every hand by hardship and danger. Exposure and privation continually tried the man who was out with the great herds; accidents, stampedes, and other dangers continually threatened his life; horse and cattle thieves continually harassed him with fears for the safety of his mounts and his charge.

A little item which appeared in the "Dodge City Times," of April 6th, 1878, read like this: "Mr. Jesse Evans and his outfit, consisting of fifty men and five four-mule teams and a number of saddle horses, started for the southwest yesterday. They go to New Mexico to gather from the ranges about twenty thousand cattle that Mr. Evans has purchased and will bring to Dodge City for sale and shipment." This expedition appeared simple and easy enough, from the tone of the item, but it gave no idea at all of the real facts in the case.

The fifty men were picked up in Dodge City. They were all fighters and gun-men, selected because they were such, for, in gathering these twenty thousand head of

cattle, they did so from under the very noses of the worst
set of stock thieves and outlaws ever banded together,
who were the Pecos River gang, with the famous "Billy
the Kid" as leader. But they took the cattle without
much fighting, and delivered them safely at Jesse Evan's
ranch just southeast of Dodge.

These men suffered incredible hardships on the drive
up. Before they were half way back, winter overtook
them, and their horses necessarily being thin from the
terrible work they had done, could not survive the cold
storms, but lay down and died. There was scarcely a
mount left. The men were all afoot, and barefooted at
that, and had to often help draw the mess wagon by hand.
They lived for weeks on nothing but fresh beef, often
without salt; no sugar, no coffee, no flour, no nothing,
but beef, beef, all the time, and they were the most woe
begone, ragged, long-haired outfit I ever saw—scarcely
any clothing except old blankets tied around them in
every fashion; no shoes or hats; indeed, they were almost
naked. But I tell you what they did have a plenty; it
was "gray-backs." With their long hair and long beards,
these little "varmints" were having a feast, and the men
bragged about these little pests keeping them alive and
warm, for, in scratching so much, it gave good circulation
to their blood. But notwithstanding their long hair and
naked, dirty, lousy bodies, the men were in splendid
health. They wandered into Dodge, one and two at a
time, and, in this manner, it was two days and nights
before they all straggled in.

Perhaps the most dangerous, most dreaded, and most
carefully guarded against phase of cattle driving was the
stampede, where all the skill, nerve, and endurance of the
drivers were tested to the limit. A common dark lantern
was often a feature at such times. The part it played in
quelling and controlling a stampede, as well as some
features of the stampede itself, is well described, by a
writer of cattle driving days, in this wise:

FIRST SOD HOUSE IN DODGE CITY

"One of the greatest aids to the cowboys during a stampede, on a dark stormy night, is the bull's-eye lantern, and it is so simple and handy. We all know when a stampede starts it is generally on a dark, stormy night. The cowboy jumps up, seizes his horse, and starts with a bound to follow the noise of the retreating herd, well knowing, as he does, the great danger before him; oftentimes encountering a steep bank, ten to twenty and sometimes thirty feet high, over which his horse plunges at full speed, to their certain death. For he knows not where the cattle, crazed by fear, will take him, but he does know it is his duty to follow as close as the speed of his horse will take him. This friend of his, the bull's-eye lantern, was discovered by accident. The flash of the lantern, thrown upon the bewildered herd, restores it to its equilibrium, and, in its second affright, produces a reaction, as it were, and, being completely subdued, the stampede is stopped, during the most tempestuous raging of the elements. The old-fashioned way was to ride to the front of the herd and fire their guns in the faces of the cattle. Now, they throw the flash of the lantern across the front of the herd and flash the bull's-eye into their faces, which is much more effective. The courage of the cowboy is demonstrated frequently on the long trail, but few of the cowboys are unequal to the emergencies."

As a result of the widespread stealing of cattle and horses, especially horses, which went on in connection with the great cattle traffic, the papers of the day abounded with notices like the following from the "Dodge City Times," of March 30th, 1878:

"Mr. H. Spangler, of Lake City, Comanche County, arrived in the city last Saturday in search of two horses that had been stolen from him last December. He described the stolen stock to Sheriff Masterson who immediately instituted search. On Monday he found one of the horses, a very valuable animal, at Mueller's cattle ranch on the Saw Log, it having been traded to Mr. Wolf. The horse was turned over to the owner. The sheriff has trace of the other horse and will endeavor to recover it.''

Many were the stories, of many different sorts, told about stock stealing and stock thieves. Some of these even took a humorous turn. One such, as told in early days, though funny was, nevertheless, true, and some do say that the man only took back what was taken from him, and it was (honestly or dishonestly) his horse. The reader may form his own opinion after perusing the story, as follows:

"Mr. O'Brien arrived in Dodge City last Sunday, August 30th, 1877, with the property, leaving, as we stated, our hero on the open prairie.

"We can picture in our minds this festive horse-thief, as he wandered over this sandy plain, under the burning sun, bereft of the things he holds most dear, to-wit: his horse, his saddle, and his gun. His feet became sore, his lips parched, and he feels, verily, he is not in luck. At last he can hold his pent up passion no longer. A pale gray look comes into his face, and a steel gray look into his eye, and he swears by the great god of all horse-thieves (Dutch Henry) that he will show his oppressors a trick of two—that he will show them an aggrieved knight of the saddle knows no fear. His resolve is to recapture his horse or die in the attempt. A most noble resolve. The horse is his own by all laws known to horse-thieves in every land. It is his because he stole it. Now, be it known that this particular horse was a good horse, a horse whose speed was fast and whose wind was good, so to speak. This horse he loved because he was a fast horse and no common plug could run with half as much speed. Seated in the saddle on the back of this noble animal, our hero feared not even the lightning in its rapid career. As we said before, his determination was fixed and his eye was sot. He would recapture the noble beast or he would die in the attempt. It was a go on foot and alone. He struck out. At the first hunters' camp he stole a gun, a pair of boots, and a sack of flour. He stole these articles because he had to have them, and it was a ground-hog case. On he came toward our beautiful city. His knowledge of the country led him direct to the farm of a rich farmer. As he approached he primed his gun, dropped lightly on hands and knees, and, with the demon glowing in his eye, stole silently through the tall buffalo grass to the house. Just at this time Mr. O'Brien happened to be riding out from town. He was riding directly by the place where our hero was concealed, and his first intimation of the presence of anyone was the sight of the man he met the Sunday before, with his gun cocked and pointed at him. 'Throw up your hands,' said the horse-thief; you have a small pistol in your belt— throw that down.' Mr. O'Brien obeyed. 'Now march to the stable before me, get my saddle and gun, and curry and saddle my horse which is picketed yonder, and await further orders.'

"Now, it so happened that the wealthy farmer was walking out that evening with his shotgun on his arm. He came to the stable, but, just as he turned the corner, the muzzle of a gun was placed near his head and the word, 'Halt!' uttered. The rich farmer said, 'What do you want?' 'My horse, saddle, and bridle.' 'What else?' 'Nothing.' The farmer made a move as if he would use his gun. The horse-thief said, 'Do not move or you will be hurt.' Silence for a moment, then, 'Lay down your gun.' The gun was laid down. By this time, Mr. O'Brien came out with the saddle and gun, the gun being strapped in the scabbard. Keeping them both under cover of his rifle, the horse-thief ordered them to walk before him to his horse and ordered Mr. O'Brien to saddle and bridle the horse, which he did. Our hero then mounted his brave steed and told his reluctant companions that if they pursued him their lives would be worthless, and then he sped off like the wind.'' Reader, ''such is life in the far west.''

Besides stock thieves and stealing, the cattle trade of early Dodge was attended by many other desperate characters and irregular practices, that were long in being stamped out. No better way of describing these desperate characters and irregular practices is at hand than by introducing a few specimens, for the reader's consideration.

Two of the greatest gamblers and faro-bank fiends, as well as two of the most desperate men and sure shots, were Ben and Billy Thompson. Every year, without fail, they came to Dodge to meet the Texas drive. Each brother had killed several men, and they were both dead shots. They terrorized Ellsworth county and city, the first year of the drive to that place, killed the sheriff of the county, a brave and fearless officer, together with several deputies, defied the sheriff's posse, and made their ''get away.''

A large reward was offered for them and they were pursued all over the country; but, having many friends among the big, rich cattle men, they finally gave themselves up and, through the influence of these men who expended large sums of money in their defense, they were cleared. Ben told the writer that he never carried but one gun. He never missed, and always shot his victim through the head. He said, when he shot a man, he looked the crowd over carefully, and if the man had any close friends around or any dangerous witness was around, he would down him to destroy evidence. The last few years of his life, he never went to bed without a full quart bottle of three-star Hennessey brandy, and he always emptied the bottle before daylight. He could not sleep without it.

Ben was a great favorite with the stock men. They needed him in their business for, be it said to their shame, some of them employed killers to protect their stock and ranges and other privileges, and Ben could get any reasonable sum, from one hundred to several thousand dollars, with which to deal or play bank.

Ben Thompson was the boss among the gamblers and killers at Austin, and a man whose name I have forgotten, Bishop, I think, a man of wealth and property, who owned saloons and dance halls and theaters at San Antonio, was the boss of the killers of that town. Great rivalry existed between these two men, and they were determined to kill each other. Word was brought to the San Antonio gent that Ben was coming down to kill him, so he had fair warning and made preparations. Ben arrived in town and walked in front of his saloon. He knew Ben was looking for the drop on him and would be sure to come back the same way, so he stationed himself behind his screen in front of his door, with a double-barreled shotgun. Whether Ben was wise to this, I do not know, but when Ben came back, he fired through this screen, and the San Antonio man fell dead with a bullet hole in his head, and both barrels of his gun were discharged into the floor.

Ben was now surely the boss, and numerous friends flocked to his standard, for "nothing succeeds like success." Some say that this victory made Ben too reckless and fool-hardy, however.

Some time after this, the cattle men gathered in Austin at a big convention. At this convention, Ben was more dissipated and reckless than ever, and cut a big figure. There was a congressman who resided at Austin, who was Ben's lawyer and friend (I won't mention his name). After the convention adjourned, thirty or forty of the principal stock men and residents of Texas remained to close up business and give a grand banquet (and let me say right here, these men were no cowards). That night, Ben learned that they had not invited his congressman, to which slight he took exceptions. The plates were all laid, wine at each plate, and just as they were about to be seated, in marched Ben with a six-shooter in his hand. He began at one end of the long table and smashed the bottles of wine, and chinaware as he came to it, making a clean sweep the entire length of the table. Let me tell you, before he got half through with his smashing process, that banquet hall was deserted. Some rushed through the doors, some took their exit through the windows, and in some instances the sash of the windows went with them and they did not stop to deprive themselves of it until they were out of range.

This exploit sounded Ben's death knell, as I remarked at the time that it would, because I knew these men.

Major Seth Mabrey was asked, the next day, what he thought of Ben's performance. Mabrey had a little twang in his speech and talked a little through his nose. In his slow and deliberate way, he said: "By Ginneys! I always thought, until last night, that Ben Thompson was a brave man, but I have changed my mind. If he had been a brave man, he would have attacked the whole convention when we were together and three thousand strong, but instead, he let nearly all of them get out of town, and cut off a little bunch of only about forty of us, and jumped onto us."

After this, the plans were laid to get away with Ben. He was invited to visit San Antonio and have one of the good old time jamborees, and they would make it a rich treat for him. He accepted. They gave a big show at the theater for his especial benefit. When the "ball" was at its height, he was invited to the bar to take a drink, and, at a given signal, a dozen guns were turned loose on him. They say that some who were at the bar with him and who enticed him there were killed with him, as they had to shoot through them to reach Ben. At any rate, Ben never knew what hit him, he was shot up so badly. They were determined to make a good job of it, for if they did not, they knew the consequences. Major Mabrey was indeed a cool, deliberate, and brave man, but he admitted to outrunning the swiftest of them.

Major Mabrey would hire more than a hundred men every spring, for the drive, and it is said of him, that he never hired a man himself and looked him over carefully and had him sign a contract, that in months after he could not call him by name and tell when and where he had hired him.

The Major built the first castle or palatial residence on top of the big bluff overlooking the railroad yards and the Missouri River, in Kansas City, about where Keeley's Institute now stands.

One of the most remarkable characters that ever came up the trail, and one whom I am going to give more than a passing notice, on account of his most remarkable career, is Ben Hodges, the horse-thief and outlaw.

A Mexican, or rather, a half-breed—half negro and half Mexican—came up with the first herds of cattle that made their way to Dodge. He was small of stature, wiry, and so very black that he was christened, "Nigger Ben." His age was non-come-at-able. Sometimes he looked young, not over twenty or twenty-five; then, again, he would appear to be at least sixty, and, at the writing of this narrative, he is just the same, and still resides in Dodge City.

Ben got stranded in Dodge City and was minus friends and money, and here he had to stay. At about the time he anchored in Dodge City, there was great excitement over the report that an old Spanish grant was still in existence, and that the claim was a valid one and embraced a greater part of the "Prairie Cattle Company's" range.

While the stock men were discussing this, sitting on a bench in front of my store (Wright, Beverly & Company), Nigger Ben came along. Just as a joke, one of them said: "Ben, you are a descendent of these old Spanish families; why don't you put in a claim as heir to this grant?" Ben cocked up his ears and listened, took the cue at once, and went after it. As a novice, he succeeded in a way beyond all expectations. By degrees, he worked himself into the confidence of newcomers by telling them a pathetic story, and so, by slow degrees, he built upon his story, a little at a time, until it seemed to a stranger that Ben really did have some sort of a claim on this big grant, and, like a snowball, it continually grew. He impressed a bright lawyer with the truthfulness of his story, and this lawyer carefully prepared his papers to lay claim to the grant, and it began to look bright. Then Judge Sterry of Emporia, Kan., took the matter up and not only gave it his time but furnished money to prosecute it. Of course, it was a good many years before his claim received recognition, as it had to be heard in one of our highest courts. But, in course of time, years after he began the action, it came to an end, as all things must, and the court got down to an investigation and consideration of the facts. It did not last but a moment, and was thrown out of court. Not the least shadow of a claim had Ben, but it was surprising how an ignorant darkey could make such a stir out of nothing.

Now, while this litigation was going on, Nigger Ben was not idle, for he started lots of big schemes and deals. For instance, he claimed to own thirty-two sections of land in Gray county, Kansas. About the time the United States Land Office was moved from Larned to Garden City, Kansas, the Wright-Beverly store at Dodge burned, and their large safe tumbled into the debris in the basement, but the safe was a good one and nothing whatever in it was destroyed by the fire. This safe was used by the Texas drovers as a place in which to keep their money and valuable papers. Ben knew this, and, when the government land office was established at Garden City,

— 274 —

Round-up of Red Polled Cattle

Ben wrote the officials and warned them not to take any filings on the thirty-two sections of land in Gray county, minutely describing the land by quarter sections. He told them that cowboys had filed on and proved up all these tracts and sold them to him, and that he had placed all the papers pertaining to the transactions in Wright, Beverly & Company's safe, and that the papers were all destroyed by the fire. Now, to verify this, he had written to the treasurer of Gray County to make him a tax list of all these lands, which he did, and Ben would show these papers to the "tenderfeet" and tell them he owned all this land, and instanter attached them as supporters and friends, for no man could believe that even Ben could be such a monumental liar, and they thought that there must surely be some truth in his story.

He went to the president of the Dodge City National Bank, who was a newcomer, showed him the letter he received from the treasurer of Gray County, with a statement of the amount of tax on each tract of land, and, as a matter of course, this bank official supposed that he owned the land, and, upon Ben's request, he wrote him a letter of credit, reciting that he (Ben) was said to be the owner of thirty-two sections of good Kansas land and supposed to be the owner of a large Mexican land grant in New Mexico, on which were gold and silver mines, and quite a large town. He then went to the presidents of the other Dodge City banks and, by some means, strange to say, he got nearly as strong endorsements. As a joke, it is here related that these letters stated that Ben was sober and industrious, that he neither drank nor smoked; further, he was very economical, his expenses very light, that he was careful, that he never signed any notes or bonds, and never asked for like accomodations.

On the strength of these endorsements and letters, he bargained for thousands of cattle, and several herds were delivered at Henrietta and other points. Cattle advanced in price materially that spring, and the owners were glad that Ben could not comply with his contracts to take them.

Quite a correspondence was opened by eastern capitalists and Omaha bankers with Ben, with a view to making him large loans of money, and, in the course of the negotiations, his letters were referred to me, as well as the Dodge City banks and other prominent business men for reports, here.

It is astounding and surprising what a swath Ben cut in commercial and financial circles. Besides, he successfully managed, each and every year, to get passes and annual free transportation from the large railroad systems. How he did it is a mystery to me, but he did it. If he failed with one official, he would try another, representing that he had large shipments of cattle to make from Texas and New Mexico, Indian Territory, and Colorado. He could just print his name, and he got an annual over the Fort Worth & Denver, and the writing of his name in the pass did not look good enough to Ben, so he erased it and printed his name in his own way. This was fatal; the first conductor took up his pass and put him off the train at Amarillo, Texas, and Ben had to beat his way back to Dodge City.

John Lytle and Major Conklin made a big drive, one spring, of between thirty and forty herds. They were unfortunate in encountering storms, and on the way, a great many of their horses and cattle were scattered. Each herd had its road brand. Mr. Lytle was north, attending to the delivery of the stock; Major Conklin was in Kansas City, attending to the firm's business there; and Martin Culver was at Dodge City, passing on the cattle when they crossed the Arkansas River. Mr. Culver offered to pay one dollar per head for their cattle that were picked up, and two dollars per head for horses; and he would issue receipts for same which served as an order for the money on Major Conklin. Ben Hodges knew all this and was familiar with their system of transacting business. Ben managed to get to Kansas City on a stock train, with receipts for several hundred cattle and a great many horses, supposed to be signed by Culver (They were forgeries, of course). The receipts were for stock of the firm's different road brands, and Major Conklin was astonished when he saw them. He did not know Ben very well and thought he would speculate a little and offered payment at a reduced price from that agreed upon. He asked Ben what he could do for him to relieve his immediate necessities, and Ben got a new suit of clothes, or, rather, a complete outfit from head to foot, ten dollars in money, and his board paid for a week. In a few days Ben called for another ten dollars and another week's board, and these demands continued for a month. Ben kept posted, and came to Conkling one day in a great hurry and told him that he must start for Dodge City at once, on pressing business, and that he was losing a great deal of money staying in Kansas City, and should be on the range picking up strays. The Major told Ben that Mr. Lytle would be home in a few days and he wanted Lytle to make final settlement with him (Ben). This was what Ben was trying to avoid. John Lytle was the last person in the world that Ben wanted to see. He told Conkling this was impossible, that he must go at once, and got twenty dollars and transportation to Dodge City from Conkling.

A few days afterwards, Lytle returned to Kansas City, and, in a crowd of stock men, at the St. James Hotel, that were sitting around taking ice in theirs every half hour and having a good time, Major Conkling very proudly produced his bunch of receipts he had procured from Ben in the way of compromise, as above related, and said: "John, I made a shrewd business deal and got your receipts for several hundred cattle and horses for less than half price, from Ben Hodges." Enough had been said. All the cattle men knew Ben, and both the laugh and the drinks were on Conkling. He never heard the last of it and many times afterwards had to ",set up" the drinks for taking advantage of an ignorant darkey. He was completely taken in himself.

One time Ben was in a hot box. It did look bad and gloomy for him. The writer did think truly and honestly that he was innocent, but the circumstantial evidence was so strong against him, he could hardly escape. I thought it was prejudice and ill feeling towards Ben, and nothing else, that induced them to bring the suit; and, what was worse for Ben, his reputation as a cattle thief and liar was very bad.

Mr. Cady had quite a large dairy, and one morning he awoke and found his entire herd of milch cows gone. They could get no trace of them, and, after hunting high and low, they jumped Ben and, little by little, they wove a network of circumstantial evidence around him that sure looked like they would convict him of the theft beyond a doubt. The district court was in session, Ben was arrested, and I, thinking the darkey innocent, went on his bond. Indeed, my sympathies went out to him, as he had no friends and no money, and I set about his discharge under my firm belief of his innocence.

I invited the judge down to my ranch at the fort to spend the night. He was a good friend of mine, but I hardly dared to advise him, but I thought I would throw a good dinner into the judge and, under the influence of a good cigar and a bottle of fine old wine, he would soften, and, in talking over old times, I would introduce the subject. I said, "Judge, I know you are an honest, fair man and want to see justice done; and you would hate to see an innocent, poor darkey, without any money or friends, sent to the pen for a crime he never committed." And then I told him why I thought Ben was innocent. He said, "I will have the very best lawyer at the bar take his case." I said, "No, this is not at all what I want; I want Ben to plead his own case." So I gave Ben a few pointers, and I knew after he got through pleading before that jury, they would either take him for a knave or a fool.

I was not mistaken in my prophecy. Ben harangued that jury with such a conglomeration of absurdities and lies and outrageous tales, they did not know what to think. I tell you, they were all at sea. He said to them:

"What! me? the descendent of old grandees of Spain, the owner of a land grant in New Mexico embracing millions of acres, the owner of gold mines and villages and towns situated on that grant of whom I am sole owner, to steal a miserable, miserly lot of old cows? Why, the idea is absurd. No, gentlemen; I think too much of the race of men from which I sprang, to disgrace their memory. No, sir! no, sir! this Mexican would never be guilty of such. The reason they accuse me is because they are beneath me and jealous of me. They can't trot in my class, because they are not fit for me to associate with and, therefore, they are mad at me and take this means to spite me."

Then he would take another tack and say: "I'se a poor, honest Mexican, ain't got a dollar, and why do they want to grind me down? Because dey know I am way above them by birth and standing, and dey feel sore over it." And then he would go off on the wildest tangent you ever listened to.

You could make nothing whatever out of it, and you'd rack your brains in trying to find out what he was trying to get at; and you would think he had completely wound himself up and would have to stop, but not he. He had set his mouth going and it wouldn't stop yet, and, in this way, did he amuse that jury for over two hours. Sometimes he would have the jury laughing until the judge would have to stop them, and again, he would have the jury in deep thought. They were only out a little while, when they brought in a verdict of not guilty.

Strange to say, a few days afterwards that whole herd of milch cows came wandering back home, none the worse for their trip. You see, Ben had stolen the cattle, drove them north fifty or sixty miles, and hid them in a deep canyon or arroya. He had to leave them after his arrest and there came up a big storm, from the north, which drove the cattle home. I was much surprised when the cattle came back, for I knew, then, what had happened and that he was guilty.

I could fill a large book with events in the life of this remarkable fellow, but want of space compels me to close this narration here.

The life of the cowboy, the most distinguished denizen of the plains, was unique. The ordinary cowboy, with clanking spurs and huge sombrero, was a hardened case, in many particulars, but he had a generous nature. Allen McCandless gives the character and life of the cowboy in, "The Cowboy's Soliloquy," in verse, as follows:

"All o'er the prairies alone I ride,
Not e'en a dog to run by my side;
My fire I kindle with chips gathered round (*),
And boil my coffee without being ground.
Bread, lacking leaven, I bake in a pot,
And sleep on the ground, for want of a cot.
I wash in a puddle, and wipe on a sack,
And carry my wardrobe all on my back.
My ceiling's the sky, my carpet the grass,
My music the lowing of herds as they pass;
My books are the brooks, my sermons the stones,
My parson a wolf on a pulpit of bones.
But then, if my cooking ain't very complete,
Hygienists can't blame me for living to eat;
And where is the man who sleeps more profound
Than the cowboy, who stretches himself on the ground.
My books teach me constancy ever to prize;
My sermons that small things I should not despise;
And my parson remarks, from his pulpit of bone,

That, 'The Lord favors them who look out for their own.'
Between love and me, lies a gulf very wide,
And a luckier fellow may call her his bride;
But Cupid is always a friend to the bold,
And the best of his arrows are pointed with gold.
Friends gently hint I am going to grief;
But men must make money and women have beef.
Society bans me a savage, from Dodge;
And Masons would ball me out of their lodge.
If I'd hair on my chin, I might pass for the goat
That bore all the sin in the ages remote;
But why this is thusly, I don't understand,
For each of the patriarchs owned a big brand.
Abraham emigrated in search of a range,
When water got scarce and he wanted a change;
Isaac had cattle in charge of Esau;
And Jacob 'run cows' for his father-in-law—
He started business clear down at bed-rock,
And made quite a fortune, watering stock;
David went from night herding and using a sling,
To winning a battle and being a king;
And the shepherds, when watching their flocks on the
    hill,
Heard the message from heaven, of peace and good will.''

(*) "Chips" were dried droppings of the cattle. Buffalo "chips" were used as fuel by the plainsmen.

Another description of the cowboy, different in character from the last, but no less true to life, is from an exchange, in 1883.

"The genuine cowboy is worth describing. In many respects, he is a wonderful creature. He endures hardships that would take the lives of most men, and is, therefore, a perfect type of physical manhood. He is the finest horseman in the world, and excells in all the rude sports of the field. He aims to be a dead shot, and universally is. Constantly, during the herding season, he rides seventy miles a day, and most of the year sleeps in the open

— 281 —

air. His life in the saddle makes him worship his horse, and it, with a rifle and six-shooter, complete his happiness. Of vice, in the ordinary sense, he knows nothing. He is a rough, uncouth, brave, and generous creature, who never lies or cheats. It is a mistake to imagine that they are a dangerous set. Any one is as safe with them as with any people in the world, unless he steals a horse or is hunting for a fight. In their eyes, death is a mild punishment for horse stealing. Indeed, it is the very highest crime known to the unwritten law of the ranch. Their life, habits, education, and necessities have a tendency to breed this feeling in them. But with all this disregard of human life, there are less murderers and cut-throats graduated from the cowboy, than from among the better class of the east, who come out here for venture or gain. They delight in appearing rougher than they are. To a tenderfoot, as they call an eastern man, they love to tell blood curdling stories, and impress him with the dangers of the frontier. But no man need get into a quarrel with them unless he seeks it, or get harmed unless he seeks some crime. They often own an interest in the herd they are watching, and very frequently become owners of ranches. The slang of the range they always use to perfection, and in season or out of season. Unless you wish to insult him, never offer a cowboy pay for any little kindness he has done you or for a share of his rude meal. If the changes that are coming to stock raising should take the cowboy from the ranch, its most interesting features will be gone.''

Theodore Roosevelt gave an address, once, up in South Dakota, which is readable in connection with the subject in hand. ''My friends seem to think,'' said Roosevelt, ''that I can talk only on two subjects—the bear and the cowboy—and the one I am to handle this evening is the more formidable of the two. After all, the cowboys are not the ruffians and desperadoes that the nickel library prints them. Of course, in the frontier towns where the only recognized amusements are vices, there is more or less of riot and disorder. But take the cowboy on his native heath, on the round-up, and you will find in him the virtues of courage, endurance, good fellowship, and generosity. He is not sympathetic. The cowboy divides all humanity into two classes, the sheep and the goats, those who can ride bucking horses and those who can't; and I must say he doesn't care much for the goats.

"I suppose I should be ashamed to say that I take the western view of the Indian. I don't go so far as to think that the only good Indian is the dead Indian, but I believe nine out of every ten are, and I shouldn't like to inquire too closely into the case of the tenth. The most vicious cowboy has more moral principle than the average Indian. Take three hundred low families of New York and New Jersey, support them, for fifty years, in vicious idleness, and you will have some idea of what the Indians are. Reckless, revengeful, fiendishly cruel, they rob and murder, not the cowboys who can take care of themselves, but the defenseless, lone settlers of the plains. As for the soldiers, an Indian chief once asked Sheridan for a cannon. 'What! do you want to kill my soldiers with it?' asked the general. 'No,' replied the chief, 'Want to kill cowboy; kill soldier with a club.'

"Ranch life is ephemeral. Fences are spreading all over the western country, and, by the end of the century, most of it will be under cultivation. I, for one, shall be sorry to see it go; for when the cowboy disappears, one of the best and healthiest phases of western life will disappear with him."

Probably every business has its disadvantages, and one of the great pests of the cattle man and cowboy was the loco weed. This insiduous weed, which baffled the skill of the amateur, was a menace to the cattle and horse industry. The plant was an early riser in the spring season, and this early bloom was nipped as a sweet morsel by the stock. Once infected by the weed, stock never recovered. The government chemist never satisfactorily traced the origin of the supposed poison of the weed. Stock allowed to run at large on this weed, without other feed, became affected by a disease resembling palsy. Once stock acquired a taste for the weed, they could not be kept from it, and never recovered, but, by degrees, died a slow death.

Like its disadvantages, every business probably has its own peculiar words and phrases, and in this the cattle business was not deficient. For instance, the word, "maverick," is very extensively used among stock men all over the country, and more particularly in localities where there is free or open range. I am told the word originated in this way. A gentleman, in very early times, soon after Texas gained her independence, moved into Texas from one of our southern states, with a large herd of cattle and horses, all unbranded. He was astonished to see everyone's stock branded and ear-marked, which was not the custom in the country he came from; so he asked his neighbors if they all branded. Oh, yes, they all branded, without an exception. So he said, "If everyone brands but myself, I will just let mine go, as I think it is a cruel practice, anyway, and you all will know my stock by its not being branded." His neighbors thought that was a good idea, but it did not work well for Mr. Maverick, as he had no cattle, to speak of, after a few years; certainly, he had no increase.

The "dead line" was a term much heard among stock men in the vicinity of Dodge City. As has been stated, the term had two meanings, but when used in connection with the cattle trade it was an imaginary line running north, a mile east of Dodge City, designating the bounds of the cattle trail. Settlers were always on the alert to prevent the removal or extension of these prescribed limits of driving cattle, on account of danger of the Texas cattle fever. An effort being made to extend the line beyond Hodgeman county, was promptly opposed by the citizens of that county, in a petition to the Kansas legislature.

The long-horned, long-legged Texas cow has been dubbed the "Mother of the West." A writer sings the song of the cow and styles her, "the queen," and, in the "Song of the Grass," this may be heard above the din that "cotton is king." A well known Kansan has said that grass is the forgiveness of nature, and, truly, the grass and the cow are main food supplies. When the world has absorbed itself in the production of the necessaries of food and clothing, it must return to the grass and the cow to replenish the stock exhausted in by-products.

At Dodge City now, however, the open range and the cattle drive have been supplanted by the wheat field and the grain elevator. In the early times, cattle men and grangers made a serious struggle to occupy the lands. But destiny, if so it may be called, favored the so-termed farmer, "through many difficulties to the stars." The time and the occasion always affords the genius in prose and rhyme. The literary merit is not considered, so that the "take-off" enlivens the humor of the situation; so here is "The Granger's Conquest," in humorous vein, by an anonymous writer:

"Up from the South, comes every day,
Bringing to stockmen fresh dismay,
The terrible rumble and grumble and roar,
Telling the battle is on once more,
And the granger but twenty miles away.

"And wider, still, these billows of war
Thunder along the horizon's bar;
And louder, still, to our ears hath rolled
The roar of the settler, uncontrolled,

Making the blood of the stockmen cold,
As he thinks of the stake in this awful fray,
And the granger but fifteen miles away.

"And there's a trail from fair Dodge town,
A good, broad highway, leading down;
And there, in the flash of the morning light,
Goes the roar of the granger, black and white
As on to the Mecca they take their flight.
As if they feel their terrible need,
They push their mule to his utmost speed;
And the long-horn bawls, by night and day,
With the granger only five miles away.

"And the next will come the groups
Of grangers, like an army of troops;
What is done? what to do? a glance tells both,
And into the saddle, with scowl and oath;
And we stumble o'er plows and harrows and hoes,
As the roar of the granger still louder grows,
And closer draws, by night and by day,
With his cabin a quarter-section away.

"And, when under the Kansas sky
We strike a year or two that is dry,
The granger, who thinks he's awful fly,
Away to the kin of his wife will hie;
And then, again, o'er Kansas plains,
Uncontrolled, our cattle will range,
As we laugh at the granger who came to stay,
But is now a thousand miles away."

THE OLD BURRELL FARM AND SOD DWELLING OF OLDEN DAYS
Located 12 Miles Southwest of Dodge City

CHAPTER XVI

Now I want to tell you something of the great officers who came to Fort Dodge in the early days.

General Phillip Sheridan first came to Fort Dodge in the summer of 1868. He pitched his camp on the hill north of the fort and next to my house. I saw a good deal of him while fitting out his command against the Indians, and he dined with me several times, together with the officers of the post. On one of these occasions, about noon, on the hills to the southwest, we saw with strong field-glasses what seemed to be a body of horsemen or a bunch of buffalo. But they moved so straight and uniformly that we finally came to the conclusion that they must be Indians. As the apparition came nearer we discovered that it was but one ambulance with a long pole lashed to it, with a wagon-sheet attached to the pole for a flag of true. It was the largest flag of truce ever used for such purpose. The driver proved to be Little Raven, chief of the Arapahoes, who had come in to have a peace talk with General Sheridan. As a result of the long talk, Little Raven badly out-generaled Sheridan (as has been related in another chapter). He said all the time he wanted was two sleeps to bring in the whole Arapahoe tribe. General Sheridan said to take a week and see that all came in. The old chief insisted that he only wanted two sleeps. He started out the next morning loaded down with bacon, beans, flour, sugar, and coffee. Little Raven told me afterwards it was a great ruse to avoid the soldiers until they could get the women and children out of danger. When Little Raven set out for Dodge, the women and children had started south, to get into the broken and rough country that they knew so well, and with which our soldiers were so little acquainted at that day. It was really laughable to hear his description of how he disposed of his ambulance after getting back to the tribe. He said the soldiers followed the tracks of the ambulance for days, so his rear-guard would report at night. The other Indians were for burning it or abandoning it; but Little Raven said he prized it so highly that he did not want to lose it. So they took off the wheels, and hung them in some very high trees, and concealed the body in a big drift in the river, covering it with driftwood.

The last visit General Sheridan made at Dodge was in 1872. He brought his whole staff with him. General Forsyth was his aide-de-camp, I think, and his brother, Mike, was along. I had known Mike for some time before this, when he was captain in the Seventh Cavalry. I was also well acquainted with the other brother, who held a clerkship at Camp Supply—a most excellent gentleman. During his stay, General Sheridan and his staff, with the officers of the post, were dining at my house. They had all been drinking freely before dinner of whisky, brandy, and punch, except Mike Sheridan. These liquors were all left in the parlor when we went in to dinner, and there was an abundance of light wine on the dinner-table. When dinner was nearly over an important dispatch came. The General read it and handed it to General Forsyth, requesting him to answer it. With that Captain Sheridan jumped up and said to General Forsyth: "You are not half through your dinner yet, and I am; so let me answer, and submit to you for review." He then requested me to get paper and pen and go with him to the parlor. As soon as we reached the parlor the Captain grabbed me by the arm, and said, "For God's sake, Wright, get me some of that good brandy, and say not a word about it." I replied, "There it is. Help yourself." He took two generous glasses and then wrote the dispatch.

The last time I had the pleasure of seeing General Sheridan was at Newton. I was on my way to Kansas

City, and stopped there to get supper. I was told that General Sheridan was in his private car. I called on him as soon as I got my supper. He knew me in a minute and received me most graciously. Not so with the brother, Captain Mike, whom I had taken care of many times and seen that he was properly put to bed. He pretended not to know me. "Why," said the General, "You ought to know Mr. Wright. He was the sutler at Fort Dodge, and so often entertained us at his home." I responded to the General that I was surprised that he knew me so quickly. "I knew you as soon as I saw you," he replied, and then began to inquire about all the old scouts and mule drivers, and wanted to know what they were doing and where they had drifted, including many men whom I had forgotten, until he mentioned their names. He said that he had been sent down by President Cleveland to inquire into the Indian leases entered into by the cattle men. We talked about old times and old faces way into midnight, and even then he did not want me to go.

In the fall of 1868 General Alfred Sully took command of Fort Dodge and fitted out an expedition for a winter campaign against the Plains Indians. He was one of the grand old style of army officers, kind-hearted and true, a lover of justice and fair play. Though an able officer and a thorough gentleman at all times, he was a little too much addicted to the drink habit. When General Sully had gotten the preparations for the expedition well under way, and his army ready to march, General Custer was placed in command by virtue of his brevet rank, and the old man was sent home. This action, as I am told, broke General Sully's heart, and he was never again any good to the service.

General Custer carried out the winter campaign, persistently following the Indians through the cold and snow into their winter fastnesses, where never white man had trod before, not even the trusted trader, until he surprised them in their winter camp on the Washita, south of the

Canadian. There was a deep snow on the ground at the time. The scouts had come in soon after midnight with the report of a big camp. "Boots and saddles" was sounded, and soon all were on the march. The command reached the vicinity of the Indian camp some time before daylight, but waited until the first streak of day, which was the signal for the charge. Then the whole force went into the fight, the regimental band playing, "Gary Owen." They charged through the camp and back, capturing or killing every warrior in sight. But the camp was the first of a series of Indian camps extending down the narrow valley of the Washita for perhaps ten miles, and Custer had only struck the upper end of it.

I have been told by good authority that early in the attack Major Elliott's horse ran away with him, taking him down the creek. Elliott was followed by some twenty of his men, they thinking, of course, that he was charging the Indians. It was but a few moments until he was entirely cut off, and urged on further from General Custer's main force. Custer remained in the Indian camp, destroying the tents and baggage of the Indians, until in the afternoon, and finally, after the Indian women captives had selected the ponies they chose to ride, destroyed the balance of the herd, about eight hundred ponies in all. He then left the camp, following the stream down to the next village, which he found deserted. It was then dusk. When night had fallen he retraced his way with all speed to the first village, and out by the way he had come in the morning, toward Camp Supply. He continued his march until he came up with his pack-train, which, having been under the protection of only eighty men, he had feared would be captured by the Indians, had he allowed it to have come on alone.

Now, I do not want to judge Custer too harshly, for I know him to have been a brave and dashing soldier, and he stood high in my estimation as such, but I have often heard his officers say that it was a cowardly deed to have gone off and left Elliott in the way he did. Many officers claim that Custer realized that he was surrounded and outnumbered by the Indians, and this was the reason he left Elliott as he did. The facts are that he should never have attacked the village until he had more thoroughly investigated the situation and knew what he was running into. Some of his own officers have condemned and censured him, talking about him scandalously for thus leaving Elliott. I cannot, however, see how he could have been badly whipped when he brought away with him about fifty-seven prisoners, besides having captured and killed so large a number of ponies.

This is the story of Major Elliott as told to me by Little Raven, chief of the Arapahoes, but who was not present at the time. He was my friend, and I always found him truthful and fair. He said that, when Major Elliott's horse ran away with him, followed by about twenty of his men, Elliott was soon cut off and surrounded by hundreds of Indians, who drove him some three to five miles from Custer's main body at the village, bravely fighting at every step. After getting him well away from Custer, the Indians approached him with a flag of truce, telling him that Custer was surrounded and unable to give him any help, and that, if he and his men would surrender, they would be treated as prisoners of war. Elliott told them he would never give up. He would cut his way back to Custer, or that Custer would send a detachment to his relief sooner or later. As soon as this announcement was made the young men who had gotten closer, without further warning, and before Elliott could properly protect himself, poured in volley after volley, mowing down most of Elliott's horses. He then commanded his men to take to the rocks afoot, and to keep together as close as possible, until they could find some suitable protection where they could make a stand. They did this and stood the Indians off for nearly two days, without food or water, and almost without sleep or ammunition.

They were then again approached with a flag of truce. This time they told Elliott it was impossible for him to get away, which he fully realized. They said that Custer had been gone for two days in full retreat to Supply, and that he had taken with him fifty of their women and children, whom he would hold as hostages, and that if he and his men would lay down their arms they would be treated fairly, and held as hostages for the good treatment and safety of their women and children. They repeated that Custer would be afraid to be harsh or cruel or unkind to their women and children because he knew that, if he was, Major Elliott and his soldiers would be subject to the same treatment. Elliott explained the whole thing to his men, and reasoned with them that under these circumstances the Indians could not help but be fair. The consequences was that Elliott and his men accepted the terms and laid down their arms. No sooner had they done so than the Indians rushed in and killed the last one of them. The older Indians claimed that they could not restrain their young men. I have no doubt that this is the true story, and that thus perished one of the bravest officers with a squad of the bravest men in our whole army. The only other officer killed in the fight was Captain Hamilton, when the first charge was made. He was a bright fellow, full of life and fun.

Among the other great men who came to Dodge City was "Uncle Billy Sherman," as he introduced himself. He came with President Hayes and party in September, 1879. The president did not get out of his car, and would not respond to the call of the cowboys, who felt that they deserved some recognition. It was a long time even before "Old Tecumseh," could be induced to strike the pace and lead off. But the cheerfulness, the hilarity, and the endless jokes of the half-drunken cowboys, who had been holloing for the President until they had become disgusted because of his lack of interest in them, induced the general to appear. Then they called for

Sherman in a manner indicating that they considered him their equal and an old comrade. Although half of those cowboys had been soldiers in the Confederate army, this seemed to make no difference in their regard for the old war-horse. They had an intuitive feeling that, no matter how they scandalized him, Sherman would be fair and treat them justly. I was astonished that their surmise was right, for when General Sherman appeared he handed them bouquet for bouquet. No matter on what topic they touched, or what questions they asked, he gave them back as good as they sent, answering them in the same generous humor. Before the close of the General's talk some of the crowd were getting pretty drunk, and I looked to see a display of bad feeling spring up, but nothing of the kind occurred, for the General was equal to the occasion and handled the crowd most beautifully. Indeed, it was laughable at times, when the General rose way above his surroundings and sat down on their coarse, drunken jokes so fitly and admirably, that one could not help but cheer him. He had the crowd with him all the while and enlisted their better feeling, notwithstanding more than half of them were Southern sympathizers.

President Hayes paid but little attention to the crowd the whole day, nor the crowd to him, but General Sherman kept it in good humor, and the presidential party at last left Dodge City amid strong cheers for "Uncle Billy," a long life and a happy one.

In a previous chapter mention was made of the visits of Senator Ingalls and of the Major-General who was once second in command at Gettysburg. These were fair representatives of the class of distinguished visitors who came especially for sight-seeing.

One Thursday the citizens of Dodge City were agreeably surprised by the arrival, in their midst, of the once famous political boss of the state, Ex-Governor Thomas Carney, of Leavenworth. He was observed in close communion with one of our leading citizens, Honorable R. W. Evans.

The Governor said he was buying hides and bones for a large firm in St. Louis, of which he was president, but he told some of his old-time friends of Dodge that he was here to hunt up a poker game, in which game he was an expert, and he wanted to teach the gamblers of Dodge a lesson, and give them some pointers for their future benefit. The governor's reputation and dignified bearing soon enabled him to decoy three of our business men into a social game of poker, as the governor remarked, "just to kill time, you know."

The governor's intended victims were Colonel Norton, wholesale dealer, the "Honorable" Bobby Gill, and Charles Ronan, old time friends of his, formerly from Leavenworth. The game proceeded merrily and festively for a time until, under the bracing influence of exhilarating refreshments, the stakes were greatly increased and the players soon became excitedly interested. At last the governor held what he supposed to be an invincible hand. It consisted of four kings and cuter, which the governor very reasonably supposed to be the ace of spades. He had been warned about the cuter before he began the game. He said he understood the cuter to represent an ace or a flush and was accustomed to playing it that way. The old gentleman tried to repress his delight and appear unconcerned when Colonel Norton tossed a hundred dollar bill into the pot, but he saw the bet and went a hundred better. Norton did not weaken as the governor feared he would, but, nonchalantly, raised the old gent what he supposed was a fabulous bluff. Governor Carney's eyes glistened with joy, as he saw the pile of treasure, which would soon be all his own, loom up before his vision, and he hastened to "see" the colonel and added the remainder of his funds, his elegant gold watch and chain. Norton was still in the game, and the

BATTLE OF LITTLE COON CREEK, WHERE FIVE SOLDIERS WERE ATTACKED BY ABOUT 500 INDIANS.

governor finally stripped himself of all remaining valuables, when it became necessary for him to show up his hand.

A breathless silence pervaded the room as Governor Carney spread his four kings and cuter on the table with his left hand, and affectionately encircled the glittering heap of gold and silver, greenbacks and precious stones, with his right arm, preparatory to raking in the spoils. But at that moment, a sight met the old governor's gaze which caused his eyes to dilate with terror, a fearful tremor to seize his frame, and his vitals to almost freeze with horror.

Right in front of Colonel Norton was spread four genuine and perfectly formed aces, and the hideous reality that four aces laid over four kings and the cuter gradually forced itself upon the mind of our illustrious hide and bone merchant. Slowly and reluctantly he uncoiled his arm from around the sparkling treasure, the bright, joyous look faded from his eyes leaving them gloomy and cadaverous, and, with a weary almost painful effort, he arose, and dragging his feet over the floor like balls of lead, he left the room sadly muttering, "I forgot about the cuter."

Now, the governor's old friends, R. M. Wright and R. W. Evans had warned him and pleaded with him not to try gambling here, and even watched him all the morning to keep him out of michief; but he stole away from them and got into this game which was awaiting him. Through his friends he recovered his watch and chain and they saw him safely on the train in possession of a ticket for St. Louis.

As a character figuring conspicuously in the visit of Senator Ingalls to Dodge City, I must mention my horse, Landsmann. Or better, I will let his story be told in its greater part by Miss Carrie DeVoe, who often rode with me behind the old horse, who was the only woman who would ride behind him, and who would ride behind him with no one else but me, because she had so much confidence in my driving. I would often cover seventy-five miles a day, and fifty or sixty miles a day was easy work for him, while I have driven him about a hundred miles a day more than once, and over a hundred miles in twenty-four hours. Miss DeVoe's story follows:

"Robert M. Wright, who, in the early days, possessed thousands of acres of land scattered throughout the length and breadth of the short grass region, was the owner of a horse of such strange behavior that it deserves to go on record with the odd characters of the border.

"Landsmann (a German word meaning friend or farmer) was originally the property of an officer who served under Maximillian in Mexico and afterwards wandered north into the United States, becoming, at length, a frontier county official. The horse accompanied his master through many dangers, and was spirited, though gentle and faithful. But, as he advanced in years, Landsmann was supposed to become addicted to the loco weed, for a change was noticeable. It was no easy matter to put him in the harness; he reared and plunged without the slightest provocation, and grew generally unmanageable—'full of all around cussedness,' said Joe, who usually fed and cared for him. However, because of his remarkable endurance, Mr. Wright purchased him for a driving horse.

"Invariably, when the owner essayed to step into the cart, Landsmann sprang forward, and his master was obliged to leap to the seat or measure his length upon the ground, sometimes perilously near to the wheels. When the horse came to a halt, which was difficult to accomplish, the driver was often taken unawares and hurled forward over the traces for a short bareback exhibition.

"Landsmann's chief peculiarity was his speed. He dashed over the prairies at a surprising rate, down into draws and up the banks, over dry beds of rivers, across pastures and ranches, never seeming to tire, and allowing no obstacle to stop his mad race. John Gilpin's renowned steed was tame in comparison. To be sure, this kind of travel was not without its inconveniences, as Pegasus sometimes fell in the harness; however, he always managed to pick himself up and sped onward as if possessed of the 'Old Nick,' which, indeed, many believed him to be.

"When the late Senator John J. Ingalls visited Mr. Wright, he was invited to take a drive. Not being acquainted with Landsmann's reputation, he accepted. Nothing daunted by the animal's efforts to wrench himself from the man who stood at his head, the senator reached the seat in safety, and his host, with a flying leap, landed at his side. The visitor began to wish he had not been so hasty; but there was little time for reflection. A spring—a whirl—and they were off across the plains. Spectators caught a passing glimpse of the dignified statesman, wildly clutching the seat and bending his head to the wind.

"It was an exciting experience and one hardly to be desired, but they returned in safety. The vitriolic senator was diplomatic.

"Like most of the interesting characters out west, Landsmann is dead, and though he died in the harness, maneuvering as usual, his master insisted—and perhaps with good reason—that his untimely end was caused by poison. At any rate, the old horse ought to go down in history, as he was one of the landmarks of the short grass region."

Miss DeVoe knew that no horse would attempt to pass Landsmann. The day before he died, after making more than fifty miles and coming into Dodge, he came in contact with a runaway team, and off started the old horse whom you would have thought was completely tired out. But he ran all over Dodge, at a high rate of speed, before I could stop him.

As Miss DeVoe says, I did think, at first, Landsmann was poisoned but he was loose in his stall and, in lying down, got his head under the manger, and died during the night, from the dangerous position he was in.

And here I want to interpolate a little in order to give the gist of the conversation with Senator. Ingalls before taking the ride described. There was quite a crowd in front of the hotel, to pay respects to the senator when I invited him to ride to Fort Dodge with me. The crowd followed us to the livery stable, everyone saying to the senator, "My God, Senator! don't ride behind that horse; he will kill you. I would sooner give you my horse." Others said: "Never do it. We will hire you a rig if you won't." The senator said, "Bob, what is the matter with the horse?" I replied, "Nothing." "Why, then, are they making such a fuss?" asked the senator. "Oh," I said, "they are a lot of geese and cowards! Come on." He said, "Bob, is it safe?" I said, "Ain't I taking the same risk you are?" He said, "That is so; crack your whip!" and away we went. He said, "Bob, is he so very dangerous?" "You see him, don't you?" I answered. "Yes, did he ever run away with you?" "Yes." "How many times?" "I don't know." "Many times?" "Yes." "Did he ever throw you out?" "Yes."

When we returned and were drinking a bottle of "ice-cold" together, the senator said: "Bob, that is the best G— d— horse for his looks I ever saw, and I never was more deceived in a horse. It is the fastest ten miles I ever drove."

General Miles has been frequently mentioned in these pages, as a sojourner at Fort Dodge and Dodge City. I give here a letter from Mrs. Alice V. Brown, a former resident of Dodge City and Fort Dodge and a sergeant's wife, because it reflects my ideas of the gallant General

BEN HODGES
The Great Desperado and Horse Thief

Miles. It is dated, Tongue River, M. T., May, 1867, and says:

"We have been out twelve days on a scout. On our return, General Miles had gone out on an expedition with six hundred men. We expect them back about the last of May. General Miles had a fight on the sixth of May. He returned today with four hundred ponies. He had four men of the Second Cavalry killed, and one officer and four men wounded. The fight took place near the Little Big Horn, where General Custer was killed. There were forty-seven Indians found dead on the field. The mounted infantry charged through the Indian camp. The only cavalry he had was four companies of the Second, and they fought well. They say General Miles is the only officer who ever led them yet, and speak very highly of him. We told them, before they went out, he would show them how to fight. Everything in the Indian camp was burned. This is the greatest victory yet. Red Horn, a chief of some note, made a treacherous attempt to kill General Miles. He came in, during the fight, with a flag of truce, and, as the General rode up close to him, he fired. He missed the general but killed one of the cavalry dead on the spot. That was Red Horn's last shot; he fell instantly, riddled with bullets. The general has had several close calls, but I believe this was the closest."

The writer wishes he had space to pay a much deserved tribute or compliment to General Miles, about his indefatigable trailing up of the Indians. His system is like the wild horse trailers; when he strikes a scent, he never gives up until he has trailed Mr. Indian to earth, and compelled him to fight or surrender.

Eddie Foy, one of the greatest comedians of our day, made his debut or about his first appearance at Dodge City. He dressed pretty loud and had a kind of Fifth Avenue swaggering strut, and made some distasteful jokes about the cowboys. This led up to their capturing Foy by roping, fixing him up in picturesque style, ducking him, in a friendly way, in a horse trough, riding him around on horseback, and taking other playful familiarities with him, just to show their friendship for him. This dressing up and ducking of Eddie is positively vouched for by a lady with whom he boarded, and who still lives in Dodge City. The writer does not vouch for the story of the ducking, but he does know they played several pranks on him, which Foy took with such good grace that he thereby captured the cowboys completely. Every night his theater was crowded with them, and nothing he could do or say offended them; but, on the contrary, they made a little god of him. The good people of Dodge have watched his upward career with pride and pleasure, and have always taken a great interest in him, and claim him as one of their boys, because it was here that he first began to achieve greatness. I think he played here the most of one summer, and then went to Leadville, Colorado, when and where he kept going up and up. His educated admirers here predicted a great future for him. This, the writer has heard them do, and, surely, he has not disappointed them. Here is further success and prosperity to you, Eddie, and may you live long and die happy!

In connection with noted individuals who, from time to time, honored Dodge City with their presence, usually coming from a distance and making a transient stay, it is well to mention a few of the leading residents of Dodge, to whose pluck and perseverance the town owed so much of its early fame and prosperity. No better beginning could be made, in this line, than by introducing the Masterson brothers.

William Barclay Masterson, more familiarly called "Bat," by his friends, and one of the most notable characters of the West, was one of Dodge City's first citizens, and, for this reason if no other, deserves a space in my book.

He, with a partner, took a contract of grading a few miles of the Atchison, Topeka & Santa Fe Railroad, near Dodge. He was only eighteen years old at the time; this was in the spring of 1872. He says that he never worked so hard in his life, in filling this contract, which they did, with a nice little profit to their credit, of whch he was very proud; but his partner ran off with everything, leaving him flat broke. He said it nearly broke his heart, grieving over his loss and over the perfidy of his partner, as he was only a boy, and the world looked dark and dreary. But this misfortune proved a benefit to him eventually, as he gained a lot of experience from the episode, and had many hearty laughs over it afterwards.

A stranger, hunting Bat one day, said to some persons, standing on a street corner, "Can any of you tell me where I can find Bat Masterson? I never saw him, and would not know him if I met him." A lawyer spoke up, and said: "Look for one of the most perfectly-made men you ever saw, as well as a well dressed, good looking fellow, and, when you see such a man, call him 'Bat' and you have hit the bull's eye."

Notwithstanding they have talked and published Bat as a robber and murderer and everything else that is vile, there was nothing of the kind in his make-up. On the contrary, Bat is a gentleman by instinct. He is a man of pleasant manners, good address, and mild disposition until aroused, and then, for God's sake, look out! He is a leader of men and a natural born general, always accomplishing whatever he undertook. This is the reason he was sought after by the "gang" and recognized as their general. He has much natural ability and good hard common sense, and, if he had got started right, Bat, today, would have been occupying a seat in the United States Senate, instead of being a reporter for a newspaper. There is nothing low down about him. He is high-toned and broad-minded, cool and brave.

In 1876 he became a candidate for sheriff of Ford county, of which Dodge is the county seat. Here is his announcement, as he wrote it, and as it appeared in the "Dodge City Times:"

"At the earnest request of many citizens of Ford county, I have consented to run for the office of sheriff, at the coming election in this county. While earnestly soliciting the suffrages of the people, I have no pledges to make, as pledges are usually considered, before election, to be mere clap-trap. I desire to say to the voting public that I am no politician and shall make no combinations that would be likely to, in anywise, hamper me in the discharge of the duties of the office, and, should I be elected, will put forth my best efforts to so discharge the duties of the office that those voting for me shall have no occasion to regret having done so.

"Respectfully,

"W. B. MASTERSON."

The home paper said that, "Mr. W. B. Masterson is on the track for sheriff. Bat is well known as a young man of nerve and coolness in cases of danger. He has served on the police force of this city, and also as under-sheriff, and knows just how to gather in the sinners. He is well qualified to fill the office, and, if elected, will never shrink from danger."

Owing to the life he had lived, it was urged by his opponents, during the canvass leading up to his election, and owing to the fact that Bat had grown to manhood under the free and easy conditions permeating a frontier community, that he would be too lenient with law breakers and evil doers; but his metal was tried on this, soon after he was inducted into office.

There was a train robbery committed at Kinsley, Kansas, and one Dave Rudebaugh was the main guy in the robbery. Rudebaugh was a very bold, bad man. This crime was not committed in Bat's jurisdiction, but in another county; still, he gathered a posse, consisting of Dave Morrow (Prairie Dog Dave), Josiah Webb, and Charlie Bassett, and took the trail. He caught on to a scent that led them to Henry Lovell's cattle camp. The posse remained at this camp until the next day after their arrival. A terrible storm was raging, and Bat was certain that the robbers would seek this camp for shelter, which they did, and, by the adoption of strategic measures on the part of Bat and his men, they were captured without a shot being fired, notwithstanding these robbers were desperate men and heavily armed. The pursuit and well devised and well executed capture reflects credit, good judgment, and bravery upon all who engaged in it.

The successful efforts of Sheriff W. B. Masterson in this capture, followed by other arrests remarkable in skill and judgment, entitles him to the unanimous accord of praise given him, at the time and since, and in which I join.

Bat was a most loyal man to his friends. If anyone did him a favor, he never forgot it. I believe that if one of his friends was confined in jail and there was the least doubt of his innocence, he would take a crow-bar and "jimmy" and dig him out, at the dead hour of midnight; and, if there were determined men guarding him, he would take these desperate chances. This was exemplified in his action in saving Billy Thompson. Billy and Ben Thompson, mentioned in a previous chapter, were brothers, high rollers, and desperate men, as well as gamblers. Billy was shot all to pieces in a gun play at Ogallallah, Nebraska. They wired Ben Thompson, at Dodge, about the shooting, but Ben had outlawed himself at Ogallallah, was well known there, and had many enemies in the town. He did not dare to go. Bat and Ben were friends, and Bat said: "I'll go, but he don't deserve it." But he promised Ben to bring Billy out. Now Bat was a stranger in Ogallallah, and Billy Thompson was at the only hotel there, desperately wounded and shot all to pieces. The citizens were down on him, waiting for him to get well enough to hang him. The chances were desperate, and Bat knew it and had to keep under cover. By chance, Billy's nurse was an old-timer and a great admirer of Bat. By some chance unknown to anyone, Bat got to him, and the nurse was only too glad to help him all he could, secretly, of course, for the nurse knew the chances he was taking in helping Bat. Through this nurse, Bat got word to a lot of his friends as well as friends of Thompson, who wanted to help him if they could. This was their plan, and it succeeded admirably. When the fast, west-bound express was heard to whistle at Ogallallah, at twelve o'clock that night, the friends of Thompson were to commence a sham battle at the big dance hall across the railroad track, some distance from the hotel, by a perfect fusilade of shots. Of course, everyone ran out of the hotel for the scene of action. Then Bat got the nurse to throw Billy Thompson across his shoulders and to follow with his clothes.

Bat landed Billy in a sleeper and locked the door, just as the train pulled out, and no one saw them. Their attention was attracted elsewhere, and they landed next morning at William Cody's (alias Buffalo Bill's) ranch, who happened to be at home in North Platte. Bill was kind hearted and was always willing to help the weak and needy, so they got the best of care, and Mr. Cody had several relays of teams stationed overland towards Dodge City. Mr. Cody, I think, accompanied them for the first few days. It was a long way across country for a badly wounded man, but they made it all right, without accident.

Another man worthy of note, on account of many good qualities, was Edward J. Masterson, a brother of Bat Masterson. He came to Dodge City with his distinguished brother, and, in 1877, was appointed marshal of Dodge City. He was in every way well qualified to

ill this position. He was a natural gentleman, a man of
ood judgment, cool, and considerate. He had another
ery important qualification, that of bravery. In those
ays, a man with any streaks of yellow in him could have
ccomplished nothing as such officer in Dodge.

The mayor and city council, knowing Ed Masterson
o possess all of the qualifications demanded by the times,
onditions, and the position, gave him the appointment,
o the entire satisfaction of all the business men and
itizens of the town. He served in such capacity about
. year and, during the time, acquitted himself in such
. way that his untimely death, in the performance of his
luty, was deeply and sincerely deplored by the entire
ommunity.

I here relate an attempt to perform duty at that
ime, and the result, as published in the "Dodge City
'imes," November 10th, 1877.

"Last Monday afternoon, one of those little episodes
vhich serve to vary the monotony of frontier existence
)ccurred at the Lone Star dance hall, during which four
nen came out some the worse for wear, but none, with
)ne exception, being seriously hurt.

"Bob Shaw, the man who started the amusement,
ιccused Texas Dick, alias Moore, of having robbed him
)f forty dollars, and, when the two met in the Lone Star,
he ball opened. Somebody, foreseeing possible trouble
ιnd probable gore, started out in search of City Marshal,
Ξd. Masterson, and, finding him, hurried him to the
:cene of the impending conflict.

"When Masterson opened the door, he descried
Shaw near the bar, with a huge pistol in his hand and a
ιogshead of blood in his eye, ready to relieve Texas
Dick of his existence in this world and send him to those
shades where troubles come not and six-shooters are
unknown. Not wishing to hurt Shaw, but anxious to
quiet matters and quell the disturbance, Masterson order-

ed him to give up his gun. Shaw refused to deliver and told Masterson to keep away from him, and, after saying this, he proceeded to try to kill Texas Dick. Officer Masterson then gently tapped belligerent Shaw upon the head with his shooting iron, merely to convince him of the vanities of this frail world. The aforesaid reminder upon the head, however, failed to have the desired effect, and, instead of dropping, as any man of fine sensibilities would have done, Shaw turned his battery upon the officer and let him have it in the right breast. The ball, striking a rib and passing around, came out under the right shoulder blade, paralyzing his right arm so that it was useless, so far as handling a gun was concerned. Masterson fell, but grasping the pistol in his left hand he returned the fire, giving it to Shaw in the left arm and left leg, rendering him *hors de combat*.

"During the melee, Texas Dick was shot in the right groin, making a painful and dangerous, though not necessarily a fatal wound, while Frank Buskirk, who, impelled by a curiosity he could not control, was looking in at the door upon the matinee, received a reminiscence in the left arm, which had the effect of starting him out to hunt a surgeon. Nobody was killed, but, for a time, it looked as though the undertaker and the coroner would have something to do."

The writer remembers this shooting scrape well. Someone ran by my store at full speed, crying out, "Our marshal is being murdered in the dance hall!" I, with several others, quickly ran to the dance hall and burst in the door. The house was so dense with smoke from the pistols a person could hardly see, but Ed Masterson had corralled a lot in one corner of the hall, with his six-shooter in his left hand, holding them there until assistance could reach him. I relate this to show the daring and cool bravery of our marshal, in times of greatest danger, and when he was so badly wounded.

April 9th, 1878, Ed Masterson was mortally wounded, in an attempt to make an arrest of two desperate men, Jack Wagner and Alf Walker, who had committed some crime and were terrorizing the town. A very short time after being shot he died. A few minutes after Ed was shot, Bat heard of the trouble and hurried to the assistance of his brother. It took but a glance from Bat to determine that his brother was murdered. He was greatly effected by the horrible crime, and, when Ed told him he had his death wound, he gathered the particulars, and, bidding his brother an affectionate farewell, hastily departed to avenge his death; and I have no doubt he made the murderers pay the penalty.

Ed Masterson's death shocked the entire town, and the feeling was intense against his murderers. To show the esteem in which Masterson was held, the city council and civic organizations passed resolutions of respect, and all the business houses closed during the time of his funeral. It was the largest funeral held in Dodge City, up to that time.

I present a photograph of Andy Johnson, one of the heroes of the adobe wall fight. He has gone through all the vicissitudes of life. A blacksmith by trade, but he has never been afraid to tackle anything that has come in his way. Always a busy man, he has made and lost two or three fortunes. It has been up and down, and down and up with him, but he has never been discouraged. Coming over from Sweden, at an early day, he found his way out to the great plains, when he was not much more than a boy. He was introduced, at once, to all the hardships and privations of a buffalo hunter, and came near freezing to death, when he was caught in several of our terrible snow-storms. He same to Dodge City soon after the town was started, and has rendered good service to us by his thrift and industry. He built the big storehouse, for Rath & Wright, at the adobe walls, and collected many trophies from the bodies of dead Indians, immediately after the fight; and I expect he had the largest collection of war bonnets, shields, bows and arrows, spears, white people's scalps, and other Indian curiosities, of anyone in the West. They were considered of great value, but were nearly all destroyed by the big fire in Dodge, in 1885. He worked some time in our hide yard, and says we often had forty thousand or fifty thousand buffalo hides, at a time, in the yard.

The Honorable M. W. Sutton, who deserves and ought to have more space in our book than we can possibly give him, came to Dodge in 1876, and at once, from the very beginning, struck a gait that gave him front rank as an attorney. Indeed, he was, for many years, the leading attorney of southwest Kansas, and always has held his own among the very best lawyers of our state. He was a friend of the ''gang,'' but always stood up for right and justice. He and the writer ran on the same ticket, and were always elected by overwhelming majorities. He was behind me, as adviser, in all my deals and undertaking. He held many responsible positions of honor and trust, and discharged their duties ably and satisfactorily. When Bat Masterson was sheriff, Mike (Sutton) was prosecuting attorney, and they made a great team. It was not, ''Scare 'em and catch 'em,'' as the old story goes, but it was, ''Catch 'em and convict 'em,'' which was nearly always sure to be the case. It was his ability, and not chance, that did it, as some of his enemies would try to make you believe. Unusual success, in any line, seems always attended by enemies, but, in this instance, both Sutton and Masterson were well fitted to follow Cy Leland's example toward those who cherished resentment against them. Leland said that if he were making answer to the resentful ones, he would repeat this printed poem which, for years, he carried in his pocket:

"You have no enemies, you say?
Alas! my friends, the boast is poor.
He who has mingled in the fray
Of duty that the brave endure,
Must have made foes. If you have none,
Small is the work that you have done
You've hit no traitor on the hip;
You've dashed no cup from perjured lip;
You've never turned the wrong to right;
You've been a coward in the fight.''

During our campaigns, in very early days, Mr. Sutton
and I had some funny things to occur. I regret I cannot
give them for want of space. Some of them would equal,
in fun, the electioneering adventures of David Crockett
and Daniel Boone. Mike was the making of our beloved,
talented, and greatly distinguished congressman, now
deceased. Mr. Sutton spared no labor or means in bringing him out and boosting him, all the time and in every
way possible; and, on every occasion, he would manage
to call the public's attention to the name of Ed Madison.
Mike surely was, for many years, the big political boss of
the great Southwest, and held the situation in his vest
pocket; and he certainly made one United States senator,
and came within two votes of making another, besides
figuring conspicuously in making and defeating others.
For many years, he was undoubtedly a power in politics.
He is retired now, living on the fruits of his past toil,
but still retains much of his former vigor, and retains
the respect and esteem of his community.

Of the number of old citizens of the town, whose residence began with the opening of the Santa Fe railway
and which still continues to be Dodge City, we find only
seven survivors. These are A. J. Anthony, Dr. T. L.
McCarty, Honorable G. M. Hoover, H. S. Sitler, O. A.
Bond, Andrew Johnson, and myself, R. M. Wright. Of
these, Andrew Johnson has been mentioned. A. J.
Anthony, who is now (1913) eighty-three years of age, is

a most wonderfully preserved man, as active and bright as a man of forty. He goes right along with a laugh and a song, and sometimes a dance. Nothing seems to worry him. The reason he is so well preserved is that he never dissipated; always led an even, pure life, and strictly temperate in his habits. He has filled several offices of honor and trust, such as county commissioner, and other county and township offices.

Dr. T. L. McCarty is the oldest and one of the best known physicians and surgeons in the West. He has lived to see Dodge City grow from a few houses to its present size. He and his son, Claude, have a fine hospital here, and they stand today in the front ranks of the best physicians in the state, and enjoy a large practice. His son and partner, Dr. Claude McCarty, was the first child (with the exception noted in a former chapter) born in Dodge City.

Honorable G. M. Hoover is one of our wealthiest men. He made all his money here. He has held many offices of honor and trust. He represented Ford county in the legislature two terms. He was mayor of Dodge City several times, and county commissioner several times. He owns a big bank of which he is president.

Mr. H. L. Sitler is a retired farmer and stock man, and was, for a long time, one of our leading men in the stock business.

O. A. Bond is pointed out, by the younger generation, as the great hunter and nimrod—the man who killed so many buffalo in one day, and stood in the front ranks of the mighty hunters in early days. He is now the owner of one of our largest drug stores, and is taking life easy in his old days.

Since beginning this book, I learn that my old friend, William Tilghman, Chief of Police of Oklahoma City, and mentioned several times in previous pages, is a candidate for the marshalship of Oklahoma. The president could

not appoint a better man, nor one more fitted for the place by all the rules of war. William Tilghman has spent almost a lifetime in this kind of work. He was marshal under me, when I was mayor of Dodge City, and Ben Daniels was his assistant. No braver men ever handled a gun or arrested an outlaw, and Dodge never passed through a tougher time than the year of the big fire, the year I was mayor It did seem like every bad and desperate character in the whole West gathered here; and when we would drive out one lot, another set would make their appearance But Tilghman was equal to the occasion. He had many narrow escapes, and many desperate men to deal with; and Ben Daniels was a good second. Ex-President Roosevelt told the writer, when I was walking with him from the round-house to the depot, that Daniels was one of the bravest men he ever saw. He said, during the Cuban war, he could send Ben any place and he was sure to go, no matter how great the danger; he never found him wanting, and he paid him many other high compliments, when I told him Ben was an old citizen of Dodge, and a peace officer. I regret I cannot give Tilghman and Daniels a more extended notice for want of space.

I would not feel satisfied, nor would I think my book complete, unless I made mention, in my feeble way, of my old friend and fellow politician, Honorable Nicholas B. Klaine. Mr. Klaine was not one of our first settlers (came here in 1877), but there is no man who has contributed more in building up and trying to snatch Dodge City from its wickedness, and bring about an era of Christian feeling and build-up of our churches and other religious and charitable institutions than he. He has labored hard, both day and night, with his able pen and valuable papers, for the welfare of Dodge City. He and I, I am proud to say, have always worked side by side in politics, as well as in many other things, for the common good. He was editor of the "Dodge City Times" for many years, and has filled several offices of honor and trust. He was postmaster of Dodge City for one term, and gave general satisfaction. He was probate judge of our county for several years. He has also helped me not a little with my book.

Now I can't help speaking a great big word for my old friend, Chalk Beeson, God rest his soul! and may God take a liking to him, is my fervent prayer. Had I space, I could write many pages of his good, generous deeds. He never neglected the sick and needy, and, in times of affliction, Chalk would always be on hand to give comfort, and aid, if necessary, to the stricken ones. He was an indefatigable worker at whatever he undertook, and he never went after anything that he did not succeed in getting it. It was greatly through his efforts that our fine Masonic Hall was builded, and it stands, today, as a monument to his labor. He was one of the widest and best known men in the state, and among the Masons he reached a high mark. He twice represented our county in the legislature, and was sheriff of our county a number of times. He was one of the celebrated scouts that accompanied the Grand Duke Alexis, of Russia, on his great buffalo hunt; he was also the originator, leader, and proprietor of our famous cowboy band, of which I shall presently say more; in fact, he was the "whole thing."

Mr. Beeson came to this country from Colorado, after spending several years there. At one time, he drove stage between Colorado Springs and Denver. He was compelled to reside in Dodge, for a short time, owing to loaning money on property here, to a friend, and not being able to get it back as soon as he expected; but he liked Dodge, took over the property instead of the money, and located here permanently. He had acquired a very good musical training in Colorado, playing always with the best musicians wherever he went; and at one time he played a steady engagement in Pueblo. When Dodge became the big cattle market of the central west, he invested money in a herd, and the first range he herded over was on the Saw Log. He afterwards took W. H. Harris in partnership with him, and they moved this herd to Sand Creek, about fifty-five miles south of Dodge City. During the severe winter of 1885-1886, they lost almost everything, and it somewhat discouraged him in the cattle business. He traded property on the southwest corner of Second avenue and Spruce street for eighty acres of land a mile and a half southwest of Dodge, where he resided until his death, due to a bucking horse he was riding.

This trade was unusual in the fact that Mr. Beeson and Mr. D. T. Owens, who owned the town property, traded evenly and complete, just as the properties stood, each family taking only their personal effects with them. And the peculiar fact still presents itself to us, that, after twenty-five years, the two properties still remain of equal value, as real estate.

Mr. Beeson was greatly admired by the Santa Fe railway people. At the time of his death he had acquired considerable land and town property. He was one of the heavy tax payers, and gave the right of way, through his valuable farm lands, for the building of the new railroad.

Another old friend and early comer to Dodge City I must mention is Mr. H. B. Bell. Mr. Bell, who was born in Maryland, lost his parents when very young, and, when a mere boy, came west to try his luck. From Lawrence, Kansas, his first stop, he went to Abilene, Ellsworth, and finally Great Bend, where he landed in July, 1872. There he hunted buffalo awhile, then got a position with a Santa Fe agent whose office was a box-car, and worked there till appointed assistant marshal under James Gainsford.

In September, 1874, Mr. Bell came to Dodge City, served several terms as city alderman, was appointed United States deputy marshal after the assassination of United States Deputy Marshal McCarty, and served in that capacity for twelve years. He also served as deputy sheriff under Charles Bassett and several other sheriffs, was elected to the office of county commissioner, served one year, and then ran and was elected sheriff, in which office he served for twelve years. Mr. Bell has been in office for about thirty years. He made many trips alone into No Man's Land, and brought out his man. When our Ford Bank was robbed, Mr. Bell was one of the important factors in bringing four of the robbers to trial, three of whom are now (1913) serving sentence. In all his official capacity, while very dangerous work in the old days, Mr. Bell has never shot a man, and never hit a man with a gun to affect an arrest, though I think he has arrested more people, for the warrants handled, than any sheriff in our western country. Mr. Bell is our present mayor, and is putting in his entire time, to give satisfaction to our people. Just to show that, in his energy and ability, time has not changed him, I clip, in part, the following, from the "Globe" of 1877:

"Mr. Ham Bell is the pioneer livery man of western Kansas. In addition to his large establishment in this city, he is also the proprietor of a branch establishment at Burton. He cuts his own hay, grows his own corn, puts up ice, hunts buffaloes and wolves, and keeps up several other businesses in town. But he has never anything to do, and will give you a trade for a horse, jack-knife, meeting house, or cast-iron jail, just to please you. Ham is a genuine, live western man, and keeps things moving."

Our fellow-townsman, and friend I am proud to call him, Governor W. J. Fitzgerald, has contributed largely to the building up of our town. He came here a poor boy, without money, and, what was worse, in very poor health. Indeed, it is a wonder he ever pulled through his long and severe sickness. But he is a rich man, today, and has earned it all by his indefatigable industry and enterprise. He is the owner of one of the finest farms and stock ranches in Kansas, with large and commodious barns and stables, and fine farm house. He has represented us twice in the legislature, and was lieutenant-governor of Kansas two terms. He is a gifted orator, and ranks high among the foremost and brightest young men in our state. He is a fine business man and a shrewd politician, and, mark my prediction, his voice will be heard in the halls of congress, one of these days.

Like Mr. Fitzgerald, there are others of our citizens who, though not the first settlers, have contributed largely to Dodge City's prosperity, advancement, and wealth, and Dr. C. A. Milton was at the head of this class. He is next to the oldest physician in Dodge today, enjoyed a large practice up to the time of his retirement, and now is much sought professionally, though acting only as a consulting physician. He can afford to avoid active practice, as he has made a small fortune from his profession as well as from his success as a wheat and alfalfa grower.

A. Gluck was for a long time the leading jeweler of western Kansas, and was many times mayor of Dodge City. His persistent and deep rooted faith in Dodge has made him a fortune. He has the distinction of being the only mayor ever impeached under the prohibition act, and his conduct was vindicated immediately afterwards by his being unanimously reelected by the people. He was not one of the first settlers, but has contributed largely to the building up of our city.

Of the many notable men that Dodge City has turned out, it is a pleasure to mention the names of Dr. Simpson and Dr. Crumbine. In early days, the "Romance of the West" was "Pipes O' Pan" to the restless youth, and among others who came west, in response to the "Pipes" was Dr. O. H. Simpson, whose mission was dentistry, and religion to save teeth. In his frontier isolation from the profession, he developed an individuality or style of dentistry that the dental profession has recognized by adopting much of it in their teachings and practice. Dr. Simpson was thrice appointed a member of the Kansas State Board of Dental Examiners, serving as president of that body for a period of twelve years; and, in his early efforts to enforce the new dental law, he came so near doing it that the "outlaw" dentists dubbed him the "Cowboy Dentist." The doctor always appreciated the fact that the greatest asset of life is youth; and it was through the open minds of the young men that made it possible for him to teach his methods of practice, while their added genius have developed modern dentistry. Doctor Simpson tells many funny stories of himself, when he was a tenderfoot and first came to Dodge, and they are mostly at his own expense.

Simpson and Ballou are the sole owners of the Willow Meadows Dairy, the largest and finest in western Kansas. It contains three hundred and twenty-five acres of rich meadow, and is surrounded on all sides by large alfalfa fields. They have gone to great pains and expense to make it perfect. It enjoys all the modern improvements, such as gasoline engines, pumping clear, cool water from deep wells, ice plant, electric light plant, cooling rooms; and with screens and other modern improvements, it is impervious to dirt and flies. The milk is cooled in a systematic manner. They have a large herd of thoroughbred Holstein cows, and milk over half a hundred.

Dr. S. Jay Crumbine, who came to Dodge City in the early eighties and practiced medicine for a number of years with marked success, is especially entitled to favorable mention as one of the Dodge City men who have done things. As secretary of our State Board of Health, he conceived the idea of the individual drinking cup, clean towels, inspection of hotels and restaurants, swat the fly, and many other things of a sanitary nature, that have received a world-wide recognition and adoption.

He not only thought these things out, but he carried hem into effect by his indefatigable zeal and energy, and is writings along these lines, tuberculosis, and many ther vital questions pertaining to health, should be read y everyone. Recognizing his ability, the Kansas State University elected him dean of their medical school, and le is filling this position now (1913), as well as acting s secretary of our State Board of Health, with, not only reat credit to himself, but a widespread benefit to the ublic at large.

In concluding this list of Dodge citizens, I present , few words on the Honorable Ed. Madison, our gifted, reatly beloved, and much lamented townsman and conressman. His political career was short, but he cut a ig figure and made a great reputation as a statesman nd debater, for one so young and opportunities so imited. He gave promise of big things in the future, lad he lived. We were all proud of him; and his funeral ras the largest ever seen in Dodge City, up to that time.

CHAPTER XVII

The Great Decline and Subsequent Revival

The early Dodge City boomers never cut the cloth scant when fitting the garment for general utility. They had no narrow vision of the prospect, and the perspective appeared the same width at both ends. As early as 1885 Dodge City was mentioned in the "Larned Optic" as destined to be a railroad center, which prophecy modern times has seen well fulfilled; and it was continually spoken of as a future metropolis, which surmise is still a healthy inspiration, gradually ripening to fulfillment. Electric lights illuminated the vision of the mind as well as the eyes, of the early boomer; and when the old timer set about promoting an enterprise, he had the consciousness of success. If the thing did not succeed at the time, it was the incentive for the revival of the scheme at a later date.

So, with her citizens imbued with such a spirit, and with the impetus given by the prodigious business activities of the previous ten years, it is not strange that the beginning of the year, 1886, saw Dodge City becoming modernized. Street grades had been established, with a view to future curbing and paving; a Board of Trade was organized in April, 1886, and was conducted with all the grave formality of later times and older communities, and with the same earnestness in promoting enterprises; about the same time, the first electric light company was organized, and also a telephone company, though the latter did not fully succeed in working out all its plans till some years later. Free mail delivery was promised from Washington, as soon as the local post-office receipts reached ten thousand dollars yearly, but this promise did not materialize till the spring of 1910, twenty-four years after it was given.

In this same year (1886), a waterworks system was so installed, and was first tested in the latter part of January, 1887. The "Globe" says: "There were six hose attached to six hydrants, in different parts of the city, all throwing water at the same time. The hose was three inches in diameter, and the nozzle one inch. At the hydrants in the south part of the city, it is estimated that streams, ranging from eighty to one hundred feet high, were thrown; while on the hills north, the power was not so great, the streams reaching a height of only fifty or sixty feet. The water was kept on for twenty minutes, and the people were well satisfied with the test. With this excellent system of waterworks, and with our three hose companies and hook and ladder company, which are in constant training, Dodge City can defy the fire fiend, in the future."

Dodge had cause to feel pride and security in her new fire fighting equipment, as she had experienced two disastrous fires before the establishment of the waterworks system. The first of these fires occurred in January, 1885, and it almost totally destroyed the whole block on Front street, between Second and Third avenues. The buildings were mostly frame, but a small brick building, on the west of the postoffice, was the means of checking the flames. The loss was estimated at sixty thousand dollars, on which the insurance was twenty-five thousand. The "Globe" tells of the heroic work of the volunteer firemen in preventing a general fire.

Dodge City's second great fire, occuring December 1st, 1885, was again on Front street, in the block between First and Second avenues, which was completely destroyed. With the exception of the R. M. Wright building, which was of brick, all the buildings were of frame. The loss was computed at about seventy-five thousand dollars. The origin of the fire is supposed to have been a coal oil lamp, exploding, or breaking from a fall, where it was suspended, upstairs over Sheridan's saloon. The fire occuring at seven in the evening, gave opportunity to save much inside property; but, owing to inadequate means of putting out fires, the entire block was soon consumed. As the "Globe" describes it: "Ladders were soon run up to the roof of the Globe building; and just as many men as could get around to work, started in, passing buckets of water, wetting blankets and spreading them on the roof and keeping them wet, while others kept the roof well covered with salt. At each of the upstairs windows were stationed one or two men, who kept the scorching, blistering building from taking fire. It was a hard and well fought battle with the fiery element." The damage by moving stocks from the buildings on Chestnut street, besides houses that were scorched and damaged by water, amounted to considerable. There was no wind, and the evening was quiet and damp.

Such were the conditions and events leading to the establishment of facilities for fire protection. And one of Dodge City's institutions, of which she was particularly proud, was her little fire company. It was the pride of the village, and the pet of western Kansas and Colorado. Wherever our fire boys went, Wichita, Newton, Denver, Leadville, Pueblo, Colorado Springs, and Trinidad, they were feasted, wined and dined, toasted and given the place of honor; and never did they fail to bring home one of the first prizes for fast runs and all around efficiency, while their conduct away from home was an honor to our town, and always mentioned as such by the town of which they were the guests. Their trim, neat, and gentlemanly appearance was also universally remarked, and favorably commented upon.

It is a notorious fact and worthy of note that the climate around Dodge City is conducive to speed. Parties from Dodge, Mr. Sam Stubbs, William Tilghman, and others, have gone east and bought up and brought back to Dodge, old, broken down race horses. Under good reatment and care, these horses would not only regain heir former speed, but would way yonder surpass it, and ould be taken back east and beat their former record nd win many races. It was the same way with young thletes. They would come to Dodge, join our fire comany, and many of them turn out even-time men; and hat is why our little fire company was always to the ront. Dodge was also the home of some of the speediest ild animals on earth; for instance, the antelope, the ttle red, swift or prairie fox, the wild horse, deer, elk, nd, last but not least, the jack rabbit. Perhaps speed as in the air—or climate.

The close of Dodge City's first great epoch of proserity was further marked by many projects for railroad uilding, most of which, however, fell through to a greater r less extent. When the Bucklin branch was built, he intended extension of the road was through Arkanas, Kansas, and Colorado; but Ford county voted one undred thousand dollars in bonds, to aid in this enterrise, and the Bucklin branch was the limit. On September 30th, 1887, the "Globe" said arrangements had been erfected for the grading, tieing, and laying of iron on he Arkansas, Kansas & Colorado railroad, which was to e built, with a connection with the Rock Island at Buckin, to Dodge City, and "which must be completed by December 31st, to earn the hundred thousand dollars in ounty bonds, voted to said road to aid in its construcion. The president, Mr. C. D. Perry, has just returned rom the East, where he arranged for all necessary maerial, and graders have gone to work." The Wichita & Western was looked for—it was always an ignis fatuus a railroad projects—but it never appeared. About this ime the Montezuma railroad was considered, and was uilt by A. T. Soule. The road was abandoned, and the ails and ties taken up. Some traces of the old road ed are yet plain.

One of the institutions of this period, of which Dodge City was justly proud, and which carried her peculiar individuality and atmosphere from one end of the country to the other, was the famous "Cowboy Band." This band was organized with a membership of eighteen men, including drum major and color bearer. The band wore the uniform of the cowboy. A large sombrero took the place of the ordinary hat, while a blue flannel shirt was substituted for the white bosomed shirt, and a silk scarf took the place of a neck tie. Leather leggings, supported by a cartridge belt and scabbard, a navy six-shooter, and spurs on boots completed the dress of this famous band of musicians.

The "St. Louis Globe-Democrat" once printed a picture of the band, showing Professor Eastman (the director) using a six-shooter to beat the time. A reporter on the paper asked the professor what he swung that gun for, and was told it was his baton. "Is it loaded?" asked the reporter. "Yes." What for?" "To kill the first man who strikes a false note," was the professor's reply.

The Cowboy Band went over a larger scope of country and was the best advertised band of any band, east or west, that was ever organized. It attracted more attention, wherever it went, not because it discoursed more beautiful music than any other band—although the members were highly complimented for their talent as musicians—but because of its unique appearance. After its fame became known, it was invited to a great many celebrated gatherings; for instance, to Washington City when President Harrison was inaugurated, and my! what a swath the bunch did cut. People just went wild over them, I expect because many of them had never seen a cowboy before; and their uniforms were a wonder to them. With their chapps and spurs and wooly leather leggings, belts and six-shooters, quirts, etc., it was indeed a sight to the people, and crowds followed in their wake when they marched down Pennsylvania avenue. They

ked to never got home. They were taken all around
ie country, and they were actually quarreled over, as
, what city or convention they would go to next. They
ere loaded down with all sorts and kinds of trophies
id presents, and even money was forced upon them.

Colonel Hunter, president of the St. Louis stock
.en's convention, and Mr. Rainwater, mayor of St. Louis,
itertained the Cowboy Band handsomely; they dined
iem and wined them and gave them the freedom of the
.ty, and none of them was allowed to spend a cent. At
banquet, given them by Mr. Rainwater at his private
:sidence, one of the band, a tall, raw-boned, awkward,
ngainly man, George Horter by name, when they were
:ated at the banquet board, took up his finger bowl
nd drank the water. The other boys noticed this and
'ere embarrassed at it. Mr. Rainwater came nobly to
ie rescue by taking up his finger bowl, also, and drink-
ig from it to the health of the Cowboy Band.

While the band was in Topeka, they were invited to
banquet, given by the great lawyer and prince of good
ellows, Captain George R. Peck, general solicitor of the
itchison, Topeka & Santa Fe railroad. During the ban-
uet, this same George Horter said: " 'Captain Peck!'
Vhy, nearly twenty years ago my captain was named
'eck." At that, Captain Peck said: "What regiment
.nd company?" George told him, when they both jump-
:d up and hugged each other. Such a scene you never
vitnessed. They both almost wept in each other's arms.
ifter twenty years, to be brought together in this way!
:t was touching, to say the least.

"The Pueblo Chieftain," in an account of the cattle
nen's convention, held in Dodge City, April 13th, 1882,
;ays:

"The cattle men's convention adjourned yesterday,
md the proceedings wound up last night with the grand-
:st ball and banquet ever held in western Kansas. It is
:stimated that the stock men here represented over fifty

million dollars. Just think of that amount of money, in one hall, in a western town. The hall was splendidly decorated by the ladies of Dodge. Evergreen anchors, wreaths, crosses, and other emblems, with a number of fine pictures decorated the walls. Among the latter were several splendid oil paintings, the work of Mrs. Chalk Beeson. The ball was a masquerade affair. The music was furnished by the Cowboy Band, and the prompting was done by Mr. Beeson, the best in the business. The banquet was in Cox's very best style, and was a magnificent affair.''

The Kansas City papers reported during the exposition of 1886: ''The Cowboy Band elicited words of praise from fifteen thousand visitors yesterday. This band is composed of real cowboys, not soft-handed dudes in disguise, as some had supposed before seeing them.''

The Cowboy Band was organized in 1881, after which time it gradually grew into prominence until it gained for itself a world-wide reputation. The first time the boys appeared in public as the Cowboy Band was in 1881, when they furnished music for the Topeka fair. In 1884 they attended the Cattle Men's National Convention at St. Louis, where they were presented with several magnificent banners as a token of the high appreciation by the people of St. Louis for the excellent music the boys furnished them. On the trip to St. Louis they also visited Chicago, St. Paul, Milwaukee, and several other important cities, and on all occasions were received by the people in a manner which showed their love for good music.

In 1885 they made their second visit to St. Louis, and in 1886 visited Pueblo and Denver, where they were received even in a more royal manner than in the eastern cities. And the boys were often heard to boast of the kind treatment they received at the hands of our good neighbors of the State of Colorado.

The abandonment of Fort Dodge, the settlement of the military reservation, and the establishment of the

Soldiers' Home, were important steps in the seeming course of advancement, in this period of Dodge City's history. The abandonment of Fort Dodge as a military post, in June, 1882, created surprise among the Dodge City people and settlers generally. With the abandonment of the fort, the people would have no protection against Indian raids. But the troops stationed at Fort Dodge were sent, one company to Fort Reno, one company to Fort Supply, and the third company to Fort Elliott, Texas, where they could be in proximity to the Indian reservations.

Fort Dodge, after its abandonment by the military, was partially demolished, many buildings being removed. However, the rebuilding and repairing took place, and the establishment of the Soldiers' Home sustained the character of the famous post. The establishment of this Home was indicated as early as the first part of 1883, a resolution having been introduced in the Kansas legislature, memorializing congress to cede the Fort Dodge military reservation for that purpose. But it was not until 1887 that the Home was established.

Late in May, 1886, a sudden rush for settlement, on the Fort Dodge reservation was made, early one Monday morning, and a hundred or more claims staked off, between Sunday night at twelve o'clock and Monday morning before sunrise. No one appeared to know how the reservation happened to be thrown upon the market all of a sudden, and no one stopped to inquire, but went right along with settling and improving some portion of the reservation, regardless of what the outcome might be. The people were perfectly wild with the excitement occasioned by this mysterious move. Every available team in the city was employed to haul lumber; carpenters were in demand, who, after being hired to do a little midnight job in the way of erecting a claim house, refused to work for their employers, but, on the other hand, hired teams and went to the reservation with lumber, squatted upon a hundred and sixty acres of land, and erected a house for themselves.

Now all this was wholly unwarranted on the squatters' part. The reservation had not been thrown open to settlement, and the only foothold the premature settlers gained was that of "squatters' right" which gave him the first right to purchase, in case the land was put up for sale. The reservation lands were subsequently opened to settlement, on terms prescribed by the government, by purchase and priority in settlement. The original "squatters," except in a few instances, relinquished their rights, and others proved up the claims.

Not the least of the signs of modernism, in this particular epoch of Dodge City, was the somewhat uncertain, but none the less significant moves toward certain social reforms. As is usual with the beginnings of such attempts, they took the form of the suppressing of profanity in public, and the establishment of a stricter form of Sunday observance. An example of one of the first protests against profanity is that of Postmaster Reamer, who, through the "Globe" of December 21st, 1886, "protests against the profanity, and in the postoffice especially, by the ladies (?), if such they can be called; more especially those that swear just because they do not get a letter."

In early times, Sunday business was the same as week day business. In the frontier days, stores were kept open on Sundays to accommodate the cattle and plains traders. Evidently the first efforts toward changing these conditions were, at first, regarded as almost hopeless. The following is significant: "Reverend O. W. Wright has presented a petition from the citizens of Dodge City to our merchants, requesting them to close their stores on the Sabbath day. He obtained the names of a majority of the merchants, but as all will not agree to close, the present effort will stop here."

A TREE IN HORSE THIEF CANYON
Where a number of Horse Thieves were Hanged

By 1883, however, efforts along this line were more successful. A telegram from Dodge City, in the spring of that year, said of the town: "For the first time since its existence, it had, last Sunday, the semblance of Sabbath. All business houses and saloons, dance halls and gambling halls were closed. There is universal rejoicing over this, and it is felt that all measures of reform, as contemplated by the city council, will be carried out. Many of the gamblers and prostitutes are leaving, most of them going to Caldwell. Now if Caldwell could only be reformed."

With all these movements toward development, improvement, and reform, following directly after her great prosperity of earlier days, it would seem that Dodge City, in 1885, was on the certain road to further advancement, steady progress, and uninterrupted growth and prosperity. But, lo and behold! a new aspect came over the spirit of our dreams. Dodge City, once famous for its extraordinary prosperity, its lavishness in prodigality and possession of wealth, at one fell swoop was reduced to extreme poverty, almost want. The change was sharp and quick, and almost without warning. The dead line was moved to the state line, and Dodge City lost the cattle trade; she also lost a tremendous freight business by wagon, the buffalo hide and bone industry, and other business incident to a frontier country. Railroads, building on the south, had absorbed the freight by wagon route; and farmers, settling on the lands, further reduced the cattle trade. Under this pressure of civilization, the town staggered under the blow. Even the great Santa Fe railroad felt the loss, for the company was put into the hands of a receiver, and the road's operating expenses were cut in two. It was the Santa Fe railway which gave Dodge City her start in pioneer life; and with this confidence, we felt if everything else failed, the road would continue to be a source of revenue to the city. Such depression, following so closely on the heels of her great affluence, was truly paralyzing.

For ten long years, Dodge City was suspended in reverses. But during this poverty stricken period, the process of liquidation was slowly being carried out. Dodge City had had so much faith in her progress and former wealth, that a calamity was unexpected; she lost sight of the fact that the unnatural extravagance of that former wealth and progress was bound to bring a reaction, sooner or later. In this depression, property went down to five and ten cents on the dollar, in value, or you could buy it for a song and sing it yourself. People would not pay taxes, and the county became possessed of much valuable real estate, while hundreds of specula- tors were purchasers of tax titles. Many of the business houses closed, and large numbers of residences were without tenants. Parties were invited to live in them rent free, so the insurance could be kept up. And the same depression was felt in land and cattle. Good cows sold for eight to ten dollars. Land around Dodge sold as low as fifty cents per acre. The writer's land, a tract of seven thousand acres, was sold under the hammer, at less than fifty cents per acre; and some for less than that price.

A good story is told of an Irishman, passing through Dodge City, from Morton county in the southwest part of Kansas, on his way to his wife's folks in the East, with a little old team of horses, a wagon, and a small cow tied behind the wagon. He stopped to water his team, and, when someone asked him where he was from and what were the conditions out there, he said, "It is a beautiful country for prospects, bless your soul!" "Why did you leave?" he was asked. "Got tired; and my wife wanted to see her folks," he replied. "What is the price of land out there?" He said: "Come here! you see that little cow behind the wagon; I traded a quarter section of land for her, and by gobs! before I made the deed, I found the critter I sold to couldn't read, so I just slipped in the other quarter section I had into the deed, and the fellow didn't know it."

Our town and country was likened to a rich family which, through extravagance and bad management, was reduced to extreme poverty. When they were down to the lowest ebb and everything was gone, the head of the family caught the eldest son in tears. He said to him, "My son, what are you crying for?" "My God, father!" he replied, "we have nothing left, whatever." "That is so, my son; but cheer up!" the father said: "Don't you see? we are at the foot of the ladder and we can go no further down; so we are bound to climb."

Thus it was with Dodge City. She was at the very foot of the ladder, and was bound to climb; and so she did, after she started—slow, at first, but after we caught our second wind, then by leaps and bounds. We commenced to go up. Our wheat which had been selling for 40 cents per bushel went up to 60 cents; our seasons began to improve, and our farmers take fresh heart and put in a larger acreage of wheat and other crops; and cattle began to go way up. Our people sold their wheat and invested in cattle; and sold their increase in cattle and bought cheap lands; and so it went, until our country got to be the third largest wheat county, two or three million bushels each year. In the harvest of 1912, Ford county was second in Kansas, in wheat production. With the proceeds from their wheat, farmers bought more land and erected business houses in Dodge City. And now Dodge can boast of the second finest court house, if not the finest in the state, a handsome city hall, a great system of water works and electric lights in splendid buildings, while our jail is a modern building, and our schools and magnificent churches are second to none.

Out of a great conflict rises a period of prosperity. To have gone through this endurance of adversity, equipped the people with courage and a sense of stability and prudence, which not only gives them caution, but nerve, in making Dodge City the commercial city of western Kansas.

As a close to this work, in addition to what has already been said in the same vein, a glimpse of the Dodge City of today, lying in the brilliant summer sunshine of 1913, must be given, or our subject will fall short of receiving complete justice. A marked change from the feverish commotion of its first great boom, or the terrible stagnation and desolation of its time of depression, is apparent. The happy medium, in its perfection, has been struck by the town, at last. It is now a busy, bustling, city of 5,000 people, all push and energy, building up and reaching out and making every other sort of steady progress toward development and improvement, socially, financially, and esthetically, without any wild clamor about it. Nor is this general progress dependent upon any transient traffic or local condition, as was the first great era of prorsperity. It is founded on the broader, firmer foundation of the development of territory and the natural pressure of modern civilization, and must, in the very nature of things, continue indefinitely and be permanent, with nothing mushroom like in its nature.

The change is great and keenly apparent to any observer of recent years; how infinitely greater, then, it must be, and how much more apparent to us who have watched the progress of Dodge, from its very beginning. Rich, green fields of alfalfa, and others of golden wheat, now surround the town, in place of the bare prairies of old; farm houses, handsome and commodious, with orchards, gardens, and pastures, occupy the place in the landscape once filled by the humble cabins, and 'dobe or sod houses, where the pioneer settler lived so long, in daily fear for his life at the mercy of murderous Indians; the primitive fording places of the river, and their successor, the rude wooden bridge of early days, have been replaced by a steel and concrete bridge, double tracked and electric lighted, across which are continually whirring smart vehicles and elegant automobiles, in place of the lumbering ox wagon or the spur driven cow pony; the weather-worn, blood-stained, old Santa Fe trail is now being honored as a distinguished historical highway and having its course marked, at intervals, by granite tablets, and a fine automobile road alongside; even the river shows change, its channel being narrowed and volume diminished by its contribution to irrigation projects above Dodge City, but this slight defection is more than repaid by the additional verdure and bloom and wealth produced by the stolen waters.

Though enormous crops of wheat and alfalfa are raised, without artificial aid, and the bulk of these staples are produced without it, irrigation is quite common in the vicinity of Dodge City. Many of the irrigation plants are private property, consisting, mainly, of deep wells, sunk to tap the underflow of the river, and fitted with pumps to bring the water to the surface. This underflow is practically inexhaustible, and the amount of water a farmer wishes to use need be limited only by the number of wells he is able to put down.

In contrast to these small systems, is the largest irrigation project in Dodge City's neighborhood, the great Eureka Ditch. This enterprise was first conceived by the Gilbert brothers, John and George, two of the most enterprising and go ahead citizens that ever struck this or any other country; and they were backed, financially, by the great "Hop Bitters" man, Mr. A. T. Soule, of Rochester, New York, who was also the founder of our big college.

By the side of the river is Wright Park, which it was the pleasure of the writer to donate to the city, in 1897, and which, in 1880, was a piece of land newly set with young trees. It is now a large grove of magnifi-

cent trees, the only indication of their not being natural
forest being the somewhat regular manner in which they
stand. Of this park, a local paper is good enough to say:
"The Wright Park is an institution of the city, highly
valued for its use in the purposes for which it was intended. In this city park, public gatherings of all kinds
are held, free of charge. The public spirit of Mr. Wright
was manifested on many occasions, but in none, will be
surpassed that of the park donation, which will be a living
monument to his memory. The only reservation Mr.
Wright made, in donating the park, was that it was to
be called, 'Wright Park,' always. Mr. Wright also
donated thirteen acres of land where the Harvey eating
house stands, to the railroad company, on condition that
a park be established; and also that citizens of Dodge
City should be charged only fifty cents a meal. But
the latter agreement was carried out for a short time
only; and the laying out and cultivation of a park is
still deferred—now nearly seventeen years having
elapsed."

The changes and growth in Wright Park is dupli-
cated in many other institutions of Dodge City. Everywhere, brick, stone, and concrete supplant the frame
structures of former days. And even good brick and
stone structures of earlier times, have been replaced by
others of more elegant quality or design. An example is
the court house which, first built of brick and stone,
was recently torn down and replaced by the just completed elegant structure of white stone and marble, a
delight to the eye in every line and detail. The contract
for the building of the city hall, a beautiful architectural
specimen of brick and white stone, in the midst of spacious,
well kept grounds, was given in October, 1887, to Messrs.
Sweeney and Toley, for the sum of $19,800. The work on
the Methodist college was under way, at this time, upwards of thirty-seven thousand dollars being expended;
but, in the time of depression, the building was discon-

inued, and the property finally abandoned as a college. Just recently, however, it has been bought entire by the Roman Catholics, and is now being overhauled and re-fitted, preparatory to the opening of a large school there at once.

The ward school buildings of Dodge, of which there are three, are large and substantial structures of brick and stone. The handsomest, the present high school building, occupies the site of old "Boot Hill," a mute but ever present and immutable witness of how thoroughly culture and education has replaced violence and lawlessness in that locality. Roomy as are her school facilities, however, they cannot accommodate the continually growing number of Dodge City's school population, and plans are now under way for the building of a new high school building, larger, handsomer, and more strictly modern than any of the others, admirable though they certainly are.

The good old Santa Fe railroad has also redeemed itself in the public mind, and resumed its part in the up-building and advancement of Dodge City. Its great round-house and machine shops of a division are located here, a handsome station has taken the place of the box-car and small station house of early days, an elegant "Harvey House" hotel is maintained, and a ten thousand dollar freight depot of brick and stone has just been completed by the road. This last statement, alone, is proof that the freight traffic over the Santa Fe, at Dodge City, is still highly important, while the passenger service is equally important, and perfect in appointment and convenience.

Among the churches, the Christian denomination was the first to erect a large and handsome church building of brick and stone, which is an ornament to the city. The Methodists have just completed an elegant twenty-five thousand dollar edifice of brick, stone, and concrete; while the Presbyterians contemplate the erection of an equally handsome building, in the near future. The

— 333 —

Episcopal church, though small, is a little gem—the most artistic building in Dodge City. With its brown stone walls, colored glass windows, and square bell tower, it is delightfully suggestive of the chapels of rural England. The Baptist church, though large, is of frame; but it occupies the most centrally located site of any church in town. It is directly opposite the Public Library, another handsome, modern building of brick and stone, wherein a large free library is maintained for the edification and education of the people of the city.

However, among all the handsome buildings of modern Dodge City, from her perfectly appointed signal station, to her huge grain elevators, there is not one which she cherishes more highly nor of which she is more proud, than of a modest little cottage in the heart of the city. This is the oldest house in town, though it is so well preserved that no one would suspect it to be Dodge's oldest house in point of service. It is as strong and substantial as it was thirty years ago, and is still doing splendid service as a residence. I wrote a brief description of this house for the "Dodge City Globe," of November 9th, 1911, which follows. Said the "Globe:"

"It is a cold day when R. M. Wright, pioneer plainsman and frieghter, cannot get up a good story about Dodge City. His latest one is about the oldest house in the town. In writing this little sketch for the 'Globe,' Mr. Wright lets the house tell its own story, in the following language:

"'Not many houses can tell a story like mine. I am by far the oldest house in Dodge City. Mine has been a checkered career. I was first built in Abilene, then taken down and moved to Salina, and from there to Ellsworth. Nothing doing in the way of excitement up to my advent in Ellsworth. There my trouble as well as my festivities began. From that time on, I led a gay and festive life, interspersed with some sad tragedies. Many fights and eraps were inaugurated there, in the wee small hours of the night; and once a murder was committed, as well as several duels started. I said murder; in those days we called it "shooting" and the man who did not get the drop was the "unfortunate." Then I was moved to Fort Dodge and first occupied by Charles F. Tracy, who was succeeded by John E. Tappen, and he by R. M. Wright, post-trader, and he by James Langton and his delightful sister, who was a great entertainer.

"'Here is where I had a gay time, as night after night, the officers of the post congregated there, to have a good time. And they had it; never were they disappointed in this. Cards, dancing, and music were the principal programme features, ending with sumptuous repasts about midnight. There have I entertained lords, dukes, and other great men of Europe as well as America. Among those who have sat at the festive board were Generals Sherman, Sheridan, Miles, Forsythe, and Pope; and brigadiers, colonels, lieutenant-colonels, and majors so numerous to mention. Once I was graced by the president of the United States, President Hayes.

"'From Fort Dodge, I was moved to Dodge City, where I have led a very peaceful life, in my old age. I am now occupied by W. B. Rhodes and family. Under all my owners, I have never been changed, but remain exactly the same building as when I was first erected, even to the two ells and porch. I now stand on the corner of Vine street and First avenue, a venerable relic of my past days of glory and splendor.'"

But why continue further with the enumeration of the noteworthy features of our city, and the description of the transformations that have taken place on every side within her boundaries, since the time when the Lady Gay dance hall was the center of social Dodge, and Boot Hill the boundary line of the great buffalo range. Change, change, everywhere change, and for the better, is all that can be seen. Did I say everywhere? I don't quite mean that. There is one place where Dodge City has not changed; her spirit of hospitality and benevolence, of liberality and justice, of kindliness to strangers and good cheer to unfortunates, is the same today as it was when the people cheered and exulted over the privilege of sending aid to the yellow fever sufferers; or when they risked life itself to rescue some frail woman from the horrors of Indian captivity. There is an indescribable, feeling of kindliness, good fellowship, and homelikeness in the very atmosphere of Dodge. The stranger feels it, immediately upon his arrival, and no matter how long he stays, he finds it continually made good. Snobbery and arrogance are little known in her social circles. Her wealthiest and most influential citizens are simple, hearty, whole-souled human beings, with the human quality pronounced in its degree; and there is a warmth and freedom of social intercourse among her residents, or extended from the residents to sojourners in the town, that seems the very manifestation of the western spirit of our dreams, or as if Dodge City might be the ideal, "where the West begins," as described in Arthur Chapman's lovely little poem:

"Out where the hand clasps a little stronger;
    Out where a smile dwells a little longer;
        That's where the West begins:
    Out where the sun is a little brighter;
    Where the snows that fall are a trifle whiter;
    Where the bonds of home are a wee bit tighter;
        That's where the West Begins.

"Out where the skies are a trifle bluer;
    Out where friendship's a little truer;
        That's where the West begins:
    Out where a fresher breeze is blowing;
    Where there's laughter in every streamlet flowing;
    Where there's more of reaping and less of sowing;
        That's where the West Begins.

"Out where the world is in the making;
  Where fewer hearts with despair are aching;
    That's where the West begins:
  Where there's more of singing and less of sighing;
  Where there's more of giving and less of buying;
  And a man makes friends without half trying;
    That's where the West begins."

APPENDIX.

1. Robert M. Wright (see frontispiece) was born at Bladensburg, Prince George County, Maryland, September 2, 1840. His father was born at Alexandria, Virginia, in 1800, and when a mere boy was on the battle-field of Bladensburg, administering to the wounded soldiers. His great-grandfather was a Presbyterian minister, and during the Revolutionary war raised a regiment of militant plowboys, at Elizabethtown, New Jersey, of which he had command at the battle of the Meadows. The British set a price on his head and destroyed all his property. His wife was shot by a Hessian soldier, as she sat at her window with a babe in her arms. Her husband was killed by Tories. His grandfather on his mother's side was Elias Boudinot Coldwell, for many years clerk of the United states supreme court, whose residence, and private library, which had been loaned to Congress, were destroyed by the British in the war of 1812. When sixteen years old, Robert M. Wright took a notion to come West. He settled in Missouri and worked on a farm near St. Louis until 1859. He made an overland trip with oxen in that year, reaching the town of Denver in May. He crossed the plains four times by wagon and twice by coach. He worked for three years for Sanderson & Company, and then became a contractor for cutting hay, wood, and hauling grain. He was appointed post-trader at Fort Dodge in 1867. He has been farmer, stockman, contractor, postmaster, and merchant. He has four times represented Ford county in the legislature. In 1899 he was appointed commissioner of forestry, and was reappointed in 1901. He resides in Dodge City.

The July, 1912, number of the ''Santa Fe Employer's Magazine'' says of Mr. Wright:

''No account of Dodge City is quite complete without reference to R. M. Wright. Going into western Kansas in ı very early day, this gentleman was, in 1866, appointed post trader at Fort Dodge. During a long and prosperous career, he has been successively a stockman, freighter, contractor, merchant, politician, farmer, county treasurer, state forest commissioner, postmaster, and representative of Ford county four times in the legislature, and once mayor of Dodge City. No man has been more closely identified with the remarkable history of Ford county than Mr. Wright. He is now living in feeble retirement in the old town which he helped make famous, while his experiences would fill an interesting volume. The following is given as a characteristic anecdote of his early life. It happened while Bob was serving as mayor of Dodge.

"One day a cow-puncher came to town, bent on having a good time, so he sauntered into the Green Front saloon and played his money on a sure thing game. In a short time, he and his little pile were parted. Sore at his ill luck, he determined to prefer charges against the proprietor for running a gambling joint, so he hunted up the Honorable Bob Wright, at that time mayor, and after introducing himself, presented his case in this manner:

" 'A feller in that 'ere Green Front has just robbed me of more'n sixteen dollars, an' I wants ter have 'im pulled.'

" 'Been gambling, have you?' retorted the Honorable Bob. Then addressing the city marshal, Bill Tilghman, who was just crossing the street, he yelled: 'Here, Bill, is a fellow that has been gambling . Run him in.' So they hauled the prisoner to the police court, where he was fined ten dollars and costs, as an object lesson to those who might presume to violate the anti-gambling ordinance of Dodge City."

2. The Dodge City Town Company (see Chapter I, page 9) was organized in 1872, with R. M. Wright, president; Colonel Richard I. Dodge, commanding Fort

Dodge; Major E. B. Kirk, post quartermaster; Major W. S. Tremaine, post surgeon; and Captain T. C. Tupper. The county of Ford was organized in 1873. Dodge City, according to the census of 1901, had 2,199 population, and the county of Ford, 5,302, since when, however, said population has probably doubled. The town is four miles west of the site of the fort.

3. Jim and Bill Anderson (see Chapter I, page 11) killed Judge Baker and his father-in-law, George Segur, at Baker's home on Rock Creek, a few miles east of Council Grove, on the night of July 3rd, 1862. Baker kept a supply store near the Santa Fe trail. The Andersons were hard characters from Missouri. At the commencement of the war they took to the brush. On one of their marauding expeditions in the spring of the year, they stole two horses from Mr. Segur. Baker and friends gave chase, and, overtaking the party west of Council Grove, recovered the horses. Baker swore out a warrant for the arrest of the Andersons. Old man Anderson, hearing of this, swore he would take Baker's life, and, arming himself with a rifle, started for Baker's home. Baker had been informed, met him prepared, and, getting the first shot, killed Anderson. July 2nd, the Andersons skulked around Baker's home, but the latter was at Emporia. He returned on the night of the 3rd. Baker and Segur after dark, were called out, both were wounded, and, retreating into the house, took refuge in the cellar. The house was fired, and Baker burned to death, and Segur, who escaped, died the next day.

4. Fort Lyon, Colorado, (see Chapter I, page 12) was originally established August 29th, 1860, near Bent's Fort, on the Arkansas River, and called Fort Wise. The name was changed June 25th, 1862. June 9th, 1867, the post was newly located at a point twenty miles distant, on the north bank of the Arkansas, two and one-half miles below the Purgatory River, in latitude 38° 5' 36", longitude 26° 30' west.

5. Fort Larned (see Chapter I, page 12), was
stablished Octorber 22nd, 1859, for the protection of the
Santa Fe trade, on the right bank of the Pawnee Fork,
bout seven miles above its mouth, 38° 10′ north latitude,
ongitude 22° west. It was named, June, 1860, for Colonel
B. F. Larned, then paymaster-general, though first called
Camp Alert.

6. Fort Dodge (see Chapter I, page 12), was locat-
d in 1864, by General G. M. Dodge, United States volun-
eers, the site being an old camping ground for trains
going to New Mexico. It is in latitude 37° 50′ north,
ongitude 100° west. A Colorado regiment camped there
efore the establishment of the post. It was a four-com-
any post, and was abandoned in 1882.

7. Colonel Aubrey (see Chapter I, page 14), was a
French Canadian by birth, and made two trips on horse-
ack between Santa Fe and Independence; the first in
ight days, in 1850; and the second, on a wager of one
housand dollars, in five days, in 1852. He was killed by
Major R. H. Weightman, once editor of the Santa Fe
'Herald.'' See "The Overland Stage to California,''
by Frank A. Root, 1901), pages 54 and 425.

8. Fort Atkinson (see Chapter I, page 12), a gov-
rnment post on the Arkansas River, twenty-six miles
elow the crossing of the Arkansas; established August
th, 1850; abandoned October 2nd, 1854. According to
Gregg's "Commerce of the Plains,'' issued in 1845, Point
f Rocks was six hundred and ten miles out from Inde-
endence, Missouri, and the crossing of the Arkansas was
bout Cimarron station, on the Santa Fe railroad.

9. Pawnee Rock (see Chapter II, page 24). This
tory was first written for and published in "Echoes From
Pawnee Rock,'' a small book from various authors' writ-
ngs, compiled by the ladies of Hutchinson, in honor of the
istoric spot. In a letter to Mr. Wright, from one of the
adies who had charge of the book, the lady says:

"I hear many complimentary comments upon your article. A Hutchinson business man, who is something of a literary critic, bought the first copy of the "Echoes" sold here and remained away from his store in the afternoon to read the book. When he next saw me he said, 'Robert M. Wright is the whole thing in your little book.'

"If there were time I could mention other appreciative remarks about your popular contribution.

"I am very grateful for your support during the months I worked on the book. In spite of some discouragement, the work was very enjoyable, and I have been paid a thousand times by the appreciative interest of patriotic Kansans.

"I hope you may be present when the Rock is formally transferred to the State.

"Yours very sincerely,

"MARGARET PERKINS."

10. The Chivington fight (see Chapter III, page 59) occurred in the autumn of 1864. In the summer of that year a band of Cheyenne Indians, under the control of Black Kettle and White Antelope, about four hundred and fifty in all, together with about fifty Arapahoes, under Left Hand, known to be friendly Indians, came to the vicinity of Fort Lyon, Colorado, in compliance with the order of Governor Evans, acting superintendent of Indian affairs. This was done with the understanding that they were to be protected from the soldiers who were to take the field against hostiles. They remained in this camp for some time, giving up their arms, and depending upon rations for their food. Their weapons were then restored to them by Major Scott J. Anthony, who had in the meantime superseded Major E. W. Wynkoop in the command of that military district, and they were told to go into camp on Sand Creek, about thirty-five miles from Fort Lyon. This they did, relying on the hunt for food, and maintaining friendly relations with

the whites. On the morning of November 29th, about daybreak, they were surprised by United States troops, under Colonel J. M. Chivington, the commander of that district. An indiscriminate slaughter of men, women, and children followed. The three principal chiefs were killed. Many of the Indians escaped on horseback and on foot, though followed by the mounted soldiers. Of the five hundred in camp, about one hundred and fifty were supposed to have been killed, two-thirds being women and children. (See U. S. Spec. Com. on Indian tribes. Report, 1867, B. F. Wade, chairman; Official Records' War of the Rebellion, vol. 41, pt. 1, page 948.)

Rev. John M. Chivington came to Denver in May, 1860, having been assigned, the previous March, to the Rocky Mountain district, by the Kansas and Nebraska conference. He had already served that conference in Nebraska. In the fall of 1861 the first regiment of Colorado volunteers was organized; John P. Slough, colonel; Samuel F. Tappan, lieutenant-colonel; and John M. Chivington, major. April 13th, 1862, Colonel Slough resigned, and Major Chivington was appointed to the command of the regiment, in recognition of his efficient service in New Mexico. In June, 1862, he was placed in command of the southern district of New Mexico, from which his regiment was relieved at his own request and returned to Colorado the following January. November 29th, 1864, he led the Colorado troops in the massacre of Black Kettle's band of Cheyenne Indians at Sand Creek, Colorado.

In 1858 and 1859 there lived in Lecompton a harness-maker by the name of John Fribley. Years after the war the writer met Fribley, who said he was with Chivington at that massacre. He was asked why the soldiers committed such an awful thing. He responded that on their march from Denver to Lyon the command called at the house of a popular ranchman, where travelers and soldiers frequently stopped, and they found the whole family murdered, the wife and mother lying on the floor with her entrails covering her face. He said the soldiers took an oath to kill every Indian they came across.

11. Fort Zarah (see Chapter V, page 91) was established September 6th, 1864, by General Samuel R. Curtis, then in command of the military district, and named in honor of his son, Major H. Zarah Curtis, who was killed at the Baxter Springs massacre, while on General Blunt's staff, October 6th, 1863. Fort Zarah was about five miles east of Great Bend, in the present Barton county.

CPSIA information can be obtained
at www.ICGtesting.com
Printed in the USA
BVHW042024011221
622918BV00006B/141

9 781375 793025